Praise for
UNROMANCE

"A splashy debut...celebrates love stories and the possibility of magic made real." —*Entertainment Weekly*

"This sexy, swoon-worthy romance is an unputdownable debut."
—*Library Journal*, starred review

"Filled with sparkling banter, clever nods to the genre, and scorching hot scenes, Erin Connor's *Unromance* is a perfect homage to all the best romcoms." —Alicia Thompson, *USA Today* bestselling author of *With Love, from Cold World*

"Erin Connor is my favorite new voice in romance. She brings the irreverent comedy and the swoon worthy romance to her romcom debut that celebrates the tropes and cliches of this glorious genre. The perfect romance novel for lovers of romance novels."
—Alison Cochrun, author of *Kiss Her Once for Me*

"Erin Connor delivers sharp wit, deliciously steamy moments, and so much charm in *Unromance* that I was kicking my feet from the first page to the very last. I loved every second of this book!"
—Jessica Joyce, *USA Today* bestselling author of *The Ex Vows*

"*Unromance* is a funny, spicy, wintery dream of a romance book that will have you rooting for the couple from chapter one. The perfect read for rom-com connoisseurs everywhere."

—Gabriella Gamez, *USA Today* bestselling author of *The Next Best Fling*

"*Unromance* is an absolutely delightful romp that takes all of my favorite tropes and turns them upside down! Erin Connor's voice is fresh and fun—she is a debut writer to watch!"

—Falon Ballard, author of *Right on Cue*

"*Unromance* is deliciously deadpan, ridiculously charming, and features the funniest, hottest couple that ever did meet. It's like Erin Connor took all the best vibes from all the best rom-coms and weaved them together just for me. I'm obsessed!"

—Catherine Walsh, author of *Snowed In*

"Erin's writing is so fresh, so funny, and so skilled, that if you told me she was Nora Ephron reborn as a millennial, I would believe you. *Unromance* makes familiar conventions feel brand new again in this lovingly self-aware send-up of the genre—even the most jaded readers will be inspired to dash through the airport and dramatically declare their love to this book. Fans of Ava Wilder won't want to miss this very fun, very steamy rom-com!"

—Jen Comfort, author of *What Is Love?*

"A love letter to romance and its readers, *Unromance* is an impossibly charming love story that follows through on the promise of its premise. A sexy, delightful read!"

—Anita Kelly, author of *How You Get the Girl*

"From meet-cute to HEA, Erin Connor's debut *Unromance* sparkles with classic Hollywood rom-com magic—combining wickedly funny banter with chemistry that practically sizzles off the page. This one's an instant favorite."

—Andie Burke, author of *Fly with Me*

"Filled with razor-sharp banter and a happily-ever-after that will make every reader swoon in the most epic way, *Unromance* is written for those of us utterly obsessed with romcoms. Mark my words—Erin Connor is *the* romance voice to watch!"

—Chip Pons, author of *You & I, Rewritten*

"Erin Connor's words can be summed up in one: Magic. *Unromance* swept me off my feet, stole my breath, and reminded me what it feels like to fall in love. Get ready to fall head over heels."

—Courtney Kae, author of *In the Event of Love*

"Funny and deeply charming. A real love letter to romance fans that manages to take the art of the rom com seriously, while also delivering on heart and humour."

—Laura Wood, author of *Under Your Spell*

"Erin Connor's debut is a romcom lover's dream of a book, both subverting and perfectly executing all my favorite tropes. Banter for days, sizzling chemistry, and a central couple I dare you not to fall in love with—*Unromance* is a new forever fave."

—Ava Wilder, author of *How to Fake It in Hollywood*

"An immensely charming debut."

—*Kirkus Reviews*

"*Unromance* is fresh, flirty, and fun—with laugh-out-loud humor and sizzling tension that will keep you on the edge of your seat—this debut doesn't just shine, it sparkles."

—Lana Ferguson, *USA Today* bestselling author of *Under Loch and Key*

"Witty and charming, tender and unflinchingly sexy, I am utterly smitten with *Unromance* and an auto-buy fan of Connor's for life."

—Laura Piper Lee, author of *Hannah Tate, Beyond Repair* and *Zoe Brennan, First Crush*

"Swoony, smart, and hilarious."

—*Publishers Weekly*, starred review

STILL INTO YOU

ALSO BY ERIN CONNOR

Unromance

STILL INTO YOU

ERIN CONNOR

FOREVER

New York   Boston

This book is a work of fiction. Names, characters, places, and incidents are the product of the author's imagination or are used fictitiously. Any resemblance to actual events, locales, or persons, living or dead, is coincidental.

Copyright © 2026 by Erin Connor

Cover design by Daniela Medina. Cover art by Guy Shield.
Cover copyright © 2026 by Hachette Book Group, Inc.

Hachette Book Group supports the right to free expression and the value of copyright. The purpose of copyright is to encourage writers and artists to produce the creative works that enrich our culture.

The scanning, uploading, and distribution of this book without permission is a theft of the author's intellectual property. If you would like permission to use material from the book (other than for review purposes), please contact permissions@hbgusa.com. Thank you for your support of the author's rights.

Forever
Hachette Book Group
1290 Avenue of the Americas, New York, NY 10104
read-forever.com
@readforeverpub

First Edition: February 2026

Forever is an imprint of Grand Central Publishing. The Forever name and logo are registered trademarks of Hachette Book Group, Inc.

The publisher is not responsible for websites (or their content) that are not owned by the publisher.

The Hachette Speakers Bureau provides a wide range of authors for speaking events. To find out more, go to hachettespeakersbureau.com or email HachetteSpeakers@hbgusa.com.

Forever books may be purchased in bulk for business, educational, or promotional use. For information, please contact your local bookseller or the Hachette Book Group Special Markets Department at special.markets@hbgusa.com.

Library of Congress Cataloging-in-Publication Data

Names: Connor, Erin author
Title: Still into you / Erin Connor.
Description: First edition. | New York : Forever, 2026.
Identifiers: LCCN 2025039040 | ISBN 9781538759448 trade paperback | ISBN 9781538759455 ebook
Subjects: LCGFT: Romance fiction | Novels | Fiction
Classification: LCC PS3603.O5476 S75 2026
LC record available at https://lccn.loc.gov/2025039040

Print book interior design by Taylor Navis

ISBNs: 9781538759448 (trade paperback), 9781538759455 (ebook)

Printed in the United States of America

LSC-C

Printing 1, 2025

*for the elder emos,
it was never a phase*

CHAPTER ONE

"Sloane Donavan, *Alternative Press*."

Tugging my press pass from my back pocket, I hold it up for the beefy man in the overtight black shirt that reads SECURITY.

He gives his stickered clipboard a cursory glance before opening the graffitied door for me. A blast of music ushers me inside, and I return the badge to my pocket while my eyes adjust to the darkness of the venue. This is my first time here, but all backstages are roughly the same. Bare-bones, all the effort put into the part the concertgoers will see. Back here, it's all metal rigging and scuffed wooden floors covered in leftover tape from past events.

I love it. It's my second-favorite place in the world.

Once I can see, I follow the flow of bodies, weaving in and out of roadies trying to do their jobs amongst the ever-growing crowd backstage. Amidst the flurry, I find the bespectacled woman I seek.

"Robb!" I call over the crowd.

Head whipping to the side, her eyes meet mine and she gestures me over, making room for me side stage. Everything sounds terrible in the wings—too much drums and not enough of literally everything else. I never watch shows from here, but it's where we always converge beforehand, where all the latest gossip is traded. Musicians, groupies, photographers, roadies, journalists—we're all crammed in here and everyone has stories to share. I've never been big on talking, but listening? That I can do.

I wind through the clusters of people toward Robb, one of the senior writers at *Alternative Press*. That alone is enough to make me idolize her, but her effortless style—pixie cut, thick black-rimmed glasses, and Monroe piercing—would also do it. Robb oozes cool, the older sister I always wanted in a house full of brothers. With her dark blue eyes and (albeit bleached) blond hair, we could be sisters.

As soon as I reach her, I recognize the face next to her, the very person we came to Battle of the Bands to see: Hudson Chase, lead singer of Hollow Graves and the next big thing to come out of Cleveland, if my instincts are correct, and I'm usually right about these things. I don't have a musical bone in my body—save for my ear—but I know talent. Maybe it's from growing up next door to a boy who's now the drummer for Post Humorous, whose single has dominated the alt-rock charts all summer. Or maybe it's the sheer number of hours I spent in skate parks as a gangly teen, listening to the local Boston bands. Whatever it was, it got me my internship at *The Offbeat*, the alt-music offshoot of *Rolling Stone*, and now, freelancing for *Alternative Press*.

"Hudson," he says, introducing himself.

I always find it endearing when the lead act isn't too proud to introduce themselves.

"Sloane Donavan," I say for the second time tonight.

I can't help but full-name myself. It's a leftover habit from childhood. Growing up with four older brothers in a sports-obsessed Boston suburb, the Donavan name was well-known for gracing the back of a lot of jerseys. That name may not mean the same thing here, but it *does* get me in the door.

What I don't expect, however, is the spark of recognition in Hudson's eyes. It's a little too knowing. I'm not vain enough to think it's because of my prowess as a writer. I've only been out of college for two years, and while I've worked for impressive magazines, I'm no one. I'm not even a full-time staff member—*yet*. But even most veteran journalists aren't on a name-recognition level. I'm a part of this world, sure, but I'm a fly on the wall, observing, not the spectacle. I don't know why he recognizes my name, but my anxiety automatically assumes it's a bad reason.

"Sloane started at *AP* last month," Robb tells him. "You'll be seeing a lot of her, I'm sure. She's helping me with the Artists to Watch column."

Hudson's brows rise, intrigued. It's a list any up-and-coming artist would kill to be on, as it's bolstered many a band from local talent to household name. "We'll have to get you by the studio sometime."

"I'd love that." I realize a moment too late I'm talking too loud, the crowd having finally quieted in anticipation of the opening act taking the stage.

I grimace apologetically. Hudson hangs his head, wavy brown hair falling forward to hide his smile. Yes, Hollow Graves is absolutely going to blow up. In part due to their talent, which even from their demos is undeniable, but also because Hudson's boyish charm is so refreshing amongst the sea of overconfident, cocksure vocalists. I'm intrigued to see how this translates on stage.

The opening band takes the stage with a scream of "Battle of the Bands 2010, *let's fucking gooo!*" and Robb gets dragged into a conversation with someone I don't know.

I dither awkwardly in place. I hate being new. Making friends has never come easily to me. I've learned how to make small talk when I'm working—how to get *other people* talking, that is—but making actual friends on purpose is not a skill in my arsenal. I blame being grandfathered in by my older brothers, always tagging along behind them, the five of us inseparable after our mom left. Then Charlie—my neighbor in the band—introduced me to his bandmates, who are my closest (and only) friends a decade later. I have no idea how to make friends as an adult. I think Robb and I are becoming friends, despite our eight-year age gap. I've got an old soul and resting bitch face, and I think she kins with that.

Catching Robb's eye, I jerk my head in the direction of the crowd and she nods, gesturing that she'll catch up with me.

"You going into the pit?" Hudson asks with a twinkle in his startlingly light eyes.

I laugh. "Absolutely not. I'm headed to the sound booth." It's the best place to watch a show. Far enough back that you can see and hear everything, with no one elbowing you to get to the front.

"Can I come with you?" he asks earnestly.

I smile. "Sure."

We make our way around the side of the room before venturing out into the crowd. No one stops us or recognizes Hudson. I flash my badge and the sound technician lets us into his booth—a rectangle of metal fencing barricading the crowd from thousands of dollars' worth of equipment.

As we settle into the booth, I exhale deeply. *This* is my favorite place in the world. The constant buzz of anxiety inside me quiets when I'm at a show. I'm fully present in a way I'm normally not. I'm not five years in the past, overanalyzing everything I could have done differently, done better. I'm not five years in the future, laying bricks to follow, paving the path to my dreams. I'm here, now. I'm simultaneously anonymous and a crucial part of something bigger than myself.

Leaning over, I bring my mouth close to Hudson's ear so he can hear me. "You won't be able to do that much longer."

"Do what?" he asks with a smirk, already knowing full well what I'm going to say. The humility is incredibly charming.

"Walk through a crowd undisturbed."

He tries and fails to contain a grin. This is why I still spend so much time at smaller venues, skulking around skate parks I'm starting to feel too old to visit. I love being the first person to discover a talent. I know some people find it insufferably snobby—*I knew them before they were cool*—but watching the crowds at their shows get bigger, the venues growing larger to accommodate them, until the crowds are bursting at the seams there, too... It fills me with proud papa bear feelings.

It's my job now, sure, but being a small part of someone else's journey to actualizing a dream—that's not work to me.

The band playing isn't bad. All female, which piques my interest. Even one woman or person of color in a band is a welcome sight on the punk scene. These girls are young, high school age at most, but they're talented. Musically, at least. They haven't quite figured out their stage presence yet. They look like they all saw the same photo of Courtney Love and said, "Yeah, that's the look." I can't help but find it endearing, because I did the same thing—albeit with her other half.

My mom left when I was in kindergarten. Growing up in a household of only men and cargo-short hand-me-downs, I was predestined to be a grungy tomboy. But by the power of Kurt Cobain and Winona Ryder, I scrapped together some semblance of a personal style—even if it is just the same jeans and band tees over and over, like a cartoon character with a closet full of one outfit and one outfit only.

As the headliners, it's obvious Hollow Graves will be winning tonight's Battle of the Bands and thus the prize—a feature in *Alternative Press*—but I make a mental note to put something together for these girls, too, before the next pitch meeting. Unlike the writing staff, freelancers aren't guaranteed assignments, so I'm constantly on the hunt for my next article—and my next paycheck.

At the end of their set, the band leaves the stage to lukewarm applause. Robb joins me in the sound booth and Hudson takes his leave to warm up with his bandmates backstage.

"Get ready," Robb warns.

"For what?" I ask in alarm, pivoting to the side to scrutinize her and her odd greeting.

She doesn't clarify, but I already have my answer. Over her shoulder is Hudson, in one of those half-hug handshakes with the lead singer of Final Revelations—hands down the biggest band to come out of Cleveland in the past decade. The lights dim as the next band takes the stage to enthusiastic applause, and it's only that which saves Dax Nakamura from being recognized by a crowd of metalheads. Over six feet tall, half Black, half Japanese, industry bad boy turned straight edge and every groupie's white whale, he couldn't blend in if he tried.

He breaks away from Hudson—who's due on stage next—and is now heading toward our makeshift sound booth. If he spotted me, recognized me, I don't know, my attention now trained straight ahead.

Robb leaves my side to open up the barricade for Dax, but because she stepped aside to let him into the tiny booth, the only place for Dax to stand is…directly next to me. My heart knocks around inside my chest like tennis shoes in a dryer.

The last time Robb, Dax, and I were in the same room was on what was supposed to be my first date with Dax. We made a pit stop at the *AP* office because Dax had merch to sign for some fundraiser.

Running errands on our date: the height of romance, I tell you. But I met Robb, and that ended up paying off for me when I decided to leave *The Offbeat* and needed an in at *AP*.

The last time I saw Dax was in my hometown of Boston, where I broke up with him. The East Coast leg of Punkapalooza was over. I was touring with Post Humorous as their PR manager (aka MySpace blog writer), and since it was their last tour stop, it was my last stop, too. As one of the headliners, Dax was continuing on. He invited me to go with him, but I had other plans. Plans to complete the final year of my journalism major and an internship in California. And what was the point of delaying the inevitable? I was in Boston, he was on tour, in lots of cities, none of them mine. That was three years ago.

And now, he's here. I'm here, in his city, with an apartment I signed a year lease on in the hopes *AP* will hire me full-time.

Once I'm sure he's watching the stage, I sneak a peek, drinking him in under the premise of tucking my hair behind my ear.

He must've spent time in the sun recently, his normally light brown skin deeper, warmer, like if I were to brush my knuckles along his unfair cheekbones, trace the line of his singular, rarely seen dimple, I could feel the sun's kiss on his skin. His hair is the same, the curls atop his otherwise close-cropped hair sticking out in every direction. A silver septum piercing winks at the bottom of his nose, drawing my attention to his mouth. I don't allow my gaze to linger there. I can't. Not when the memories of what he can do with that mouth are branded on my skin like an invisible tattoo. At the base of his throat, the chain that holds his sobriety chip disappears under the frayed collar of his shirt. I don't spy any new tattoos, but real estate on his body was already hard to come by three years ago. I can smell his soap from here, the same piney scent I mourned when it faded from his sweatshirt I stole.

I close my eyes against the flood of memories, but the smell of him wraps around me like the sweatshirt I still wear. I face forward again and stop breathing for a moment in the hopes that it clears my head. I knew seeing him again was an inevitability. I just thought I was prepared for it.

I could not have been more wrong.

He leans down, lessening the difference in our heights, his lips brushing against my hair, the evergreen smell of him surrounding me once more. "Hi, Sloane."

My eyes snap open, the low timbre of his voice like velvet, my skin tingling like static between silk sheets, something inside me waking up after a three-year nap.

The sound of my name in his mouth sends me back to when he first said it, three years ago.

CHAPTER TWO

It's 2007, the second day of Punkapalooza. I'm sunburnt, hungover, dehydrated, and lost in a parking lot. I had to trudge all the way back to the van to unearth my Nokia charger from my duffle. A simple enough task for a hungover girl with a dead phone, except the fairgrounds we're playing at today are a maze. I've been wandering amongst the towering tour buses three times the size of our dinky van for the past ten minutes trying to find the chain-link corridor that connects the parking lot to backstage. I tie my hair up so I can concentrate better.

"You lost?"

Of course I'd meet Dax Nakamura for the first time after sweating my ass off all day. I can *feel* the Georgia humidity pasting my baby hairs to my neck and forehead.

It doesn't bode well for my future in journalism that I'm completely tongue-tied, but I'd argue that I should get a pass when it comes to Dax. I didn't think people this attractive existed in the real world. The headline "Hot People: They're Just like Us!" flashes through my mind, with placeholders for images of Dax doing mundane activities like grocery shopping and taking out the trash. I can't fathom it.

Surely his trash just sets itself on fire to save him the hassle, much like I want to do right now.

After a day in the stifling Georgia heat, I look like a sad, twice-warmed-up lasagna. Dax looks insufferably perfect. The way his warm brown skin drinks up the blood orange of the sunset has my cheeks reddening worse than my sunburn. I've been silent way too long, staring—gawking—at him. To my horror, I realize my mouth is hanging slightly open. A moment longer and I may be drooling.

His whiskey-colored eyes, which have been so intent upon my face, flick down, assessing me briefly. It's like breaking a spell, the instant he relinquishes me from his gaze. The sounds of the festival come rushing in, as if it, too, had been holding its breath. I breathe shakily, and my tongue unsticks. Unfortunately, it chooses to form a completely nonsensical response to his question.

"I'm allowed to be back here," I hear myself saying like a dolt.

The corner of Dax's mouth twitches up, not quite a smile. "I know."

His response makes even less sense than my statement. He couldn't possibly know. Tour started yesterday, and I've only seen him 1.5 times—from a distance. (Not that I'm counting.) There's no way he knows me. He must have glimpsed the VIP badge hanging from my back pocket.

He jerks his head in the direction of the festival. My desire to get out of this parking lot maze overrides my desire to get away from him before I can embarrass myself again. I nod, falling into step with him as he confidently begins cutting through the rows of buses.

I can't help but try to smooth over my weird proclamation. "It's just, I left my badge in the van this morning and security had me escorted out. It was a whole thing."

I'm boring myself with this line of conversation. I can hear myself talking, droning on, but I can't stop, can't find more interesting words to say to this industry icon who will forget this entire interaction in a matter of hours. I, on the other hand, will spend the rest of eternity cringing about The Time I Met Dax Nakamura and Was a Complete Wet Blanket. This is not the way it goes in my daydreams. In those, I always have the perfect quip, some scintillating story where the punchline always lands. This is...not that.

He nods. I don't know him well enough to know if he's also bored by me or if that's just his face. "You're with Post Humorous, right?"

I trip, barely recovering before I face-plant.

He gestures down, and I realize my shoes are untied. Kneeling, I pray he keeps walking so I can't embarrass myself further. Alas, his beat-up black Vans stay firmly pointed in my direction as I make bunny ears out of my laces, a rote task that shouldn't feel as mortifying as it does.

I try to remember what he said before I tripped. Dax speaking to me, I can wrap my head around. Dax knowing who I am? That doesn't make sense at all. But it does remind me that I'm not some groupie trailing after him. I am here of my own merit. (Okay, a slightly fudged merit that I'm my friends' band's PR manager.) Despite being escorted out earlier today, I *am* allowed to be here. When I straighten, my posture is less slouchy than usual.

"You didn't have to wait on me," I tell his shoes because I cannot meet his gaze.

"It's not like they can start without me."

There's that famous Dax ego. Alas, he's not wrong. Glancing up, he looks abashed for half a second before shrugging it off. He doesn't care if some random girl thinks he has an ego—earned or not. He jerks his head, taking off again. I fall into step with him and try to reconcile the guy I've heard about—a diva, a lush, a liability—with the guy who patiently waited for me to tie my shoes before safely seeing me back to the venue. It doesn't feel like I'm talking to one of the most famous people on the tour. He's just... a dude.

"Besides"—he speaks as languidly as he walks—"I could use the company."

We're through the chain-link tunnel now, reentering the fray of backstage. I glance meaningfully at the crowd we're weaving through. "Yeah, company must be so hard for you to come by at such a massive festival."

Dax scoffs, something akin to surprise flickering across his perma-bored expression.

As the youngest of five and the only girl, petulance is in my DNA. Based on the way he's eyeing me, I don't think he minds.

Our steps slow to a halt as we near the main stage—time for us to go our separate ways.

His gaze is sharper, like he wasn't fully paying attention before, but he is now. "I'm Dax, by the way."

As if I don't know that. *He knows* I know that. "I know."

Brilliant, Sloane. You make words in the right order so good.

Dax shakes his head, looking away and laughing under his breath. I want to drown in the deep, husky sound of it. "I figured, but—" His full attention is on me now, the corner of his mouth quirking up in another not-quite-smile. This time, a ghost of a dimple winks at me. Is he— *Oh my god, is he flirting?* Or is he just hot and talking? Do I *want* him to be flirting? God, no. I've barely made it through this laughable excuse of a conversation. I have no desire to continue mortifying myself in front of this man. "I was trying to get your name."

"Ah" is all I can manage, still struggling to wrap my head around the concept that Dax Nakamura could maybe, possibly, be flirting with me.

Surprise flickers across his face once more. He's losing the fight against his smile, one corner creeping higher and higher the longer we drag this out. "Are you...are you really not going to tell me your name?"

My mouth twists off to the side in a show of consideration. I don't know why giving it to him feels so big. As an aspiring journalist, I *should* want one of the biggest names in the industry to know my name. But...if he knows it, he can forget it, and in this moment, nothing feels more tragic than telling him my name, crossing paths with him again in a year, two years, and he's forgotten it, forgotten me. I don't want to invite the opportunity to be so devastatingly disappointed, so I shake my head.

If I thought I had his full attention before, I was wrong. Challenge lights his irises from within, his pupils dilating.

I fear I've only made him more interested, somehow. Before I can figure out how to assure him I am a lot more effort than I'm worth—just ask every single guy I've ever dated—I'm enveloped in a sweaty, sticky hug that smells like cheap beer. My friends have found me.

"SLOOOOOOOOANE!" my friend Drew bellows from across the backstage area before hugging whoever is hugging me from behind. Soon, all five of my friends are squeezing the ever-loving shit out of me.

To his credit, Dax is completely unfazed by the spectacle. Worse, he's smirking. "See you around"—he says each word like it's delicious, savoring each syllable—"*Sloane*."

Goddamnit, Drew. But god bless Drew and my friends for hugging me so tight right now because my knees are inexplicably weak.

"Let's hope not." I was aiming for snark, but it comes out on a wheeze thanks to the sheer number of limbs still squeezing me like a long-lost husband returned from war.

Oh, fuck me. There it is. Dax's full smile. A quick flash of white teeth, a singular dimple in his left cheek. As quickly as it appeared, it's gone. He hums thoughtfully, giving me a curious once-over, like he's memorizing me, like we'll be doing this again.

I don't know what to make of that. When he turns and waves two fingers lazily over his shoulder, I breathe fully for the first time since we crossed paths.

I blink back to the present, the noise and smells of the venue rushing back in. Dax's voice echoes in my ear and I shiver, goose bumps rising on my skin.

Hi, Sloane.

Three years ago, he won my name. Three years later, he still says it like a prize.

♪ ♫ ♬

I'm not a coward for hiding in the alleyway between sets.

I'm not.

It's been three years with no contact. I don't know Dax anymore, but too much has happened between us to make small talk like strangers. So, after the final supporting act's set ended, I feigned needing to use the restroom, slipping out of the sound booth that was much too tiny for all that history, and retreated to the alleyway to do breathing exercises. I don't actually know how to *do* breathing exercises, but now seems like an ideal time to start.

The alley smells like stale beer and cigarette smoke. I get far enough away from the ragtag group of people clustered out here and rest my forehead against the brick wall, still warm from the sun that set a while ago. For half a second, I'm ashamed for hiding back here, but the idea of exchanging bland pleasantries with Dax—as if we didn't spend a summer stealing moments together behind tour buses with desperate hands and pleading noises—sounds like my own tailor-made purgatory.

The crowd roars, and I shake my head to clear it—once, twice—before heading back inside. Hollow Graves will go on soon, and I don't want to miss the start of their set. The sound tech lets me back into the booth, and Dax takes half a step back—as much as he can in the cramped space—so I can squeeze by to be next to Robb. A well-intentioned gesture, except my ass brushes up against Dax's front as I pass, and even the opening notes of the Hollow Graves set can't drown out the groan Dax fails to muffle.

I can see the band on the stage, I know there's music playing, but all I can hear for the entirety of the first song is *that moan*. The applause that follows the opening song jars me out of... whatever that was... and I shove it all down. I will not let my nostalgia for that summer get the best of me. I know all too well the specific pain of waiting for someone who's never coming back, but I'm not a five-year-old girl anymore. I have a job to do. If I want *Alt Press* to offer me a full-time position and, thus, keep my five-year career plan on track, I need to focus—not get swept away.

When the Hollow Graves set ends, Dax is out of the booth before I can blink. I'd be offended if I weren't so relieved. It'll be easier to concentrate on work without wondering if he's sneaking glances at me like I'm sneaking glances at him. It *should* be easier, except I blink and I'm backstage, with no memory of how I got there, going through the postshow interview on autopilot. I'm supposed to be leading this interview—Robb wants to hand off the Artists to Watch column to me so she can finally launch the vertical she's been gunning for—but Robb has to jump in a couple times with follow-up questions that I like to think I would have thought of were my mind not half on a man who's not even here. I hate that it's affecting me this much, but *fuck*.

Seeing him, hearing his voice, the smell of him that evokes memories of his soap resting on my shower caddy for that one perfect weekend before everything fell apart—

"And how's working with Final Revelations?" Robb asks, cutting off my trip down memory lane and bringing Dax into the present.

I blink over at her. She didn't share that fun fact about Hollow Graves with me. She's avoiding my gaze, and I know the omission was intentional.

Hudson glances at me before answering, and my chest flushes as I realize why he recognized my name earlier. Not many people know about Dax and me. Our "relationship"—for lack of a better word—was brief and bright and burned out quickly. Whatever it was, it's not a part of my past that I like to flaunt.

While Robb knows I knew Dax—Dax introduced us, after all—I don't think Robb knew we were more than a tour fling. But there's no way she doesn't know now. The tension in that sound booth could've been cut with a knife.

Thankfully, Final Revelations doesn't talk to the press, so the likelihood of our history ever getting out, of that summer being used against me, is slim. *It's fine.*

But tell that to my inner monologue. If there's something to overanalyze and nitpick until three a.m., then I'm wide-awake, alternating between the highlight reel of Dumb Shit Said by Sloane Donavan and my favorite think piece, All the Ways Anything and Everything Could Go Wrong.

So when Robb asks if I want to go for a drink after the interview, I say yes even though I don't really want to. Well, I kinda want the drink, but I'm tapped out as far as being social goes, even though I can't remember the last time I just *hung out* with someone. My new apartment doesn't feel like home yet, but I still long to return to it, a place where I can't be blindsided by the appearance of the only man who's ever made me come.

"I'm sorry," I blurt as soon as Robb reappears with two beers in hand. This dive bar's minimal decor isn't nearly distracting enough to drown out the heady turn of my thoughts.

Robb hands me one of the beers before promptly downing half of hers. "For what?"

"I was unprofessional back there. I'm sorry, I...I was off my game. I swear I'm normally better at this."

Robb smiles knowingly over at me. "Sloane, this isn't our first time working together. You think I'd be handing off my column to you if I didn't know that? You think they'd even *let me* give it to a freelancer if they didn't also know that?"

I take a deep breath, nodding. "Yes. Thank you, I needed that reminder." I begin absentmindedly picking at the label on my bottle. "I guess...I didn't expect it to be this hard."

"Choosing art as a career?" Robb asks, brows arched high above her glasses.

The laugh comes out of me in a snort, which makes Robb laugh, which makes me laugh harder, and soon, I'm lightheaded. Rubbing my brow, I try to pull it together. "Thank you, I needed that, too."

"Besides," she says quietly, rolling her beer back and forth between her hands contemplatively. "I owe *you* an apology. I should've told you Dax gave me the tip on Hollow Graves, but I didn't think he was coming, so it didn't seem relevant. When I met you, I suspected you two were"—she wiggles her eyebrows suggestively—"but I didn't know it was..." Her eyes widen. "Like that."

I take a long sip of my beer to delay answering. "We dated for, like, a month."

Technically, a month and a half, but it's what I always say if someone asks about it. A month is nothing. Unless you're on the same tour. Then there are multiple cities, thousands of miles, all day, every day, isolated from the real world so it's nothing but you and them and *music*. It's all-consuming.

It's the only relationship I've ever had that's actually worth talking about, except for the fact that I absolutely do not want to talk about it.

So, I downplay it. A few weeks. Small potatoes. Conversation moves on.

"Must have been an intense month."

Goddamn Robb and her pitch-perfect journalistic instincts.

I can't look back on that summer and not blush. I went from having done nothing more than kissing with a side of heavy petting to realizing I'd put my underwear on inside out after hooking up with Dax in the back of an empty tour bus. I met a side of myself I hadn't known existed. On the road, suspended from reality, the summer before my final year of college, my postgraduation internship at *Offbeat* already lined up. For perhaps the first time in my life, I felt secure enough to let loose. It's not that I didn't like that version of myself—it's that I *did*. And that scared me. I finally understood how my mom once thought building your life around another person could be enough. It was the antithesis of everything I've ever worked toward. So, at the close of that magical summer, I ended it. He let me go with two mumbled syllables, and I knew it had been the right thing to do, even if, three years later, the ache refuses to fade.

Bracing my elbow on the dingy pub table, I rest my face in one hand, tracing the condensation rings on the surface with the other. "It was, yeah. Off the record, though, please," I say with a grimace.

Robb huffs a laugh. "Dating Dax isn't exactly a story." She flinches. "Sorry, I didn't mean that how it sounded."

I shrug. She's not wrong. I wasn't Dax's first or last, never mind that he's both for me. "I would appreciate it if no one else at work knows, though."

Robb tilts her head to the side. "Okay, but...knowing Dax is a good thing. Networking is everything in this business."

Before I can shove the words back in, they come spilling out. "I wouldn't call what Dax and I were doing *networking*."

Robb throws her head back and laughs, attracting the attention of a few nearby tables. "I meant if it's possible for you and Dax to move past, well, *the past*, he knows a lot of people. You've got connections—use them."

"A girl using her ex to get ahead in her career? Yes, everyone will think, *Aw, poor Sloane, so brave, getting her heart pulverized but still soldiering on.* Not, *Ah, she slept her way into her career.*" I fix her with a frown.

Robb grimaces but doesn't contradict me, knowing I'm right. I don't name-drop Dax for a reason.

"One last thing—and then I won't mention it anymore," Robb hedges carefully. "But I think he was just as thrown seeing you as you were at seeing him."

I frown. Dax said hello and not a single thing more. Never mind I did the same.

"He asked about you," Robb continues. "When you left between sets. He tried to be subtle about it, asking why *Offbeat* was here. I told him you were with *AP* now."

I wait for Robb to continue, but she only studies me with a knowing look before draining the last of her beer. She won't tell me more unless I ask—and we both know I'm too proud to do so.

"Anyway," I say around a heavy sigh, steering the conversation back to shoptalk. "I don't care if it takes me longer, or if I have to work harder, but I'm going to earn this on my own merit. Well"—I gesture between us—"besides utilizing you to get the job in the first place. Which I still owe you for." I laugh self-deprecatingly, kneading my brow. "I still can't believe we met because Dax ran errands on our date."

Robb makes a noise of disbelief, methodically peeling the label off her bottle.

I don't need a journalist's intuition to tell me she's holding something back. "What?"

She smirks. "That wasn't chance. He was supposed to come by the day before with the rest of the band but asked to come that day, with you, and for me to be there and pretend it was chance because he didn't think you'd accept the networking help."

I blink, sitting back in my seat. That considerate, genius asshole.

"Don't overthink it, babe." She swats me lightly on the arm, bringing my attention back to her. "We needed more women on the team, and I'm sorry all I could get you was freelance for now, but knock it out of the park with the Artists to Watch column and you'll be on staff soon enough."

I sincerely hope so. With the inconsistency of freelance paychecks, and rent eating up the entirety of my meager internship pay, I have no savings to speak of, no cushion to fall back on. I need this to work out. I've already left one dream behind in California. I'm not ready to give up on this one, too.

CHAPTER THREE

I've barely gotten a word in during the past half hour of our Buncha Punks Skype call, but I hardly care.

I miss my friends so much. My laptop screen is divided into six squares, my own face in the bottom right corner, the other five occupied by my friends, best known as the band Post Humorous. Even when they tour, they don't miss our weekly chat, and I appreciate that, even if seeing them all cuddled up on one screen while I'm all alone on mine makes me jealous—and guilty for feeling jealous. It's hard being on the outside of all their stories when I was once a key actor in them. I romanticized moving away from home, going somewhere no one knew me, somewhere I could find myself and chase my dreams. No one warns you how lonely choosing yourself can be. These weekly Skype calls are a lifeline back to myself.

Charlie is in the top left corner. With his soft brown hair and even softer brown eyes, he's all boy-next-door charm and "aw, shucks" attitude. I've known him since I was in diapers. There were two loose boards in the fence that separated his backyard from mine (literally the boy next door). After his mom caught us sneaking back and forth, squeezing through the slats, my dad put in a gate. Charlie's house is as much home to me as my actual home.

In the bottom left of the screen is Reid, who is probably the only person on this call who has said fewer words than me. The curtain of his straight dark hair hides his face as he cleans under his nails with a guitar pick. All of my friends bring something different—but equally necessary—to the table. Reid is the one you go to when you want to angst it out without actually talking about anything. Reid and Charlie make up Post Humorous's rhythm section, bass and drums, respectively. While they may be the quietest members of the band, they're its heartbeat.

In the middle of the screen, exactly where they'd want to be: Brooklyn and Drew. B has foregone her usual armor of impeccable makeup today, the Chu family freckles on full display, her thick mane of black hair in a topknot that's more chic than messy—an art I've never quite mastered. Brooklyn is the only person who could rival Charlie for the title of my best friend. We met when we were sixteen, at a show. I'd seen her in the corner of the venue, looking slightly out of place in her too-colorful clothes, but when she got on stage to sing a duet with one of the bands...there was no question where she belonged. I begged the boys to record a song with her. After years of playing incrementally larger venues, that single blew up, playing on all the local Boston radio stations. She didn't officially join the band until after she finished college, but there's no doubt she's an integral part of the group, because:

Drew. Our frontman and lead guitarist. With dark brown hair whose life mission is to defy gravity, arching over his head in clashing waves, and eyes the gray of the ocean before a storm, he's the quintessential sexpot frontman. He could have chemistry with a wall, and his onstage presence with Brooklyn is mesmerizing. Their will-they-won't-they energy is no doubt responsible for a large part of their fan base. The two of them are currently finishing each other's sentences as they recount a story we've rehashed a million times, becoming more and more embellished with each retelling.

The only person who can match their energy is Tyler. Sweet, golden-retriever-in-human-form Tyler, our keyboardist. His hair is held in a perfect swoop across his forehead with an elastic headband, and between the thick blond hair, dark blue eyes, and chin dimple, we could easily pass as twins.

"I didn't suck his dick *at* Disney World," Tyler interjects. "It was the Disney *hotel* our fans got us a discount at so we didn't have to sleep in the van with Reid's smelly ass."

"That was Drew," Reid drawls. He's now painting his nails with black polish, seemingly distracted, but he provides his expected response on cue, nonetheless. "You're the one who insisted on Indian food, knowing damn well—"

I look to Charlie because my spidey sense tells me he's looking at me. We share an eye roll while our friends bicker.

"I saw that," Brooklyn chastises us. "And while we're taking a walk down memory lane, anything you'd care to share with the class, Sloane Marie?" She fixes me with a glare through the screen. I cannot believe she middle-named me.

For the first time since we all logged on, everyone in the chat shuts up, waiting for her to continue. She was born to be a leading lady.

"No," I say simply. Turning away from the laptop camera, I dump my ramen packet into the now-boiling pot of water.

"Wait, what happened?" Tyler stage-whispers. "What did Sloane do? Sloane never does anything."

"Hey," I call over my shoulder. "I do things."

"Yeah, like ditch us and move across the country," Drew says with a pout.

I splutter. "Brooklyn lives in LA! I'm so much closer now," I remind him. "But if you don't wanna crash at my place next time you tour—"

"Ignore Drew," Charlie insists. "That's just his way of saying he misses you."

I flash them all a smile as I stir my ramen. "I miss you all, too." *So much*, I don't say, my heart squeezing.

"Okay, but what's the drama?" Tyler cuts in, done with this heartfelt moment. I love him, but damn it. I know exactly what Brooklyn is going to grill me for, and frankly, I'm surprised it's taken this long. The article came out a week ago.

Brooklyn clears her throat dramatically, holding up the latest volume of *Alternative Press*. "Artists to Watch, curated by Sloane Donavan." She pauses as all the guys whoop and cheer for me, my name in print for the first time ever. She rattles off the first few bands, omitting the short blurbs I wrote for each one, until—"Hollow Graves. Ohio has a long history of producing household names, and under the tutelage of *Final fucking Revelations*, with their heavy riffs and Hudson Chase's powerhouse vocals, Hollow Graves is primed to be the next big thing out of Cleveland."

I clear my throat. "I didn't say 'fucking.'"

Brooklyn purses her lips.

"So what?" Charlie shrugs, twirling a pen between his fingers like a drumstick. "We know half the bands in Boston. It's not weird they'd know the Final guys."

"True, but I find the choice to name-drop her ex interesting."

Reid snorts. His half-lidded eyes always give the impression that he's perma-stoned, but the slight redness around his green irises gives away that he definitely smoked before this call. "B, if I was working with Dax or any of the Final guys, I'd want everyone to know."

"So, you're not trying to bat signal to Dax that you're living in his city now?"

Broth sloshes everywhere as I pour my ramen into a bowl. I delay responding by cleaning up my mess. "Dax already knows I'm here. I saw him at Battle of the Bands a few weeks ago."

It sounds like the words were literally strangled out of me. Weirder yet is the complete silence that meets them. I can count on one hand the number of times I've seen this group speechless. They always have words. And feelings. Or worse: feelings words.

I tap my laptop trackpad. "Did you guys freeze? Is my Wi-Fi...?"

"We're here," Brooklyn says, ruffling her pile of jet-black hair in disbelief. Her eyes flutter shut as she takes a controlled breath, lashes casting a shadow on her freckled cheeks. "You've been holding this back for *weeks*?" She screeches the last word, glaring daggers at me through the screen. "Details, Sloane! What happened when you saw him?"

"The usual," I say, shoving noodles into my mouth. "I feigned indifference. Showed zero emotion whatsoever."

"Yeah, that checks," Drew mutters, running a hand through his already mussed hair.

"Smart," Reid says, endorsing me.

Brooklyn waves off their commentary. "Did he see you? Did you talk?"

"We were trapped in a sound booth together."

Tyler makes a noise of intrigue. "Like, in a sexy way?" He bites down on his fist, eyes rolling back into his skull in feigned orgasmic ecstasy.

I snort into my ramen, broth flying everywhere and speckling the counter. "No. In a terse-silence kind of way. We said hi and I'm pretty sure that's it."

Brooklyn sighs. "You're a travesty, you know that?"

"I'm aware." I grin goofily, a curly noodle hanging from the corner of my mouth.

"Do you think you'll see him again?" Charlie asks cautiously. I did my best to hide how much the breakup with Dax fucked me up, but as my neighbor, Charlie was definitely privy to how many nights I spent sitting on my roof, crying and blasting My Chemical Romance's "I'm Not Okay (I Promise)" on repeat through my bedroom window. He had the decency not to comment on my lack of subtly in song choices, but a few nights in, he did note, *It sounds really good through a wall.*

I avert my gaze, dragging my spoon through the bowl of broth as I consider, as if I haven't been wondering the exact same thing. "I'm writing a bigger article on Hollow Graves, so I might run into Dax again, depending on how hands-on he is."

"And are you hoping to get 'hands-on' with him again, or...?" Tyler asks with a not-so-innocent affectation.

I choke on my noodles as Charlie utters, *"Jesus, Tyler."* As I struggle to dislodge ramen from my windpipe, I gesture for them to move on. "I'm done being the main character of this chat. What's the plan for Halloween—y'all still coming out for the *AP* show on the thirtieth?"

Brooklyn arches a brow. "Anyone we know on the bill?"

I sigh heavily. "Yes, Final Revelations is headlining. Dax will be there."

On the screen, Brooklyn presses her lips into a thin line. She'll be texting me as soon as this call is over, wanting to hash this out further. Thankfully, she knows I won't want to do that on a call with all the guys, and heartily embraces the subject change: them coming out to see me for *AP*'s Halloween show. But because she's my best friend and because I'm hers, I know her next word is intentional:

"Okay," she says simply, a dull affectation to her tone so unlike her usual chipper one. It's a message for me and me alone, the guys oblivious, happily chatting about their plans to road-trip out in the van rather than fly. I barely hear them, knowing Brooklyn will email me all the important trip details in the form of a color-coded Excel spreadsheet. It's her subliminal message that has my full attention, echoing hollowly in my brain.

Okay.

Three years ago, at Punkapalooza. The memory I do my best to bury, the one that haunts me, nonetheless. I've just told Dax we should end things, and I'm waiting for him to say something—*anything.* The muscle in his jaw twitches like he's preparing to fight me on it, but when he opens his mouth, all he says is *Okay.* I wait for him to say more. He doesn't. I want to provoke him until he does fight me on it. I don't. Because what's the point? I'm going back to finish my degree, and Dax is continuing on tour. I'm not going to follow him around and we both know it, and yet…

And yet.

That haunts me, too. Because it wasn't just the distance that scared me. The distance is the excuse I tell everyone, knowing it gives little room for rebuttal. Mostly, I was just scared. Dax was like gravity. I feared that if we tried to make it work long-distance, the gravity would win out. That I wouldn't finish my degree, that I'd follow Dax around on tour, settle down in Cleveland, get a job at *AP*, and never know if I was doing it for me or for him.

It's why my mom left. I spent my angsty teenage years hating her, but the older I get, I understand her more and more. And I hate her for that, too. She married my dad at nineteen, had my oldest brother, Nate, at twenty. Her entire identity was being a mother, no life outside of us. She put her dreams on hold to settle down with my dad, and it slowly ate at her until she felt she had no other choice but to leave, to find herself.

I rub the tiny scar on my ring finger. My brothers all have an identical one. When Nate dragged his heartbroken self home from college—his third-choice school, having chosen to follow the girlfriend that dumped him two weeks into the first semester—we crawled onto the roof outside my bedroom window and made a blood pact: to never repeat our mother's mistake, to never give up our own dreams for another person, because those people can leave. I was ten. I didn't fully understand the promise I was making, but I cut my ring finger and spilled a few drops on the scratchy roof tiles anyway. And for the next eleven years, I kept my promise, made big plans for myself, and couldn't imagine ever giving up on them for a boy.

And yet...

I chose my dream that summer, and that dream later blew up in my face. And now, I'm back in the same city as the love I left behind. A more romantic person than I might call it fate. *Brooklyn* would call it fate. Instead, she's reminding me of how, with two syllables, that relationship ended. We spent months overanalyzing that one word, the monotone way in which he said it, picking apart those measly four letters for any hidden meaning. Three years ago, she'd championed me and Dax, how good he was for me. Both of us have changed since that summer—*because* of that summer. I don't regret Dax or anything we did, but I can't have rose-colored glasses about it. Not right now. Not when I know, without a doubt, I will run into him again. Soon. Possibly this week.

The noodles in my stomach turn leaden. I talk a big game, pretend like it doesn't bother me, that I don't feel anything anymore. But the truth is, Dax is the only person who has ever made me feel, well, anything. Discovering I could feel those things was important to me, special. How do you hold all of the good inside the same heart they shattered?

⚡ CHAPTER FOUR ⚡

I see Dax again sooner than I thought.

I've been in and out of the studio with Hollow Graves the past few days, interviewing them for their article. Despite my wariness that I'd run into Dax, the closest I've come to any member of Final Revelations is the near-reverent way each member of Hollow Graves speaks about them. The lack of run-in has lulled me into a sense of security. Maybe Dax and I can orbit the same scene without actually colliding as often as I'd feared.

When the studio's receptionist kicks Hudson and I out at closing time and asks us to leave through the side door, I wish she'd mentioned who else she'd just sent that way.

As I push open the alley door, October night air rushes in and steals my warmth and I regret leaving my jacket in my car. In the alleyway, the haze of cigarette smoke greets us, hanging like a cloud over—of fucking course—the entirety of Final Revelations. My gaze skips over Dax, and I drink in the sight of Marcus, Jonah, Cain, and Barrett—an absolute bear of a man who I have to actively resist the urge to hug.

Barrett's face lights up as he exhales a stream of smoke. "Boston, is that you?"

I can't help but return the smile, my feet dragging me over to him automatically. He squishes me into his side in a one-armed hug, his '80s rocker curls tickling my cheek. "It's me." I hope the thickness in my voice is disguised by its natural raspiness and my face being half-smothered in Barrett's massive barrel of a chest. God, when was the last time someone hugged me?

"Thought you were in LA," Jonah asks in his nonasking way. In his knit sweater, he looks more like he just clocked out of a day at the office than a guy in a metal band. "At *Beatoff*."

"*Offbeat*?" I correct.

"That's what I said."

I purse my lips to keep from laughing. The band's beef with *Offbeat* predates my internship by a few years. "I was in San Fran, but not anymore. I'm freelancing for *AP*." I moved to California a year after Dax and I broke up, so I have no idea how Jonah knows that.

"You live here now," Jonah clarifies, shaking his shaggy black hair out of his face as he exhales a cloud of cigarette smoke.

I nod, and I'm acutely aware that while Dax and I were ignoring each other last time, he's definitely paying attention now. I can't bring myself to look at him, but his gaze bores into the side of my face. I'm not entirely sure why. Robb told him all this at Battle of the Bands last month when he asked, though *why* he asked, I don't know.

"Anyway," I say slowly. I peel myself out from where Barrett still has his arm around my shoulders, hitching my backpack higher. "Good to see—" The words get stuck in my throat, my eyes bouncing between all of them and then back to the studio door. The reason they're all here hits me over the head like a brick. "You're recording." The words come out of me on a breathy exhale, and I'm unable to stop the grin spreading across my face.

None of them confirm or deny anything. Of course they don't.

Final Revelations recording a new album is *massive* news. Five albums and over a decade in, it's been years since they last toured, even longer since they released anything new.

"I'm not asking for an interview—I know that's a nonstarter. Just...whenever you're ready to announce"—I begin backing out of their little circle so they can't immediately shoot me down—"let me have the exclusive that there's gonna be a new album. That would be huge for me." I'm not really sure what weird movements I'm making with my hands, but I'm trying to convey how *no pressure* I'm being despite how intensely I want this. "Please."

I aim the last word at Dax in a Hail Mary. If there's even a shred of affection for me left in him—

Our gazes meet for the first time in three years. The alley's atmosphere shifts, every particle separating me from him crackling with electricity. Overhead, the sky thunders out a promise and a warning. Even in the low lighting, I can see on his stupidly beautiful face that he feels it, too. He glances away, a muscle at the corner of his jaw twitching, like he's forcing himself not to speak—or smile.

Tearing my gaze off of him is like prying two magnets apart. To the group at large, I say, "Think about it?" I back up until I'm out of the halo of light over the alley door, safely wrapped in darkness. Once my back is turned, a dopey grin spreads across my face. If I can snag that exclusive, it might not be enough to make *AP* hire me full-time, but it would be a huge step toward getting that offer.

"Sloane!"

I turn, disappointed to find that it's Hudson and not Final Revelations chasing after me. I really need to hedge my expectations when it comes to them. They don't need the press—need *me*—and they know it. I need to know it, too.

I rub the scar on my ring finger subconsciously. It was a long shot, but at least I tried.

"Walk you to your car?" Hudson offers. Before I can tell him that's not necessary—it's dark out, but it's only seven o'clock and there are plenty of people milling around—he continues. "I can talk to them for you."

I shrug. "We both know they won't do anything they don't want."

Hudson laughs under his breath. "True." He glances at me sidelong, and I don't know how I know it's coming, but I do.

I want the ground to open up and swallow me whole. Our interview went really well, and it wouldn't be the first time a subject confused Actual Conversation with flirting. And now... He's going to ask me out. But I know how this goes. We go on one date—maybe two if they're feeling chivalrous—before they try to sleep with me. They're going for a home run, and I haven't even decided if I want to step up to the plate.

Before Dax, I was half-convinced I was asexual, that I simply didn't have those feelings like other people. Now I know that I do—it just takes time, trust, and attraction, three things that rarely collide for me. Normally, I'm grateful my demisexuality weeds out the ones who only wanted one thing from me. Other times, I resent it, wishing my body's wants could be fulfilled without my heart and brain needing to be so involved. I *want* to be wanted, but this isn't some video game I can speed run my way through. It's as frustrating for me as it is for them. They call me a tease. Say I'm too much effort. They leave. I let them. It's never worth the headache.

Well... once. It was worth it once.

"Hey," he says softly, a hand at my elbow to stop my quick gait, as if I can run away from the question. "Maybe this is weird, considering your history with Dax and all, but would you... would you wanna grab a drink sometime? Off the record," he adds with a cheeky smile. When I don't immediately answer, he continues. "It's just, I've enjoyed talking to you this week. You're not like other girls I know, and I just—" He shrugs, and I know he genuinely thinks he's flattering me when he says *not like other girls*.

I force myself not to cringe, not to tell him that I've got mommy issues up to my eyeballs, and as such, I'm literally the amalgamation of every woman I've ever thought was cool.

"Hudson…" I have no idea how to gently let him down, how to explain that he enjoyed our conversation because that's my job, that asking out someone who's writing an article about you puts that person in an impossible position, that we've spent the past few days talking about him, that *that* is what he likes. He doesn't actually know anything about me.

My attention snags on approaching footsteps behind us, and instinctively, I take a step back so we're not blocking the walkway.

Hudson grumbles under his breath as Dax slows to a stop in between where Hudson and I now stand on opposite sides of the sidewalk. In the low light of the streetlamp, Dax's gaze bounces from Hudson to…not to me, more like everything *but* me, the negative space of me. "What?" Dax grunts.

Hudson shakes his head, glancing over at me. I have no idea what expression I'm making, but it must convey a lot, because he presses his lips together and nods. "Have a good night, Sloane."

I nod back. "Thanks, uh, I'll be in touch about the article." Mentally, I pat myself on the back for salvaging this awkwardness into something remotely professional.

Hudson is still nodding, each of us reduced to bobbleheads with how uncomfortable this has become. He turns and waves over his shoulder as he walks back in the direction of the studio.

Dax raises his eyebrows at Hudson's retreating form, saying nothing—looking at nothing—when he turns and gestures for me to lead the way.

Right—I was going to my car. "Are you just trying to get me alone to murder me?"

"Only one way to find out," he says dryly.

I press my lips together to keep from smiling. He's not supposed to still be funny after we've broken up. And what? We haven't spoken in three years, but we're supposed to banter like old friends?

Are we friends? I have no idea. I can feel his gravity drawing me in, but it's not the same quiet tether that bonded us three years ago. This magnetic pull is Stage Dax, the version of him that crowds can't look away from. The real Dax, the one most people never meet, hopes you never look too close. I don't know how to act around this version of him, to be on the other side of his walls when there was once a time I felt at home inside them.

I resume the trek to my car, but my legs refuse to take up their normally quick gait. Dax falls into step, matching my leisurely pace with no complaints, despite having an even longer stride than mine.

I glance at him sidelong as he tugs the zipper of his hoodie higher, and I shiver as we pass out of the warmth of the streetlamp.

I'm beginning to wonder if he's really going to ignore me the entire way to my car when he speaks.

"I didn't know you were freelance." Three years of no communication, and those are his first words to me? Saying hi doesn't count. But this? This question was premeditated, intentional. I just don't know why he cares. It's such an odd thing to comment on after everything.

"Yeah," I say simply. If he wants to talk to me, he's going to have to *talk*.

It takes him a moment to extrapolate, each slow step like he's buying time. "So, will you leave—if they don't hire you full-time?"

"Don't sound so hopeful," I grouse.

He barks out a laugh, the sound short and sharp, swallowed instantly by the night.

Does he hope I leave? I don't know how to interpret his laugh. I can't help but search for clues that this is as weird for him as it is for me. Just a hint, and then I'll let this go. I need some hair of the dog for this heart hangover I didn't know I had. I have no interest in rekindling anything. The part of me that loved him feels like an entirely separate person, a side of me that bloomed for him and only him and hasn't reared its head since. *And yet...*

I wrap my arms around myself, thinking longingly of the jacket I forgot in the back seat of my Jeep.

Somehow, without looking at me, Dax registers my chill, shrugging out of his jacket and holding it out to me.

"I'm fine," I lie.

"California spoiled you."

I purse my lips stubbornly. It's barely cold and yet I'm shaking like a leaf. It's embarrassing how quickly San Francisco stole my Boston-born imperviousness to cold.

"Take the jacket, Donavan. You're fucking shivering."

The wind picks up, rushing along the sidewalk and stealing the last of my warmth. I grit my teeth together before sliding my arms through the proffered jacket and zipping it all the way up.

"Thank you," I say stiffly, melting into his warmth still clinging to the jacket. I should be relieved things are becoming marginally less awkward with us, but I don't feel relief at all. I feel *undone*, the ghost of what we had like a phantom limb.

We walk in silence for a bit, resuming our pace that is far more leisurely than is natural for two tall people. I don't know who set the pace this time—him or me.

"Do you miss it—California?" Dax says unexpectedly, cutting through my gross overanalysis of our gait.

I shrug. "I miss the sunshine, but I missed being somewhere with seasons more."

I'm trying and failing to follow his train of thought. At least we're talking this time—even if it is painfully contrived, a stark contrast to our easy conversations three years ago.

Realization dawns on me. This is *exactly* like three years ago. When we first met, our stilted conversations were so at odds with our complete inability to stay away from each other. Brooklyn said we were like alley cats, circling each other, sizing each other up. I have no idea what we're dancing around this time, but I know this game. Pulling each other closer with one hand while pushing each other away with the other. Dax ignoring me at Battle of the Bands. *Push.* Dax walking with me to my car. *Pull.* The guarded questions. *Push.* Giving me his jacket. *Pull.*

"Did I accidentally interrupt back there—with Hudson?"

I snort. "No. Well, yes." I time my words to land as we pass beneath another circle of light to catch his reaction. "He asked me out."

The timing was unnecessary because Dax doesn't react at all, his face completely blank. This Dax is so unlike the Dax I fell in love with three years ago, the man whose expressions I knew like a well-loved book, with pages dog-eared for my favorite ones.

"I said no," I tell him.

He turns to me as we slow to a stop at the crosswalk, still looking around me and not really *at* me. "You should, if you want."

Push.

He's so goddamned neutral about it that I want to shake him. How is he so nonchalant when I'm *all* chalant?

"I wasn't asking your permission."

The corners of his mouth turn up slightly at the annoyance in my tone. I don't know what it says about us that we always revert back to this needling, that we *enjoy* it. "Hudson did—ask for permission." His voice is raw, like every word he gives me is half-thawed, wrecking him on the way out.

My brows shoot up toward my hairline in surprise. "And you gave it?" It's the wrong question to ask. I don't *belong* to Dax. No one has to get his damned blessing, but it blurts out of me anyway.

For the second time today, he looks at me.

It's dark, so I can't wholly make out his eyes beneath the shadow of his brow, but that magnetic pull is back. I can feel his attention as it slides from my head to my toes and back up, goose bumps following in the wake of his gaze. "What else was I supposed to say?" he asks softly, his voice like smoke. "That you're mine, and no one else can touch you?"

It should sound possessive and have me rolling my eyes, but the way he says it is like silk, wrapping around me and melting the tension from my limbs. It's everything I wanted him to say three years ago, to fight for me, for us, because I was too damn scared to.

His eyes trace every curve of my face, memorizing every lash, every freckle. The way he's drinking me in with this tortured expression is making it hard for me to breathe.

Pull.

I wish I were wearing something better than yesterday's skinny jeans, [redacted] days ago's hair, last night's mascara, and my high school Chucks that can no longer be called white.

I can't tear my gaze from his, fearing that once I do, that wall of his will go back up. I'm equal parts desperate for it to go back up and ready to shred it to pieces. I refuse to break our stare-down—not even when the wind picks up a strand of my hair and swats me in the eye with it.

Before I can react, Dax is there, his fingers brushing my brow, guiding the lock of hair out of my face and gently tucking it behind my ear. His knuckle ghosts along my jawline in a gesture that I'm not sure was intentional. For a moment, I'm hurtled backward through time, to when that searing touch would have ended with my chin pinched between his thumb and forefinger, guiding my mouth to his.

I swear his gaze drops to my lips for a fraction of a second, as if he's remembering, too.

Pull, pull, pull.

The crosswalk beeps in warning as the signal turns to a flashing red hand.

I jump, crossing the street quickly, chastising myself for nearly missing the chance because I was getting moon-eyed over my ex giving me an iota of attention. With a heavy exhale, I let it go. I've spent enough time overanalyzing this man. It would've been nice to have some indication about how he feels—felt?—but for what? Dax is a part of my past, and now my present, but I have no delusions about a future with him. My thumb rubs absentmindedly over the smooth scar on my ring finger. I will not, under any circumstances, catch feelings for Dax Nakamura. Again.

Despite our hurried crossing of the street, our pace slows once we're on the other side. Any slower and we'd literally be dragging our feet.

Pull.

I stuff my hands into the jacket's pockets, and a whiff of Dax's piney scent wafts up to me on the chilly October air. I definitely don't take a second hit of it off my shoulder on the pretext of brushing away a stray hair. "So, you're recording again?" I ask to break the silence.

"That's off the record." He doesn't say it unkindly; he just says it like fact.

Push.

"Fine," I huff, not bothering to hide my disappointment. Breaking that news would've been a massive get for me. I knew it was a long shot, so I shouldn't be disappointed, and yet... "But if you ever wanted to go on the record—"

He glances at me sidelong, giving me a nearly imperceptible noncommittal shake of the head. He's so *Dax* in this moment that I nearly laugh. Not my Dax, but the one everyone knows. He's such a little shit when he doesn't want you to get too close.

I nudge his side with my elbow, and the gesture is both overly familiar and foreign all at once, like a memory passed down from a previous life.

He elbows me back with a barely repressed grin. I prod him again, and he feigns falling like I've shoved him. I scoff under my breath. Drama king, that one. He snaps back to my side like a magnet, the shadow of his dimple winking at me.

I sigh wistfully, letting the exclusive go for now, changing tactics. "The mentoring, like with Hollow Graves—do you do that a lot?"

"We try to," he says. "Mentor," he adds, like he's weighing every word on his tongue slowly before voicing it. For someone who screams into a microphone for a living, he's incredibly soft-spoken. But it's all there if you know how to listen for it. Even after all this time, I'm still dialed in to him like a favorite radio station. "We wouldn't be where we are if other bands hadn't helped us. It seems like the least we can do to pay it forward."

"That was a lot of words all at once. Are you okay?"

Dax snorts, his eyes cutting to me again. Even in the dark, I can feel the warmth in his wry gaze. This is our game, an old dance we never forgot the steps to. We poke, we prod, we push each other.

He opens his mouth to speak, and I cut him off. "Off the record, I know."

The corner of his mouth pinches, his cheek dimpling. "You can use me."

I raise my eyebrows at him, but he's not looking at me, his attention fixed straight ahead.

"Yeah?" I ask in disbelief.

"Yeah." He says the word like it carries the weight of the universe.

I want to ask him more. And try as I might to pretend, it's not *just* for the article. But he's already given me more than he's given any journalist in eight years, so I don't want to push it. I might have been able to once, but now... We're not there. I don't know if we'll ever be there again, and the thought breaks my heart a little bit all over again.

That summer, once we got past our initial push/pull phase, we talked nonstop. It was one of my favorite things about Dax. I got to start with a blank page. I'd never had that before. I'd always been known as "one of the Donavan kids" or "Charlie's/Brooklyn's friend." For the first time, with him, I got to be Sloane—just Sloane. An unknown. I spend most of my time telling other people's stories, and it wasn't until I met Dax that I realized how much I wanted to tell my own.

We reach the intersection where I parked, and my steps slow to a stop. I can't help but feel like we didn't finish our conversation.

I have nothing left to say.

Push.

I have everything left to say.

Pull.

Dax will always feel like unfinished business. I just have to get used to it.

I jerk my head toward my old Jeep, its white paint rusting at the seams from too many Boston winters. "This is me."

He nods, taking a step back and gesturing to the other side of the intersection. "I'm that way."

I wonder if that's the truth or a lie. I hate that I want it to be a lie, that I want him to have gone out of his way to spend time with me—stilted conversation or not.

"Well—" I wave awkwardly, taking a half step back.

"Sloane," he calls, his gravelly voice wrapping around my name like a river rock worn down from years trapped in the undertow.

He closes the distance between us easily. He closes nearly *all* of the distance between us. My posture straightens as if struck by lightning. There's no way he doesn't clock the way my breath hitches at his proximity.

I tip my head back to meet his gaze, trying desperately to decipher his rapidly shifting moods. Backlit by the streetlamp, his face is all harsh angles and shadows, his expression impossible to make out.

When his hand comes between us, for a second I think he's going to grab my chin, tip it up, aligning our mouths the way he used to. But he doesn't. What he does instead is somehow worse.

Pinching the jacket zipper between his fingers, he slowly drags it down, his knuckle grazing along my front. He doesn't break eye contact the entire time, like now that he's given himself permission to look, he's going to fucking *look*. It's a struggle to keep my face impassive, hoping against hope he can't hear the thundering of my heartbeat.

Pull.

The zipper snags at the bottom, and he gives it a tug so the two sides of the jacket fall open. The motion rocks me forward, our fronts almost colliding. I catch myself, resuming the minuscule distance between us. This is just our game.

Push.

His fingertips graze my collarbone, an indulgence before his hands slide under the jacket and ease it back off my shoulders. The movement brings us closer, his front brushing mine. The friction of my T-shirt against my skin is more erotic than it has any right to be. It seems I'm not alone in that, his Adam's apple bobbing as he swallows thickly. It's not the cold giving me goose bumps as he guides the jacket down my arms, his touch like a match dragged too slowly along a strike pad to ignite, but the promise is there.

Dax standing this close to me, teasing me, pushing my buttons... My body's response to him is Pavlovian, as are the words that slip out unbidden: "I cannot fucking stand you."

It's what I said to him before he kissed me for the first time. It's what I said to him again and again that summer as he infuriated and enthralled me in equal measure. He memorized the script of our first kiss word for word the same way I did, because those rare moments when real life is better than any movie—you don't forget that. It's tattooed on your heart.

I cannot fucking stand you.
Stop flirting with me.
I would never.
That would be disgusting.
Completely abhorrent.
And then he'd shut me up with a kiss.

Dax's face is still concealed in shadow, and it's unfair because I'm certain an embarrassing, bald hope is illuminated on mine. I can't help it.

He dips his head, his lips a ghost along my scalp. "I know," he breathes. "Me, too." With that, he steps back, a grin and that damned dimple hitting me like a blow to the chest. "See you around, Donavan." He turns and jogs across the street.

He doesn't say his line.

He... forgot.

Push.

Whatever game we were playing, it wasn't the Getting Back Together Game, and I didn't just tip my hand; I spilled it all over the table. It would be tragic if it weren't so goddamn mortifying.

A slew of curses rush to the tip of my tongue, and I suck them all back in, reveling in their bitter taste. Nothing can happen with Dax, because of the very thing he's doing right now: walking away. Like it's nothing.

Push, push, push.

He passes beneath a streetlamp, shrugging on his jacket and flicking the hood up before disappearing into the night, looking like a goddamned music video as I'm left standing here, alone and shivering.

I'm rooted to the spot, reeling, seething, half hoping he'll glance back.

He doesn't.

I loose a few of my withheld curses as I let myself into my car and tug the hoodie from my back seat over my head. It's the one I stole from Dax three years ago, the one that no longer smells like him. I hope my scent clings to the jacket I borrowed tonight. Then I hope it fades, haunting him the way he haunts me.

CHAPTER FIVE

To get home, I have to drive back the way I just walked.

As I pass by the studio, I spy someone slipping into a car parked at the mouth of the alleyway.

Dax.

He went out of his way to walk with me.

That motherfucker.

Pull.

⚡ CHAPTER SIX ⚡

"How'd your presentation go?"

Robb makes a noise of malcontent.

"No," Denise gasps, abandoning picking at her green hair's split ends. "How could John say no? A Modern Classics vertical would be brilliant."

Robb sighs. "He didn't say 'no,' not really, just 'not yet.' It's 'under consideration.'"

I lean back slightly, out of the danger zone of her overzealous finger quotes, my shoulder squeaking against the glass conference room wall. The Monday pitch meeting ended half an hour ago, but as the only women on staff, Robb, Denise, and I always congregate in the hallway after to bemoan whatever pitches we didn't get approved and celebrate each other's wins. Before I can press Robb for details, the door to John's office opens.

"Donavan, a word, please," he barks.

I straighten automatically, feeling like a kid about to be grounded. Mentally, I run back everything I could have done wrong, ever.

I exchange a nervous look with Robb, who shrugs in a way that says, *Your guess is as good as mine.*

Crossing over to John's office, I poke my head in trepidatiously.

"Come in," he calls, already settled back behind his desk. "Take a seat. Shut the door. Not necessarily in that order."

I close the door behind me, but with the glass walls, it does little to provide privacy beyond muffling our voices to passersby.

Settling into the leather chair that, to my horror, squeaks like a fart as I sink into it, I suppress a childish giggle as John surveys me over his steepled fingers.

"Donavan," he says. I think he intends it to sound fond, almost paternal, but the alarm bells in my head remind me this is how my father used to sit us all down before extracting truths out of his five half-feral children, who might or might not have been colluding on a lie about what really broke the oven door / couch / bunk beds / you name it.

I smile weakly at him, unsure what the purpose of this meeting is. I scan his face for clues, but I've never really been able to figure John out. With his salt-and-pepper hair, he's like the George Clooney of music journalism. His light blue eyes are always twinkling with a scintillating story that he'll tell a little too close to your face, enveloping you in his ever-present cigarette-and-coffee aura.

John shakes his head at me, and I have no clue why.

"What do you have on your plate right now?" he asks, taking a sip of his coffee with one hand and clicking his computer mouse with the other.

Am I being fired?

I open my mouth to speak but no sound comes out, panic throttling my vocal cords. Swallowing, I take a deep breath before trying again. "Just the next Artists to Watch piece," I admit pathetically. He could totally be firing me. Robb could take back that recurring piece, and I could be let go, my five-year plan blown to smithereens. Before my thoughts can spiral further, John speaks.

"Good," he says with a grin. Surely that's not an *I'm firing you* grin. "Your Hollow Graves piece is doing really well online," he tells me.

I know this already. It was my first big online article with *AP*, and I check its stats every morning from bed in a way that I'm entirely aware is unhealthy. I feel bad for Hudson, his band's article completely overshadowed by who I quoted, the internet abuzz with conspiracy theories about why Dax has come out of the woodwork, most of them correctly deducing the band would be announcing something soon.

"Good work getting that Dax Nakamura quote," John says with a slight widening of his eyes. "I thought I was hallucinating when I read your draft."

I nod, forcing a small smile. Not hallucinating hard enough that he didn't eviscerate my draft with his red pen. His repeated note of *Voice?* over and over in the margins still haunts me, affirming my fears that my previous mentor beat it out of me.

"More importantly," he continues, entirely comfortable being the only one really speaking in this conversation, "you impressed Hollow Graves' manager. Do you know who else they manage?"

"Final Revelations, Nocturnal Creatures, Undead Kings," I rattle off, unsure where this is going.

John leans across the desk, light blue eyes sparkling as he nods slowly. He beckons me closer with one finger, like he's about to let me in on some big secret. This man is dramatic as all hell, a true storyteller.

"Final Revelations," he echoes in an awestruck whisper, his coffee-cigarette breath clouding my senses.

"I don't understand," I whisper back.

John's Cheshire grin widens. "They want you to write another article."

I blink, still confused. "About...who?"

John slaps his hands against the desk like he's playing the drums, an outlet for the boyish cheer now crinkling the corners of his eyes. "About Final Revelations."

I understand what he's saying, in theory. I know the words, but what he *means* doesn't make sense. Final Revelations doesn't speak to the press. They haven't in eight years. There's no way Dax agreed to this, much less agreed to do it with *me*. A quote is one thing, but a whole article?

John's face falls. "Donavan," he says, clearly disappointed by my lack of reaction. "This is the article of the fucking decade. Why are you not jumping out of your chair? Are you in shock?"

My jaw moves, an attempt to speak is made, but I have no idea what to say.

"She's in shock," John says to what I presume is his ever-present invisible audience. Then his reporter instincts must kick in, his eyes narrowing. "Or is it something else? Something I should know?"

His gaze pins me to the spot. If this is really happening, if Final Revelations wants to do their first interview in eight years, then our history is absolutely a conflict of interest. Right? Or is there a statute of limitations on such things? Does three years of silence undo six weeks of Technicolor? An article of this caliber was in my five-year plan, not my five-month plan. I'd be a fool to pass this up.

The memory of Dax walking me to my car replays in my mind, the false stops and starts as we attempted to make conversation. Conflict of interest aside, I'm not convinced we *could* pull this off. I should say no. John should give the article to Robb. She's been here longer, is friends with the Final guys, could write this in her sleep. The words get stuck in my throat.

"Could I think about it?" I manage.

John looks like his eyes are going to bulge out of his head. "Is there," he says slowly, emphasizing each word, "something I should know?"

I'm hurtled back in time to being sat down by my father at the kitchen table, the shattered oven door over his shoulder. Him asking me if the story my brothers and I all told about the barstool falling over and shattering the glass was true, how I wiped the memory of Bryce and Nate playing WWE with the folding chair, the oven door a casualty of their animated wrestling match. I take all my memories of Dax from that summer, the box I've kept them in, and shove them inside another box, and another, like the Christmas prank my brothers pull on my dad every year. My face impassively blank, I tell John the same thing I told my dad about the oven door, the basement couch, and the bunk beds' suspiciously early demise. "No. Nothing you need to know."

John's eyes flick over me inscrutably, and I shrug. I'm perhaps a bit too good at lying after all my brothers' shenanigans. "I met them, the Final guys, a few years ago at Punkapalooza. They were nice." The trick to a convincing lie is to tell as much truth as you can. If I gave him the full truth, I'd only be confirming what everyone thinks of female music journalists anyway—that we're groupies, starfuckers, not actual journalists. "It's just...like you said, this will be huge. I wouldn't pitch you something I hadn't done my research on first. I want to make sure I'm the right person for this, that I have an angle, before I say yes. Otherwise, it should go to Robb. She knows them well."

John finally leans back, swiveling side to side slightly in his desk chair. "They said to give it to her if you passed," John admits, and I realize his inquisition was not spur-of-the-moment but intended to catch me off guard.

"That's fair," I say diplomatically.

"But they asked for you," John continues, suspicion still present in the downturn of his mouth.

"They believe in paying it forward," I say, referencing my Dax quote in the Hollow Graves piece, sending up a silent thanks to him for such a perfect cover. "I haven't spoken to them in years"—mostly true—"but maybe they just want to give me a leg up." True? I have no idea why they're doing this—*blindsiding me* with this—but I will be finding out as soon as I'm free of John's too-piercing gaze.

He hums noncommittally. "Well, it would be quite a leg up, to be sure." He folds his arms on the desk. "Full transparency? If we weren't on a hiring freeze right now, I'd have brought you on full-time already. Nailing this article is how I can make a case to get you on board. I believe you can do this," he says emphatically. I want to believe him. "But I'm not going to kick you out of the nest either. I want you and Robb to work together on this. She brought you in, vouched for you. The two of you work together well, and she's been wanting more responsibility. I think this would be a win-win for both of you."

Having Robb in my corner does instill a modicum of confidence in me. Especially after how John massacred my last piece. I blink, and his chicken-scratch notes of *Voice? Voice? Voice?* flash before my eyes. I shake my head on the pretext of getting my hair out of my face, and the red pen clears from my vision.

"I'll let you know before the end of the day," I promise. I need to get out of the office, the air suddenly heavy in my lungs, the walls too close and too glass, too visible.

John hesitates for a moment before conceding with a nod.

Gathering my bag from my feet, I slip out of the chair, pausing at the door when John speaks.

"Donavan," he calls softly. "Don't pass this up because you're afraid to be great."

I nod once, blinking rapidly at the pinpricks stinging my eyes. I'm not used to having a boss who believes in me. If I can pull off this article, perhaps I'll believe in me again, too.

♪ 🎵 🎶

The moment I'm clear of John's glass office doors, I'm tugging my phone from my backpack's side pocket, avoiding everyone's gazes so I don't get pulled into a conversation. I don't know that I breathe until I'm outside.

I scroll through my contacts until I find his name, my thumb bouncing between the dial and message buttons. The same ones I stared at for weeks after we broke up, never mustering the courage to use either, until eventually the urge dulled, too much time passing for my pride to allow me to use them. Those old feelings sharpen, intertwining with my insecurities about the opportunity being laid at my feet, then twist into anger. How dare he. I asked him for an exclusive outside the studio, and he said no. Now he changes his mind, dangling the interview of the century in front of my boss's face without talking to me about it first?

I slam the dial button, bringing the phone to my ear, pacing back and forth on the gravel parking lot. It rings and rings before going to voicemail. I don't bother listening to the message, hanging up and dialing again. After the first few redials, I realize I'm being slightly unhinged about this, but before I can hang up, the call connects.

"'Lo?"

My knees give out. It's definitely the gravel shifting underfoot and not my body's innate reaction to Dax's raspy morning voice.

"Hi," I breathe, all the anger and fight whisked away on the slight breeze.

"Someone better have died for you to be calling this early," he grumbles.

"It's nearly noon, Nakamura."

He grunts, and I can hear the rustling of sheets on the other side of the line. I don't *try* to picture him in bed, but it's hard not to when the memory is seared into my brain like graffiti I can't remove. Him turning to watch me across the pillows, the curls atop his head sticking out in every direction, his crooked septum piercing reflecting the early morning light, his tattoos dancing as his muscles ripple beneath them. My fingers twitch, longing to trace the lines of the Ghibli-esque dragon that wraps around his left arm, from the face on the back of his hand up to the tail at his shoulder, where it disappears into the tangled branches that form a canopy over the reaper at his back before joining the tree on his right side, the skulls nestled amongst the tree's roots, which wrap around his right hip and disappear into the dip there—

I'm grateful for the breeze that coasts along my now-overheated skin.

Banishing the image, I wrap my arm across my chest like armor. "Anything you want to ask me?"

A beat of silence, and then, "Oh, fuck." I am definitely not thinking about him saying those words in bed, in a very different context. "Sloane," he murmurs.

I close my eyes against him first-naming me. I'm so used to being called Donavan by everyone that it feels overly intimate.

"I was going to talk to you today—"

"Great," I say, cutting him off. "Meet me at Grindcore. You're paying."

A startled laugh crackles over the line. "Of course." A moan of pleasure escapes him as he stretches like a cat in sunshine, his morning habits still seared into my mind. The sense memory of it all has me sweating somewhere that's not my armpits. "I'll be there in fifteen."

I hang up without saying anything, because my tongue is in knots at how he can't help but be indecently sexy, even when half-awake. It doesn't bode well for my ability to professionally interview him.

Why am I even considering this?

But...how can I not?

CHAPTER SEVEN

While I wait for Dax, I claim one of the available tables, extracting my laptop from my dingy yellow JanSport and connect to Grindcore's Wi-Fi. Grindcore is the kind of coffee shop that could only exist next to somewhere like *AP*. It's less soothing hues of latte browns and acoustic guitar covers and more slap-tagged tables and industrial decor, its baristas more concerned with flipping the vinyl every four songs than expediting drinks.

The excuse I gave John for wanting to think it over isn't without merit. Messy history aside, I *love* this band, but I'm not sure where I'd even begin. What angle would make for the most interesting read? As a fan of their music, what would I want that's not already out there?

Opening a new browser window, I search "Final Revelations."

When the results populate, my heart aches. Below the expected links to the band's website and a YouTube video of their infamous screamo cover of Cher's "If I Could Turn Back Time" are a handful of articles popular enough to make the first page.

A *Billboard* link states, "Final Revelations' Frontman Makes a Fool of Himself, Band Somehow Redeems Reverie Fest Performance."

Then, Mike Song's *Offbeat* article from eight years ago—the one that launched my mentor's career and made Final Revelations stop talking to the press. My mouse hovers over it, but then I chicken out.

Toggling over to the images tab, my frown turns into a fond smile. There are the quintessential metal band photos, all five of them in incredibly dark settings, backlit. There are photos of them playing festivals, and seeing them in daylight feels wrong by comparison. There are a lot of photos of Dax—some lifted from his now-deleted MySpace, while others are grainy screenshots from the band's YouTube tour vlogs. There's a photo of a young Dax that catches my eye. He's squatting against a graffitied wall, grinning as he chews on his hoodie string. It takes me a moment to realize what's off about it: He doesn't have his dimple yet. His dimple that's not a dimple. I scroll farther down, my stomach in knots. If I were still at *Offbeat*, I know how Mike would ask me to write this piece, the gossip he'd want, that readers would devour, making my interview instantly more iconic than his. But because I know the Final Revelations guys, I know that's not what they'll want. What kind of article is John expecting? And can I deliver it?

Another photo catches my eye, another picture of Dax. He looks... Well, he looks incredibly fucking sexy. His chin is tilted up, and he's looking down at the camera with a cocky, lopsided smirk, dimple on full display. Next to him is a photo of Heath Ledger from *10 Things I Hate About You*, playing with a Bunsen burner fire. Someone captioned it "same energy." I laugh before toggling back over to the main page, Mike Song's article staring back at me. Mustering my courage, I click on it.

♪ ♫ ♬

[Excerpt from The Offbeat *archives]*

The Misrevelation of Final Revelations: Are We Already in the End Times?

By Mike Song for The Offbeat
November 17, 2002

The last time I saw Final Revelations live, they were a mess. If it weren't for lead guitarist and original frontman, Marcus Bailey, their Reverie Fest performance would've been a complete shit show, as their "replacement" lead singer went from sounding like a demon to battling his own.

Dakota "Dax" Nakamura was only seventeen years old when he replaced Marcus Bailey as lead vocalist for the explosively popular Final Revelations. Three years later, not only have Bailey's vocal cords recovered from the laryngitis that caused him to relinquish his spot as frontman, but they're covering for Nakamura. What was once the most promising band on the metal scene, poised to become one of the greats, is on the precipice of fumbling right before they can cement themselves as one of the rare metal bands to cross into mainstream popularity without alienating their original fan base.

But have they reached too high too fast?

After the band's performance at Reverie Fest during which Nakamura wandered around the stage seemingly unaware of where he was or that his guitarist was providing the bulk of his vocals for him, Nakamura checked himself into rehab.

Six months later, the band announced they would resume their postponed Euro tour.

I had the chance to sit down with the band and sit in on a rehearsal. If you, like me, were wondering if claiming your suspended ticket is worth the effort or if you should sell it before it loses all its value, read on.

The rehearsal venue has that haunted air that all venues do sans crowd, a fact amplified by the near-demonic noises Nakamura is making over the microphone. My affinity for metal has always been lukewarm at best, but even I'm unable to deny the appeal of Final Revelations, the range of Nakamura's vocals, from his growls to his cleans. It's rare for a metal band to have a frontman with a range that seamlessly translates live, and in the empty venue, as Nakamura lets out an impassioned "fuck" after a particularly taxing melody, I breathe a sigh of relief.

Final Revelations is back.

But—can they maintain it?

Fresh out of rehab, Nakamura is holding a bottle of water the way you'd hold the neck of a fifth of vodka. He winces as he takes measured sips, which makes you wonder if there's something else in the bottle, but that wouldn't align with the narrative they're now pushing about rock's favorite bad boy—that he's gone straight edge.

If you've read my work before, you know my qualms with the term. Most who claim it don't actually abide by all three X's—no drinking, no drugs, no sex. I don't waste any time in pressing him on his interpretation of the term—particularly the latter of the three, where most fall off the wagon. He fingers the sobriety chip around his neck, avoiding my question by delivering one of his own, "You interested?"

While Nakamura looks healthier than the last time we crossed paths, I am not a twentysomething girl; thus, I'm not interested. I ignore his question as he ignored mine and move on. When I ask him how his sobriety is going, he simply says, "Fucking peachy." The newly twenty-one-year-old isn't particularly known for being loquacious—nor does he seem all that worried about cleaning up his image.

I begin to wonder why I'm even here. If this interview was arranged to set the record straight about the band being on sure footing once again, I'm not convinced. None of the band members want to talk about what happened six months ago—maybe because even *they* aren't convinced they've turned over a new leaf?

If anyone had hopes that Nakamura would become the poster boy for sobriety, I'm here to tell you, don't expect him to be giving inspirational speeches in school gymnasiums anytime soon.

The band only wants to talk "about the music," with little regard for what the fans want to know: What happened at Reverie Fest? Was the rehab stint a PR stunt? Is Final Revelations really back? Or are we setting ourselves up for yet another disappointment?

After a few hours of grunted two-word answers from Nakamura, it's apparent only Marcus Bailey was willing to talk, but even then, I only got one answer to the above that was longer than one word:

Nothing.

No.

Yes.

Fuck off.

Make of that what you will. Being in a band isn't only "about the music" anymore. Just ask their label, Dropkick Records—who, rumor has it, will be "parting ways" with the biggest band on their roster after only two of their three contracted albums. Make of *that* what you will.

♪♫♬

By the time I finish reading the article, my hands are shaking with barely suppressed rage. I can't believe I ever considered Song my industry idol. Nor that, after all this time, his article is still one of the first things to populate when searching "Final Revelations." That this, one of their lowest moments, will become their legacy.

I click on a few more articles, and even the ones praising their work are threaded with the same incorrect rumors and assumptions. *Their label dropped them for being impossible to work with. Dax's rehab stint was a publicity stunt. Marcus and Dax can't stand each other.* Final Revelations may have stopped speaking to the press, but that didn't stop the press from writing about them—and Mike Song's article set the tone for how they would be talked about for eight whole years.

I'd hoped the research would enlighten me, give me an angle to write from, but I'm more lost than ever. The task at hand feels insurmountable. How am I supposed to undo nearly a decade of false narratives?

The door to the coffee shop opens, and Dax prowls in. There's no other way to describe how he moves, lithe like a jungle cat, unfairly graceful for someone so tall. His eyes scan the shop, his gaze somehow cutting and indifferent all at once. He's in full stage mode right now, the persona he sinks into when he doesn't want to be approached. If it weren't so effective, I'd find it pretentious. A few people clustered around mismatched tables exchange knowing looks and nudges, but no one gets up or says anything. I probably should have picked a coffee shop that wasn't a favorite haunt of metalheads, but it was the most convenient for me, and at the present, I'm not inclined to inconvenience myself for Dax Nakamura.

Spotting me, he gives me a slight jerk of his head in acknowledgment before approaching the register. My chest pangs unexpectedly, the greeting so different to how his mask used to melt into something softer for me, his gaze always finding mine backstage, whether to roll his eyes or share in a secret smile from across the room.

After ordering, he weaves between the haphazardly placed tables and chairs to my spot against the far wall, balling up his receipt and dropping it on the table with his phone and a blueberry muffin.

"No, I didn't want anything, thanks for asking," I say with heavy sarcasm, fixing him with a look.

I swear the corner of his mouth twitches, but his resting bitch face refuses to crack. He wanders over to the pickup counter and grabs the cup the barista just set down. Returning to the table, he places one hand on the back of my chair, hovering over me as he sets the insulated cup in front of me.

"You were saying?" he says with an arch of his brow, close enough that his words coast over my cheekbone.

My breath hitches, and I wrench my gaze from his, staring down at the cup as he goes back to grab the iced coffee now waiting for him.

Trepidatiously, I bring the coffee to my lips, blowing on the inky-black contents before taking a sip. The sweet, warm liquid slides down my throat, and my muscles relax.

Three years later, and he still remembers my coffee order.

Granted, I've only ever drunk my coffee one very simple way. With five kids to wrangle, my dad's quiet morning routine was sacred, a moment of peace before the chaos of *Nate, stop locking your sister out of the bathroom* and *Bryce, Austin, no soccer in the house* and *Gray, if you're not out of bed in the next three minutes*—I was a part of the chaos until one morning I discovered how nice it was to start my day in silence with my dad. He made me hot chocolate until he decided I was old enough to try coffee. I hated the bitter taste, adding sugar to it so it still *looked* like his black coffee.

Dax sinks into the chair opposite me, clinking his plastic cup against my insulated one. "What's so important you had to call me seventeen times before noon?" he asks around his straw before taking a long pull.

My face screws up in disbelief. "It wasn't seventeen," I protest.

He gives me a disbelieving glance, flipping his phone over and unlocking it before flashing me his call log.

My throat goes tight, not at the embarrassing number of times I called him in my rage, but at the name he still has for me in his phone:

sloane <3

The phantom limb of what we were aches. I read once that stabbing a phantom limb reminds your body that it's not really there. The only reason the heart is still by my name is because he hasn't used my contact info in three years. The ache subsides to nothingness.

I clear my throat. "I only count seven, not seventeen."

His jaw wiggles as he fights a smile. In the end, something soft wins out. "I'm sorry," he says sincerely, and every bratty fiber in my body dissipates. "I asked our manager to let me talk to you before he went to *AP*, but I think he wanted to lock it in before I could change my mind."

His gaze roves over me, to my crossed arms and the grip on my coffee that I've been taking tiny sips of. "How pissed are you? Should I grovel?" The corners of his mouth turn up slightly, and I hate that I'm not immune to being charmed by him.

Reaching between us, he methodically peels the paper from the muffin, his fingertips digging into the squishy bread, tearing it in half and sliding the larger half over to me.

Dax knows how to get his way with me—feed me—and I should have known reaching out to him would only end one way, but I wouldn't be me if I didn't make him work for it, at least. My mind was made up as soon as I read the Mike Song article, but if we're going to do this, we have to address the elephant in the room. I've given Dax so many pieces of myself, and I don't regret any of it, no matter how it hurt once it ended. But tying my career to him...I rub the scar on my ring finger as a reminder to myself to tread carefully.

"As much as I'd love to see you grovel..." I'm going for wistful, but the words ring a little too true, sticking to my ribs and scraping my throat raw on the way out. Thankfully, my voice has been five-packs-a-day raspy since forever, so I don't think he can tell. It's too little, too late for him to give me the grovel I wanted three years ago and never got. I shake my head to clear it. "I called you because I need to know this can work, that *we* can work together."

Dax nods slowly, picking a blueberry out of his half of the muffin and rolling it between his fingers like a magician with a coin. I throw all my life plans and goals out the window. All I want in this moment is to be that blueberry. *Move over, Violet Beauregarde.*

"Are you interviewing me to interview me?" His dimple winks at me before he stifles the smile.

"Yes," I say simply.

He makes a noise of intrigue. "How am I doing?"

"Not great."

A full grin breaks across his face for half a moment. "I'm rusty," he says, pouting attractively.

I take a slow sip of my coffee, studying him over the cup. He's still in Stage Dax mode, which is precisely why I'm unsure if we can do this. But it *is* easier being around him when he's Stage Dax. It allows me to be Reporter Sloane. In this context, we know what we are to each other. But if he can't be real with me, I'll never get anything out of him worthwhile. Sure, I could write some surface-level shit, and readers would guzzle it down, grateful for a drop after an eight-year drought. But I could write that article without Dax. I don't want to write that article. Not only is this my chance at a full-time job offer, health insurance, benefits, but also at making a name for myself in this industry, catapulting my career plan forward. This is my golden ticket to any job I want. I can't fuck this up or I may as well quit now.

"I can handle rusty," I say, carefully placing my cup down, studying it instead of him. "I'm not worried about that."

"What are you worried about?"

I meet his gaze, a glimmer of Real Dax peeking through. Something inside me cracks, all the sugarcoating falling away from my words. "That Robb should be the one writing this. That someone who's not your ex would be able to get a better interview out of you. If you can't be open with me, then it should be her, not me."

His expression shifts into something unreadable, like he's thrown everything he's feeling at the wall like spaghetti, and what stuck is impossible for me to disentangle. He stares off into the middle distance for a moment before speaking. I'd hoped when he looked at me again, it would be as himself, but there's still that sparkle of Stage Dax mischief.

"Remember when we dated?"

"We dated?!" I ask in disbelief, half-heartedly playing along. I do my best to hide my disappointment that we're still playing games when I desperately need him to be sincere, to prove that he still can be with me.

"I know," he stage-whispers. "Don't tell anyone or I'll never live down biffing it when I was majorly outkicking my coverage, but—" He waves this off like *me* being out of *his* league isn't backward, but I'm glad we're on the same page about our history needing to remain secret for this to work. "You kept trying to break up with me before we were even together, and then the next day you'd come back like"—he bats his eyelashes and pitches his voice into something softly feminine—"*Hey*."

I scoff. "That is not what I sound like."

Undeterred, he continues. "You wanted me." I make a show of clutching my throat like I can't breathe, and he fixes me with a frown. "My ego is suffocating?"

Flashing a smile in confirmation, I take a satisfied sip of my coffee.

"As I was saying," he continues with a prim purse of his lips that's so comical I have to stifle my laugh. "You wanted it—us—but you were scared because it was new, and you needed me to meet you where you were."

My eyes flutter shut as I realize where this is going. Lurching forward in my chair, I lean across the tiny table. My voice is half admonishment, half laughter. "You are not seriously trying to compare me giving you my virginity to you giving me an interview."

"Virginity is a patriarchal construct," he says, quoting me from three years ago.

I work my jaw back and forth to keep from smiling before caving to the laugh I've been repressing. "This is not even close to the same!"

"My body is a temple, Sloane."

"Oh, shut the fuck up," I say around a laugh.

He grins. "Go easy on me, babe. I'm a born-again interview virgin."

I throw his balled-up receipt at him, and he swats it away. It flies across the room, and we both duck our faces because if we make eye contact, it's over. I shake my head at the ground, ignoring the way I can see him shaking with barely suppressed laughter out of the corner of my vision.

Dax slips out of his seat, scooping up the receipt and recycling it. Once we're both certain we won't burst into hysterics, our gazes lock from across the table. It's not Stage Dax looking at me now, but the real him. My heart squeezes in recognition. *Ah, there he is*, it seems to say. This version of him, without the mask he wears for everyone else, is the version I fell in love with—even if we never said that four-letter word.

"Jokes aside," he says, softly serious. "Sometimes you want something, but you're scared of doing it because you've been burned before, and you just need the other person to be patient with you until you can open up again."

Now that his facade has cracked, my own crumbles, my next words coming out less factual and more pathetically honest, tinged in self-doubt. "And Robb could do that." Everything I've ever wanted is at my fingertips, but I can't reach out and grasp it, because I'm bleeding insecurity everywhere. You think when opportunity knocks, you'll answer, but I'm standing on the other side of the door, paralyzed with doubt.

He concedes with half a nod. "She could, but... I trust you more."

My gaze bounces across his face, searching for some hint of a lie. How? How does he still trust me so implicitly after all this time? How is it everyone believes in me, but I can't? And would they still, if they knew how I'd spent the past two years?

When I don't say anything, a pinch appears between his brows. "Why did you leave *The Offbeat*?"

I glance away, failure burning my cheeks, unnerved at how he seems to be reading my mind, even though there's no way he knows. "Just say it."

The furrow between his brows deepens. "Say what?"

"I told you so," I say in a poor impersonation of him. I gesture for him to get it over with.

It was always a point of contention between us. I'd had my sights set on *Rolling Stone* ever since I first decided on this career path. I combed every volume for Mike Song's articles, reading them before diving into whatever else was on the cover. And I wasn't the only one. It's why *Rolling Stone* chose him to launch *The Offbeat*—and why I chose him to be my mentor, step one in my five-year plan to get to *Rolling Stone*. Even knowing what he'd written about Dax, seeing firsthand the impact Song's salaciously addicting writing style had on his subjects... Sometimes, I kick myself, thinking I should've known he wasn't going to be the mentor I'd hoped. But I was young and naive, and I let my hero abuse his mentorship, all because I thought I was paying my dues. If I wanted my name on a byline, I had to earn it. I had to do the grunt work, the invisible work. In reality, it wasn't my work that was invisible. Just me.

Dax studies me, reading my body language like a book. He nods at my arms crossed over my chest, knows I don't want to talk about this, and drops it.

"Fuck Mike Song," he says instead.

I laugh sadly. Song is no longer my personal paragon of success, but losing that has left me adrift, no North Star to guide me.

"Say it," Dax whispers.

"Say what?"

"Fuck Mike Song," he repeats, savoring each syllable like it's delicious. "C'mon. It feels good."

I watch him through narrowed eyes. "I didn't even tell you what happened."

"You don't have to. If you left before getting to your dream job, then…" He shrugs, toying with his straw wrapper, winding it around the tip of his finger until it turns purple. "He fucked up." He releases the tense hold he has on the paper and it unfurls, drifting lazily to the tabletop. "Say it," he eggs me on.

With a sigh, I mumble, "Fuck Mike Song."

"Like you mean it, Donavan," he all but growls, curling over the tiny table between us.

I match his stance, leaning in so he can hear the contempt in my voice. "Fuck"—the hard snap of the consonants against my tongue is cathartic—"Mike Song."

It's only then I realize how close our faces are, giving me a front-row seat to the pride softening his gaze as he watches my mouth form the words. His lips quirk up in a wicked smile, like the venom on my breath is a palpable thing and he likes the taste.

"That's it," he says encouragingly, his voice low and deep.

And just like that, my mind is hurtling back in time to when he used to say those same two words to me in a *very* different context, the same purr in his voice and pride in his eyes.

I jolt backward, my chair scooting away from the table a fraction with the force of it. I clear my throat, my right hand coming up to fidget with my earrings, twirling each piercing half a turn until I've rotated all seven of them, a calming mechanism I've tried to break but that reappears occasionally.

"Well," I say, taking a deep breath, resurfacing from being caught in the undertow of Dax's presence. "As wonderful as this interview foreplay has been," I begin, reverting back to our previous metaphor and cursing that it was so sexual, "I will have a deadline, so you will have to seal the deal eventually."

Dax slips back into his stage persona seamlessly. "I'll give it up to you. Don't worry." He winks.

I huff a laugh, and I realize he's not the only one having trouble being vulnerable here. But maybe we can figure it out together. For whatever reason, he believes in me. Despite everything, I believe in him implicitly. Maybe we can believe for each other, until we can believe in ourselves again. Happily ever after may not have been in the cards for us, but maybe we can give each other a happier ending.

"So," he says, cutting across my thoughts, a flicker of the real Dax peeking through. "We doing this?"

There's an edge of desperation to his voice, and I realize how badly he wants this, needs it, even. I forget, for a moment, about myself and what this could mean for me. My journalistic instinct hums as, for the first time, Dax gives himself away, just a little bit. The question isn't *Why me?* but *Why now?* What changed for him?

It's a risk, to be sure. I could write the best article of my life, but if our past gets out, it'll all be for nothing. I'll forever be the girl who slept her way into the exclusive of the decade. My integrity is already in the gutter after my *Offbeat* internship, so I have nothing to lose— and everything to gain if we pull this off. The question isn't whether I can undo nearly a decade of bad press, but rather *Could I live with myself if I don't try?*

I extend my hand to him, and he grins as he slides his hand into mine. His thumb ghosts over my knuckles, and the unconscious habit sends a jolt through me. His grip tightens, like he felt it, too. He gives a perfunctory pump before taking his hand back, flexing his fingers like they're waking up from having gone numb, the same electric sensation pulsing through my own.

We share a glance, and I know my expression mirrors his.

What have we gotten ourselves into?

If we want to walk away, now is our chance. But neither of us says anything. We're in this together now. For better or for worse. His legacy, my name—they're ours for the reclaiming.

Setting my phone face up on the table for Dax to see, I pull up John's contact and compose a two-word email.

I'm in.

[Excerpt from Sloane Donavan's Final Revelations interview transcript]

1997: Semi-Somebodies

MARCUS BAILEY, VOCALS/GUITAR: I'm not saying I started the band, but—

BARRETT JOHNSON, DRUMS: I got everyone together.

CAIN WILLIAMS, BASS: I introduced Barrett and Marcus, which was kinda how it all started. Marcus was this scrawny little Jewish kid with something to prove, and Barrett was just... serious? Not a word typically used to describe Barrett [*laughs*], but he takes drumming and being in bands seriously. You just knew he wasn't the guy who'd be selling you carpet or whatever in five to ten years. He was going to do this for life.

MARCUS: The first time I saw Barrett was at The Lot. It wasn't a venue—it was just the gravel lot behind this Mexican restaurant where they let bands set up a stage made out of pallets between the dumpsters. Real highbrow shit.

BARRETT: Oh god, yeah. I used to play a lot of shows at The Lot with my old band—one of them, anyway. We were shit. [*laughs*]

MARCUS: Barrett is an absolute monster on drums. The band I was in at the time was alright, but it was college and I knew once we graduated, they'd all go off and get "real jobs," and I wanted to keep making music. I knew I needed to link up with someone like Barrett. Didn't think I'd ever actually get *him*. He was older, a staple on the scene. He'd actually done tours—national tours. I didn't know anyone else who'd done that. The rest of us were just local semi-somebodies.

CAIN: Barrett's from California. You could tell because of the girl jeans. Everybody wears them now, but back then, we were all still wearing JNCOs so big you could fit an entire laptop in the pockets—not that anyone had laptops back then. But yeah, Barrett was cool. Barrett wore skinny jeans. So, every band dude in Cleveland started wearing women's jeans.

BARRETT: Yeah, you could say I'm a style icon. [*chokes, laughs*]

JONAH JACOBS, GUITAR: No one would call Barrett a style icon. He was a damn good host, though. His house had a basement and a backyard good for putting on shows, and extra bedrooms that bands would crash in when passing through Cleveland. Back then, before the internet became more than just a few message boards, we were so isolated. The only bands you knew outside of the mainstream pop stuff were your local bands. So, if you were part of the Cleveland punk scene in 1997? Barrett's house was the place to be, to party. It's how you met bands from other cities. What were they doing? What was their sound? What were they writing about?

MARCUS: Girls. Every band, everywhere. We were all writing about—whining about—girls. Well, some of us were writing about guys, too, but that's when you conveniently stopped using gendered pronouns in your lyrics. The punk scene's always prided itself on being political—progressive, but it wasn't there yet back then.

CAIN: I was in a couple of bands. That was pretty normal. There were too many bands and not enough musicians. Or too many ideas and not enough bands. So, some days I was in this band that sang about girls they were too scared to talk to, and other days I was in this band whose every show ended up with the cops getting called because we were talking about politics, raging against the machine and all that, and our frontman liked to pick fights with people in the audience. Anyway, the guys in the hardcore bands hated the guys in the feelings bands, but really, guys talking about feelings was pretty radical stuff, too. Neither of those bands lasted long.

JONAH: Who started Final Revelations? No idea. I just knew my current band's infighting was so bad I would've said yes to anyone. I just wanted to play, and I knew Cain and Barrett from, y'know, around. They're both massively tall and take up space, so you can't exactly miss them. Marcus…Marcus was pretty. The Cleveland scene was very grungy, but Marcus was super into that Brit rock look at the time. Very put together. He wore vests and rings and his hair was always perfect. He took himself a bit too seriously. But then we started writing together, and yeah, he's a bit of a control freak, but his ideas were also really fucking good.

BARRETT: Industry trends are constantly shifting, but slowly. And usually, whoever's out there pushing boundaries? Gets fucking shit on. Then, in three to five years when everyone's imitating it, everybody pretends they knew it'd be big all along. [*laughs*] But there's no way to know which way it's gonna go while it's happening. You're just doing shit that sounds cool and hope people dig it.

JONAH: I don't think I was good enough at playing [guitar] to even dream of being in a band as big as Final became. But when you're surrounded by people that talented—I didn't want them to catch on that I wasn't as cool as they were, so I got good quick.

MARCUS: I always knew we'd be big.

CAIN: Don't tell Marcus this—that first album was good—but I didn't believe we were gonna be more than a flash in the pan, at best. But then…we got Dax.

CHAPTER EIGHT

The red light over the studio door is off, so I let myself in.

Since agreeing to write the Final Revelations piece, I've been working nonstop. First, their manager sent over the NDAs—so many NDAs. Then, John lost his mind that we had secured the exclusive of the year. He texted me three times in a row, called before I could reply, and by the time we got off the phone, I had a calendar invite in my work inbox titled "Let's Fucking GOOOOOOO!" (It was later changed to the much more appropriate—but much less fun—"'Final' Discussion," which I can only assume means HR saw the original title on his calendar.)

John wants to rush the piece to make the November issue, so I'm on the tightest deadline of my life—a little more than one week to pull off the biggest article of my career. After a brainstorming meeting with John and Robb, Robb wished me good luck in a way that still haunts me. She left that meeting drawing the same conclusion I did: John and Final were going to want entirely different articles. John wants the scoop on all the rumored Final Revelations gossip—and the guys want to set the record straight, to reclaim their legacy and integrity as artists. And I have to figure out who I want to make happy—my boss or my friends.

I've spent the past week trying to figure out how to do both. At night, I interview one of the guys after they finish up at the studio, and the next day, I transcribe the interview, hoping a magical solution will come to me. Thus far, no such luck.

I only have Dax left to interview, and I'm running out of time. Originally, I had Dax slated first, but he had "a thing" and canceled. Losing one day wouldn't be a big deal if I had any idea what I was writing, but every outline I've submitted to Robb has been massacred with notes, pushing me to dig deeper, to spice it up. I know what they want from me: the kind of article Mike Song would write, the kind readers love and artists hate.

My deadline is in three days, and I have nothing to show for the past few days of work but a handful of transcripts and a recycling bin full of discarded drafts. The only thing between me and a full-on ugly panic cry is the willful delusion that interviewing Dax will unlock the article, and it'll flow out of me perfectly on the first draft.

I've arrived at the studio fifteen minutes early every single day, hoping to catch a glimpse of their upcoming sixth album, which I've yet to hear more than a few fragments of.

Today, however, when I walk in, they're not even holding instruments, and Paul, their sound tech, is scrolling through his phone. Jonah's and Cain's guitars hang limply at their sides as they chat with Barrett in the drum booth.

Marcus and Dax are standing on the other side of the window that divides the control room from the booth. They have dry-erase markers and are scribbling on the glass what I can only assume is the album's track list—and the source of their argument.

There are so many chicken-scratch song titles crossed out, then stubbornly recircled, arrows, numbers—I can't make sense of it.

"Donavan," Paul greets me.

"Getting a lot of good takes today, I see." I gesture to the scribbles. Dax spares me half a glance in greeting before jumping in to stop Marcus from making a change.

Paul snorts.

Dropping my backpack at my feet, I attempt to block out Marcus and Dax's muted bickering and decipher the board, but it's hard when it's backward from this side of the glass. "Jesus. Do they really have that many tracks?"

Paul glances up from his phone. "Nah, half of it's the sixth album. Marcus keeps trying to bring it back."

I blink, riddling through his words, which refuse to compute beyond a faint buzzing of my journalistic instinct for a juicy secret. "Oh?" I prompt vaguely.

"Great fucking album," Paul says, dropping his phone into his lap. "Can't believe they never released it. But if Marcus gets his way"—he gestures to the glass, to Marcus beyond it, the soft waves of his dark hair growing steadily more unkempt with each frustrated run of his hands through it—"maybe some of it will make a comeback."

Bing-*fucking*-o.

I check that the switch to talk into the booth is off.

"You worked with them on it?" I ask, feigning a totally normal amount of intrigue in this massive revelation of an unreleased album. I've interviewed four members of the band this week, and not a single one of them mentioned it, which I know must've been by design.

Paul nods, stretching. "Yeah."

Damn it, don't clam up on me now, Paul. I switch tactics. "Are they always like this?" I gesture to Dax and Marcus practically writing over each other.

Paul snorts. "Always. I just wait until they finish and need me to push buttons. One time, me and the guys made them a GET ALONG shirt and threatened to put them in it if they didn't stop squabbling like an old married couple." Paul grins. "They didn't think it was as funny as we did."

I smile and nod, the image of Dax and Marcus shoved into a giant T-shirt together pushed aside as a headline swims before my vision.

"All the Rumors Are True"

It practically writes itself, the way I'd approach this article if I were still working under Mike Song at *The Offbeat*. While I was his intern, he'd let me "take a stab" at whatever he was working on. Then, he'd turn around and eviscerate my draft with his red pen. I was young and dumb and didn't know yet how to advocate for myself in the workplace. I endured it with a smile, all my hopes and dreams hanging on the promise of a referral to *Rolling Stone* that never came.

The death of a mentor happens like this: You think your turns of phrase appearing in their articles is just coincidence, subconscious—a compliment, even. You think it's a sign that you're not a completely terrible writer. If you can just present your work through a lens they approve of—their voice—they'll finally let you write something for real. It works. Sort of. The slashes of their red pen become less frequent, your drafts no longer resembling a bloodbath. Your drafts no longer resemble you, either, but you're gaining their respect. Your words are peppered into their work in a way that can no longer be ascribed to coincidence. You should be mad, you *would* be mad, but they keep telling you how proud they are, how much you've grown. You think if you write something so good—their version of good—they won't be able to slap their name on it anymore. They do it anyway. When you quit, you're not surprised when they say you'll be back. After all, their voice is yours now. You don't even know what yours sounds like anymore. You leave California with nothing to your name. The scar on your ring finger burns. You chose your dream, and your dream didn't choose you back.

Dax and Marcus continue writing over each other like crabby toddlers. This is the juicy article John wants.

I couldn't want to write it less.

I don't know what I do want to write, either, but this unreleased album—and the way they hid it from me—has my fingers itching. When did they record it? Why didn't they release it? Who made that call? I suspect the answer is right in front of me, and for the first time since I started amassing my research, I have a spark, an angle I want to chase. I have to get my hands on this album.

A grin stretches across my face as I feel a sense of direction for the first time in months. I press the intercom button.

"Hi boys," I say, cutting across Dax and Marcus's terse discussion of the track list. Their eyes meet mine through the glass. "Who's gonna tell me about this secret unreleased album?"

From the drum booth, Barrett drops his stick onto a cymbal with a *ting* and a muffled, "Oh, fuck."

As one, every member of the band's attention drifts from me to Dax, who's watching me intently.

Oh, fuck indeed.

My spark turns into lead in my stomach. I'm not the betting type, but if I were, I'd wager this secret album was written in the past few years. The odds that there are unreleased songs about me? I'm all in.

"Don't all offer at once," I joke, swallowing the lump in my throat at the very real possibility of being the subject of Dax's lyrics.

Do I want there to be songs about me? Is it worse if there *aren't*? What would he write? Good things? Bad things? With his proclivity for metaphor, would I know either way?

Marcus leans one shoulder against the glass to put himself in Dax's line of sight, heavy brows raised in question. Dax cuts his eyes to his bandmate, and I watch as they have a silent argument. I press my lips together to keep from smirking. I know exactly who made the call to keep this album a secret—and who will slip me a copy.

"Ready?" I ask Dax, with a pointed glance at the clock on the wall.

He glances up at the clock on their side before meeting my gaze. "For?"

"Don't play, Nakamura."

Cain chuckles from inside the booth. "Last name. Boston's *pissed* pissed."

Dax smiles uncertainly. "No, our interview is tomorrow, on the nineteenth."

My eyes flutter shut, praying for patience. Dax told me he would need to go slow, but this isn't going slow. This is a standstill. If he's sabotaging this out of fear, if he bails on me again... My chest tightens, my deadline pressing in forebodingly.

Jonah answers for me. "Today is the nineteenth, dude."

Reopening my eyes, I catch Marcus clapping Dax on the back. "It's a good thing you're pretty."

Dax shoves him playfully, and Marcus jogs away laughing.

I cross over to the door that connects the control room to the sound booth, and it opens before I reach it. Placing a hand on Dax's chest, I try very hard not to think about how it's the same spot I claimed as my pillow during long stretches between tour stops. He gives under my touch, allowing me to guide him back into the room.

Crossing my arms, I fix him with an unamused frown. "I'm surprised, Nakamura."

From the drum booth, Barrett giggles at my continued use of Dax's last name. For such a large man, the sound is surprisingly delicate.

Dax throws his marker into a cup as the others begin packing up for the day. They'll leave most of their stuff here, camped out in studio B until they finish the album, but an attempt to tidy up at the end of the day is half-heartedly made. "That I have zero concept of what day it is? Because that shouldn't surprise you, Donavan." He says my surname pointedly.

It's so easy to fall into this rhythm with him. If only that would translate into an actual fucking interview. But I don't need banter. I need an article. "No," I quip innocently. "That you're giving up an opportunity for your favorite pastime."

The corners of Dax's mouth curl up, but I wouldn't call it a smile. "Oh yeah?" he purrs, hovering over me so I have to tilt my head back to look at him. "What's that?"

"Talking about yourself."

Marcus bursts out laughing, and I half forgot there was anyone else in the room, that they were paying any attention to us. Dax sucks on his teeth, annoyed with himself for walking into that one.

Cain claps me on the shoulder as he passes by. "God, I fucking missed you."

"It's always nice watching Dax get shit from someone else for a change," Jonah chimes in from where he's tucking his guitar back into its stand.

"Just get back together already so we can stop keeping secrets," Marcus grumbles from where he's meandering around the room with a trash can, tossing their daily damage into it.

I blink, several thoughts flashing through me at once. One, I was never sure Marcus liked me that much. Two, I'll definitely be capitalizing on that when I ask him for a copy of the unreleased album, a topic I've only allowed to drop so they'll let their guards down. Three, they think we're getting back together? That absolutely cannot be a narrative that gets around.

"Give me some credit," I scoff, hoping it doesn't sound as forced as it is. "It would take a lot more than an article for me to get back together with a guy who let me go with one word."

Everyone titters, but I regret my words immediately. I intended it as a joke, but it came out so much more bitter than that. I can feel Dax's penetrating gaze like an X-ray, and I can't bring myself to meet it, so I attempt to smooth it over. "Seriously, though, no one here knows...No one *can* know about—"

"Yeah, I wouldn't want anyone to know either," Cain teases, shrugging on his jacket and sliding a beanie atop his buzzed hair.

This time, my gaze meets Dax's before I can stop it.

His expression is impossible to read.

I blink away, the back of my neck heating. If anyone at *AP* found out how deep my history with Final Revelations runs—even if I manage to pull off this article and redeem the Final Revelations name—my own would be forever ruined. "Please?" I ask, needing confirmation that we're clear on this.

"You got it, Boston," Barrett calls from the control room, having left his drum booth.

Cain and Jonah meet my eyes and nod briefly before finishing packing up.

"More secrets," Marcus confirms with a grunt as he slings his bag onto his back. "Got it."

"Thank you," I say to the room at large before approaching Dax. "Are you seriously bailing on me again?"

He won't look at me, very intent on arranging the contents of his backpack. "I didn't bail on you. My sponsor kid called me last time."

My mouth parts slowly, and I nod jerkily. "Oh." It's weird how you can feel like you know someone so fully and still know nothing at all. How badly I want to know everything. I knew Dax on tour. I knew Dax in suitcases and hotel rooms and tour bus back rooms. I don't know Dax at home, his morning routines or social circles, the NA meetings he still goes to religiously. Swallowing around the lump in my throat that won't budge, I try again. "And today?"

He takes his time situating his dented, scratched, and stickered thermos into his bag, handling it like it's precious and not beaten to hell and back, before finally zipping his bag shut and turning to me. But whatever honesty snuck through with his admission of where he really was last Thursday, it's long gone, locked away.

"We've got something more fun than an interview," Marcus says, his hands grabbing my shoulders and jostling me. "IC show."

My mouth gapes open. "Immaculate Conceptions are playing a show?"

Marcus smirks, knowing he's got me on the hook—and Dax off the hook. "C'mon. You can grill Dax on the two-hour car ride to Columbus."

"Shiiit," Barrett rumbles. "We can do Dax's interview for him."

"Hey, I'm Dax," Jonah says in an uncanny impersonation of him. "I'm six four. My favorite color is black. I like eating my weight in noodles and writing sad emo poetry."

Dax glares at Jonah out of the corner of his eyes, a barely repressed smile tugging at his mouth. "They're called lyrics."

Ignoring him, the guys continue dropping ridiculous Dax facts like I'm a writer for *J-14* and drafting a pull-out magazine poster for girls to hang on their walls. I laugh under my breath, my gaze drifting on autopilot back to Dax, only to find him already looking at me. When our eyes lock, he shakes his head at me like, *Do you see what I have to put up with?*

They keep up their nonsense all the way through the studio and out the alley door, and I grin. God, I've missed this. Even with music constantly playing, my apartment always feels too quiet without a plethora of older brothers or bandmates to drive me up a wall. As we come to a halt outside Barrett's SUV, I pull Dax aside.

"This is great and all," I say, gesturing toward the guys holding their sides from laughing so hard at Dax's expense. "But I need your interview. Tomorrow. I'll beat down your door if I have to."

A ghost of amusement flits across his face before quickly being snuffed out by whatever melancholy has him in its grip. "What if I moved since last time?"

"He didn't!" Marcus calls.

Dax flips him off.

I raise my brows at Dax, and he concedes with a nod. "Tomorrow." His attention flicks up, his left hand going to my hair. A gentle tug, and it comes cascading down from its bun. Dax clicks the pen I'd used to secure the messy knot atop my head and gently cups the back of my hand, extending my arm. He scrawls something on my forearm, my entire being reducing not to the drag of the ballpoint but to where the side of his palm brushes against my skin as he scrawls his address. "In case you forgot," he murmurs once he's finished, his gaze drifting to mine.

I don't have time to school my face into something professional, though I don't know if it matters, given how close he's standing, in the circle of my arm, his hand still cupping the back of mine, never having dropped it. He'd see everything anyway. I pull my hand back in a daze, breaking our eye contact. It's unfair how he affects me still, even when he's so distant.

"I haven't forgotten," I breathe. I haven't forgotten a single fucking thing. This would be so much easier if I had.

"Ready?" Marcus calls with a pointed arch of his brows, gaze bouncing knowingly between the two of us.

I nod, breaking the hold of Dax's gravity and crawling into the third row of the SUV.

Marcus and Jonah are the shortest members of Final Revelations, so I expect one of them to crawl in after me, but as I'm settling into the corner of the back row, Dax plops down next to me, long limbs invading my space without actually touching me, as if learning his lesson from *whatever that was* outside the car. The entire two-hour drive, despite numerous potholes that jostle us and despite both of us possessing way longer limbs than are meant for these seats, we maintain the careful no-man's-land between us the entire two hours.

They're the longest two hours of my life.

CHAPTER NINE

Finally, after two hours of playing our weird game of back seat Twister meets Operation, Barrett pulls into the venue's loading zone. I sag, muscles aching from the effort of appearing relaxed whilst taut like a rubber band, careful not to let any part of me brush up against any part of Dax.

A security guard wanders over to wave us along, and Cain rolls down his window. They have a hushed conversation, and next thing I know, the chain-link fence is being rolled back. Barrett pulls in and parks next to the nondescript tour vans and trailers of equipment. A thrill of excitement shoots through me. I should be used to this by now, but getting VIP treatment is always cool. I hope it never stops feeling this way.

"Do you think we'll still be doing this when we're eighty?" I whisper to Dax as the other guys begin piling out of the car.

I don't know why I bother asking.

He's been withdrawn the entire drive, barely participating in the car shenanigans except for flinging the occasional wry comment, but Dax can talk shit on autopilot. I've given up any hope that I'll get anything useful out of him today for the article, but I'm trying to be patient with him, like he asked.

Tomorrow. I can be patient with him until tomorrow. Then, this needs to get serious. Tonight, I'm going to enjoy seeing one of my teenage idols perform for the first time in years.

Dax glances at me sidelong as Jonah lowers the middle row for us to climb out. "I dunno. I didn't think I'd live past twenty-seven, so..."

He gets out of the car, and I nearly double over as all the air comes whooshing out of me. It's the most real thing he's said all day and it's absolutely devastating. I'm still scrambling to put myself back together as I follow him out of the car, feeling very much like I left my stomach in the back seat.

As my feet hit the gravel, Dax shifts to make room for me, maintaining our careful no-man's-land. I spent the entire two-hour drive trying not to touch him, and now I'm gripped by the visceral need to pull him back to me, to wrap myself around him, protect him, tether him to me. I don't know how he's chatting nonchalantly with Marcus like he didn't just casually say one of the saddest things I've ever heard. I follow behind the guys on unsteady legs to the alley entrance.

Dax knocks on the rusty metal door, and it swings open.

"Final Revelations," he says to the man with the clipboard. The guy doesn't even bother checking the list. A cursory look at Dax confirms who he is, and whether they were on the list or not, you don't *not* let Final Revelations in when they show up at your door.

Dax's offhand comment left me shaken, but now I'm positively flying outside of my body. My best friends may be Post Humorous, and their songs may be on all the alt charts, but even they don't have clout like this. I need a pass, an ID check, and a name on a list to get in anywhere. I sometimes forget who Dax is to this industry in favor of who he is to me, but then something like this happens, and it bowls me sideways.

The security guard shifts his attention to me, where I'm half-hidden by Barrett.

"She's with m—" Dax clears his throat. "She's with us," he says definitively.

After checking my ID, the security guard hands us all neon-green wristbands, stepping aside to let us pass.

We slip inside and hug the wall as our eyes adjust to the dim lighting. To our right, flashlights swing back and forth, illuminating the pathway for the openers who are about to take the stage.

I fumble with the wristband, unable to get the backing off the taped end. When I try and fail for the third time, Dax takes pity on me and eases it from my grasp.

Bringing it to his mouth, his lips curl back to bite the stubborn paper, tugging it off—a move that should not feel as erotic as it does, my eyes following his every movement like a magnet. Gently, he wraps the band around my arm. My pulse flutters in response to his touch, and I pray he can't feel it. I'm sweating like a Victorian woman who just had a gentleman graze her exposed wrist for the first time. He adjusts the tightness of the band and pauses, attention drifting up to mine. "That feel good?"

"Mmph," I garble out, giving him a jerky nod because who knows what fucking word that was supposed to be.

An upward tick at the corner of his mouth is the only acknowledgment he gives that he knows his touch has rendered me completely incapable of coherent speech. He smooths down the adhesive end of the wristband, his thumb grazing over my pulse point in a move that is definitely intentional. He knows what he does to me, and he's toying with me.

I cannot fucking stand him.

Marcus clears his throat and we both jump. Dax drops my wrist like it burned him, and we step away from each other. I'm looking at nothing, everything, anything but him.

Marcus jerks his head in the direction of the other guys, who are already making their way farther backstage. As Marcus follows after them, I hesitate.

Dax watches me, nodding, because he knows I won't watch the show from back here. I never do. "Tell the pit I miss her," he says longingly.

He looks wistfully at the crowd beyond the backstage barricade, and I can't imagine only watching shows from back here, where the sound is shitty, barely glimpsing any of the bands' onstage production.

"When was the last time you watched a show from front of house—like, for fun and not work?" I ask, already grieving the loss for him.

His face scrunches up in thought. "Ten—eleven?—years ago?"

I'm bowled sideways again—and not just because he answered a question for the first time all day. I know how young Dax was when he started out, but eleven years feels too long. I don't feel old enough to have been doing anything for over a decade. Our teenage experiences could not be more different. I spent mine wondering if I'd ever get boobs, and Dax was signing other people's, probably.

"Have you ever signed someone's boobs?" I blurt.

A low, startled laugh escapes him. I love his laugh, the way the joy of it always seems to surprise him, the airiness alleviating the heaviness etched into the curve of his shoulders, the hard set of his mouth, a gasp of air after being trapped in the undertow of his own mind, which I know is not kind to him. "Hard-hitting journalist Sloane Donavan, ladies and gentlemen."

"Gotta be thorough," I say reasonably, despite wanting to die inside. I don't know that I actually want him to answer the question.

"I don't know. Maybe? I don't remember ever doing it, but that doesn't mean I didn't." The left side of his mouth curves up, a flash of dimple winking at me.

I nod. More of Dax's stark honesty. His dimple punctuates his sentence like a reminder—the dimple that's not a dimple, but rather a relic of a day he doesn't remember. He told me that three years ago, in the same baldly factual way he always does when talking about the hazy years before he got sober. It's the same affectation he used in the car when casually admitting he thought he'd become a member of the 27 Club, dying too young like so many musicians before him.

I've never been more grateful for someone to be twenty-eight in my life. It's my new favorite number.

The need for him to have twenty-seven more years, then twenty-seven more after that, and for them to be full of *this*—the feeling that lives in a crowd, the one I've dedicated my life to chasing—has my rib cage in a choke hold, a tightness gripping my lungs and other chest organs I won't acknowledge by name. An idea takes root, a plan falling into place, a feeling of rightness settling into my bones like this was always how tonight was supposed to go, interview be damned.

"Wait here," I say, placing my hands on both of his arms as if to physically plant him there. Slipping out from backstage security, I weave through the crowd to the merch tables. I ask for the first hat I see and hand over nearly all my cash. May the band spend it well.

I flash my wristband to get backstage, making a beeline for where Dax is waiting for me, right where I left him. Stretching up on my tiptoes, I situate the hat onto his head.

His brows pinch together. "Thank you?"

I step back to assess him. He's so fucking recognizable, even with a hat. I grab the two sides of his jacket, laughing through my nose when I recognize it. It's the same one he let me borrow when he went three blocks out of his way to walk me to my car. Notching the two sides of the zipper together, I make eye contact with him as I slowly, so very slowly, zip the jacket all the way up. His breath hitches and holds. Apparently, I'm not the only one hyperconscious of our every touch.

Curling my fingers under the hood of his jacket, I bunch it forward to cover the sides of his neck, but it barely conceals the oni mask tattooed on his throat—a dead giveaway. But this is as good as it's gonna get.

"Not that I don't love being your Blasian Ken doll, but what're you doing?"

At the sound of his voice, my gaze locks with his. I'm far too close to him again, his gravitational pull sucking me in without me even realizing it.

"Disguising you," I say simply, taking a careful half step back so we're not sharing the same air anymore. "I've never been in the pit. Take me?"

He blinks at me, then stares off to the side, his shoulders curling in like I gut punched him. "*How* have you never been in the pit?"

I shrug. "I mean, I've been at the *edges* of the pit while people were moshing, but I've never been *in* one. I didn't want to get my nose broken—again. But like, a nice, respectable circle pit"—I mime the circular flow of bodies with one finger—"I'd try it."

He rocks onto the balls of his feet, staring up at the ceiling. "You're not gonna get your nose broken." He hums. "Most likely," he adds under his breath. He rakes his teeth over his bottom lip as he considers. He's nodding even before he speaks, and I know I've got him. "Okay," he says with a grin.

In my best Barbie voice, I say, "Let's fucking *go*," dropping into a growl for the last word.

A surprised laugh bursts out of Dax, a flash of sunlight in the middle of a thunderstorm. "You're ridiculous," he murmurs fondly. "Let's go, Emo Barbie."

We slip out of backstage and begin making our way through the crowd. It's a risk, bringing him into a room full of people that are his exact demographic, but that grin he gave me? Worth it. This industry hasn't been kind to him, and I want to reclaim this piece of it for him, *with* him.

Whatever melancholy had him in its grips earlier is slowly melting away, and I'm trying not to think too hard about the lengths I'd go to shield him from it, to keep that spark in his eyes.

As the crowd grows more densely packed, he reaches back for me, and I slide my hand into his without thinking. Sensation zings up my arm, like we've lost this round of Operation, but it doesn't feel like losing. It feels a little too right.

As the opening song comes to a close, the lead singer jumps up onto a riser. "WHAT'S UP, COLUMBUS?"

The crowd screams back at him.

"Alright," the frontman says on a pant, kneeling down onto one knee. "As the first act, it's my job to remind y'all to take care of each other. If you see something, say something. That said..." He smiles devilishly, and we all know what's coming before he says it. "Open up that pit," he growls, the audible equivalent of a squiggly metal band font.

The crowd surges. If not for Dax's hand in mine, I would be swept away as the center of the floor opens up, bodies pressing out in all directions to make room. I sidle up behind Dax to keep from being separated, trying not to focus on all the places my body is now pressed up against his, the way his evergreen scent has me melting farther into him.

The next song begins, and the bass from the speakers reorders my heartbeats. I always watch shows from the floor, but usually near the back, where I can see and hear everything without getting pushed or shoved. It's a rare day when I venture into the crowd, but never *ever* have I gone into the pit. It's not an experience I knew I wanted until tonight. It scares me and thrills me in equal measure. But if I'm going to do it with anyone, of course it would be with Dax. I miss the version of myself I became with him. I've already had so many of my firsts with him. What's one more?

I watch as people begin entering the empty space created in the middle of the floor, an anticipatory grin spreading across my face. It looks so unorganized, all elbows and flying limbs, but yet, there's an unspoken rule, the wall of people at the edge of the pit holding the line and shoving bodies back into the melee when they get too close to the edge.

I envy their ease in their bodies. My growth spurt hit in middle school, making me half a head taller than my classmates, most of whom never caught up to my height. Most days, I still feel like that gangly preteen, my long limbs less runway-model chic and more car-dealership inflatable guy flailing in the wind.

Dax guides me in front of him so I have a clear view of the stage. We're only two bodies deep of the pit, and he keeps an arm around me, not touching me, bracing for the inevitable surge. Sure enough, when the bass drops to a slow chug and the first breakdown begins, the pit swells and expands. Dax pushes back, his other arm coming up to tug me against him, a veritable wall behind me, not letting anyone touch me. When the crowd settles, I know I should reestablish our careful distance, but... I don't. He doesn't.

I'm grateful my back is to him, my face burning with the headiness of so much of me touching so much of him, our no-man's-land blown to smithereens.

The crowd recalibrates to accommodate the growing mosh pit. The girl to my right smiles over at me, and I can't help but return it. Being in the crowd might be a sacrifice of personal space, but I'd forgotten how much fun it is to watch a show from here. Then her gaze flicks up to Dax, her mouth forming a small o. I hold a finger to my lips, and she closes her mouth, nodding once in understanding. Even with my flimsy disguise, Dax is too damn recognizable.

The song continues to build, the upcoming breakdown undeniable, the blast beats of the drums a warning to take a breath before the plunge. The pit has worked itself into such a frenzy that it's organized itself into a circle pit, the momentum of the mass of swirling bodies like a black hole, sucking you into its gravity.

"You ready?" Dax asks, his mouth pressed against the shell of my ear so I can hear him.

I tilt my head back, staring at him wide-eyed, my gaze flitting between him and the pit. I grew up wrestling with my brothers who were twice my size, but I knew I could trust them not to actually hurt me—my twice-broken nose was my own klutziness's fault both times. I've been to more shows than I can count and have rarely seen anyone hurt. It's not the strangers in the pit that I don't trust—but my own abysmal spatial awareness. I shake my head tightly, chickening out.

"I won't let *anyone* fucking touch you," he promises with a growl I feel in my toes. He punctuates his statement with a bop to my nose, and I smile weakly.

I shake my head again. "Not yet." I'm flying high out of my body from all the ways we've casually touched in the past few minutes, how very not casual I'm feeling about it. I need to center myself, to regain awareness in my limbs, before I fling myself into the fray.

He nods, and all I can see is the man I fell in love with, the one that was so, so patient, who effortlessly threaded the needle of pushing and respecting my boundaries. His gaze sweeps over me before ducking down, bringing his face to my eye level to check in with me. "You okay if I go?"

I nod.

He turns to the guy behind us. "Watch out for her," he says before pushing his way through the wall of bodies. I barely register the guy taking Dax's place, filling the gap he left at the edge of the pit.

Dax is immediately sucked into the circular flow of bodies, right as the breakdown begins to build. The venue goes dark, an audio clip from *V for Vendetta* coming through the speakers. "Beneath this mask there is an idea, Mr. Creedy. And ideas are bulletproof."

The lights come back up and their vocalist is atop the riser. In a fry scream, he yells, "You cannot fucking bury me!" A ding of the drummer's cymbal punctuates the prebreakdown callout before the rest of the band jumps back in with punishing intensity. As the mosh devolves into the chaos of a push pit, a laugh works its way out of me and I look for Dax automatically, needing to share it with him.

I don't know how I find him amidst the chaos, how he finds me after being spun around, but we do. From opposite sides of the pit, our gazes catch and lock, and he beams, dimple on full display, eyes nearly shut from the force of his smile. I can hardly breathe around my heart in my throat.

I thought my feelings for him were a phantom limb, my brain refusing to accept what we lost. But these feelings are real, *present*, my heart kick-starting with a jolt.

Of course on the fringes of a fucking mosh pit I'd realize this.

I thought we could do this and be friends. And we are friends. But we're not *just* friends. We never have been, and I don't think we can be. For me, that will always be doing it halfway, and I'm not the type to half-ass anything. I am whole-ass into this man, always have been, always will be. It's why this is so impossible, because right now, that's what we have to be: halfway.

One interview. One article. But then... *Then what?*

I'm grateful for the press of bodies on all sides to keep me upright. I'm positively buzzing with the force of everything coursing through me. Three years and he's still the first person I look to when something's funny, the one I could find blindfolded, the only one I would consider flinging myself into a pit for—just to see him smile.

Dax breaks eye contact for a moment to haul someone back to their feet, and I'm not sure what my face is doing, but from the way his smile softens, everything I'm feeling must be on full display. *I know,* he seems to say.

This. This feeling. The one I only get standing in a crowd, scream-singing my heart out with a bunch of strangers. I get it for him, too. And right now, sharing this with him... I want to feel like this always. I want *him* to feel like this always. This man's joy is my lifeblood.

I forget, for a moment, that we're in the middle of a crowded room, that there's a man growling demonically on the stage, kids throwing haymakers in the pit, pinwheeling across the venue floor. It's just me and Dax, grinning like idiots at each other from across the room.

I forget until the song ends, when someone with too much momentum flings themselves against the edge of the pit, knocking into Dax, sending his hat flying. I know exactly what's about to happen, and before I even consciously make the decision, I'm already making my way to him.

The most direct route is through the pit, so I enter the sparse space in the middle of the venue. The break between songs should've been a reprieve for me to safely cross, but the band immediately launches into their next number, and that, coupled with everyone around Dax realizing who's amongst them, begets chaos.

I elbow men twice my size out of the way as Dax politely ducks his head, trying to get to me. But he's too tall, too recognizable, heads whipping in his direction, a ripple going through the crowd as the word spreads. The first breakdown in the song hits right as I make it to Dax, my hand finding his like a magnet. The crowd surges back as the pit presses out on all sides, and we ride the wave of momentum. Hands grab at Dax, but I barrel through without stopping. The crowd spits us out near the VIP barricade, and the security guard steps aside as soon as he spots Dax coming.

Once we're safely backstage, I spin around to Dax.

"I'm so sorry—"

I don't bother finishing my apology. Dax's head is thrown back, hand on his abs as he belly laughs. I could get drunk on the sound of it.

"Fuck," he wheezes, his gaze finding mine. "You went into a pit to save me." For half a second, I think he's going to tell me that was stupid, but he just shakes his head, smiling so hard his eyes crinkle. He cradles my face between his hands. "You fucking badass. Thank you."

I don't know how to respond. Adrenaline from, well, *everything* courses through my veins, so I just nod. "Anytime," I say weakly.

We stand there, his thumb gently tracing along my cheekbone, like the moment in the pit where everything else fell away, but this time we're much, much closer. His gaze bounces all over my face, like he's collecting clues. As if it's not completely obvious.

I know we should say something, but what is there to say?

Everything.

Nothing.

He's my assignment. Nothing can happen here. We had a moment, but that's all it can be.

A tortured sound rumbles deep in his throat, and his hands fall from my face, but not before a ghost of a touch trails along my jaw, his knuckle guiding my chin higher in promise.

Dax opens his mouth, but before he can speak, we're interrupted.

"Hey," Marcus calls.

I nearly jump out of my skin. I must've invented teleportation because I blink and I'm a foot away from Dax. Marcus and Dax are having another one of their silent glaring conversations.

Marcus jerks his head for us to follow him, and we fall into step behind him. Dax guides me in front of him, his hand ghosting along the back of my T-shirt before falling away.

He doesn't touch me again for the rest of the night.

I remind myself it's for the best.

♪ ♫ ♬

"See you in a bit," Wes, lead singer for Immaculate Conceptions, calls over to us before queueing up to go on stage.

Today is one of those days that feels like an entire week. I feel alive. I feel wrung out. I've felt every emotion under the sun in the past few hours.

After the openers finished their set, the supporting act put on a divas-of-the-'90s playlist that had the entire crowd raving while the roadies flipped the stage. I longed to join in, but after I finished swapping contact info with the openers—they are without a doubt going on my next Artists to Watch list—Barrett introduced me to Wes. He gave me *his* contact info, and my fingers are buzzing to draft up a pitch to John for tonight's show. I'm not supposed to be working on anything else but my Final piece, but fuck it. It feels good to be excited to write.

A hush falls over the crowd as the lights dim, announcing the start of the last act of the night. When one of the crew members comes over to where I'm standing with the Final guys halfway through the first song, I realize Wes's comment was meant for Dax, who is now being fitted with a mic pack.

"That— He— Are you—" I inhale sharply, feeling only halfway inside my own body.

Despite my inability to form a proper question, the slow grin spreading across his face confirms he understood me completely.

Dax has done a handful of features on other artists' tracks, but this one is old. They recorded it after that first tour, when Final opened for Immaculate Conceptions, the tour that put Final on the map. IC has played the song live before—but never with Dax.

It takes a lot to make me fangirl these days, but I'm fully fangirling right now. IC paved the way for bands like Final. This is metal history in the making, the two of them taking to the stage together for the first time ever. I'm so grateful I already got Wes's contact info. John is going to kiss my feet tomorrow.

"When?" I ask Dax.

He takes one glance at how tense I am and smirks, stepping aside for me. "Next song."

I bolt. I'm not watching metal history be made from the wings. I walk as quickly as I can without raising alarm, exiting backstage just as the first song ends.

The crowd has pushed so far forward that it's empty in front of the raised sound booth in the middle of the floor, so I post up in front of it as Wes has the crowd make some noise for the opening acts.

"Columbus," Wes calls over the mic, "we're gonna play an old one for ya. Hope that's okay." Enthusiastic cheers ring out in response. "How many of you fucks are Final Revelations fans?" The sound is deafening. "Well, then: You're fucking welcome."

The band kicks in seamlessly, and the energy in the crowd is palpable. It's one of their older hits, but almost everyone in the crowd is around my age or slightly older, and this song is quintessential to the scene. They're screaming all the words along with Wes, but you can see the craning of heads to try to see into the wings as the song approaches the first chorus.

When Dax comes out, I press my back against the wall, needing the support as the explosion of sound hits me. I'm grinning so hard it's embarrassing. It's him, it's this song, it's this night, it's everything.

It takes a solid twenty seconds before the crowd calms down enough to even be able to hear Dax's low growls under Wes's clean vocals. When not singing, Dax is toying with all the other band members, playing air guitar with the bassist and kissing the drummer on the forehead in a way that's far too sweet for the impending brutal breakdown.

As Wes parts the crowd down the middle in preparation for a wall of death, Dax comes to stand beside him, one leg propped up on the riser, surveying the crowd with a cocksure expression.

My competency kink is thriving.

The lights go out, drenching the venue in darkness and silence. In time with the slow chug of guitar, the lights come back up. The crowd, which Wes split like the Red Sea, rushes out from both sides, colliding in the middle. Dax lets out a long, low note, one foot still propped on the riser as he arches his back, holding the guttural for longer than should be humanly possible.

The song pivots back to Wes, but my eyes are only for Dax. He rests his arm on his knee, surveying the crowd with a smile, the red lighting giving it a sinister glow.

He looks so happy it makes my chest ache.

The feeling refuses to subside for the rest of the night, and I'm beginning to suspect this man's happiness may be intrinsic to my own.

By the time we climb into the back of Barrett's SUV, I'm wrung out, raw. I don't have anything left in me. I can't bring myself to care about being further behind schedule on my article. The night was too perfect to worry about things like deadlines.

When Dax collapses next to me in the third row, I'm too tired to worry about our no-man's-land. When we hit the highway, he stretches sideways in the seat and opens his arms, offering me his chest to rest on. I don't have the bandwidth to overthink it, readily accepting the more comfortable option for the long drive. I'm wiped, sorer than I should be after doing nothing but standing for a few hours. This can't be the same body I used to attend dayslong festivals in.

I don't know how long we lie like that, both of us buzzing with equal parts adrenaline and exhaustion. All I can think is how right this feels, how we needed this—a night to just be Sloane and Dax, and not the reporter and her subject. A night with no pressure, no expectations, to let our hair and our walls down.

The rest of the guys are rehashing the night, and I don't know how they have so much energy, but then again, they haven't been awake nearly as long as I have.

I fall asleep, or I was about to fall asleep—I'm not sure. I'm vaguely aware of Dax speaking, his words impossible to make out over the steady thumping of his heartbeat, my ear pressed to his rib cage. I hum in question.

"Are you awake?" he asks quietly, his long fingers threading through my hair in the way he knows will put me to sleep in seconds.

"No," I mumble sleepily.

His laughter rumbles through his chest.

I try to inject faux alertness into my voice, but my tongue is heavy and the words come out slurred. "What'd you say—before?"

When he doesn't answer right away, I tilt my head back so I can look at him. I poke him between the ribs, and he grabs my hand to stop me from doing it again. I raise my head slightly, my chin poised to dig into his chest in the way that he hates, all these little quirks we had coming back to me like riding a bike.

"Don't," he pleads.

I narrow my eyes at him before resting my cheek against his chest once more. I'll give him five seconds before I make good on my threat—

"I asked," he begins quietly, the arm around my back coming up to brush my hair off my face before twirling a lock of it around his finger, "if you regret it."

"What?"

"Us."

I sit halfway upright. "What?" I breathe. Jonah and Marcus are asleep in the middle row, softly snoring, and I keep my voice low enough so as not to be heard by Barrett or Cain, who are talking quietly in the front seat, their voices indistinguishable over the music quietly emanating from the speakers. "No. Why would you—"

"You don't want anyone to know." It's not exactly a question, but I answer him anyway, his sudden shift at the studio making so much more sense now.

"Purely for professional reasons." I play back our conversation at the coffee shop, trying and failing to remember if I spelled that out.

Dax's eyes widen and he nods, not needing me to explain. "So, pull my head out of my ass next time before getting offended?"

"But you love it there," I tease. He scoffs in mock offense and I duck my head to hide my grin. Sinking back down against him, I shift slightly higher so my head can rest on his shoulder. I hold his gaze so he can see the sincerity of my words in the semidarkness, in case hearing them isn't enough. "And for the record: No, I don't regret any of it."

He's still holding my hand inside his fist, and his grip softens but doesn't let go, bringing our hands to his mouth, brushing his lips over my knuckles. My fingers twitch, longing to trace the curve of his lips the way they used to on long drives between cities, back when we couldn't get enough of each other, when lying next to him on a tiny tour bus bunk felt like the height of romance, my chest so full of him that I thought it might burst.

When the road stretches out in front of you endlessly, anything feels possible, even knowing someone completely. The long conversations we'd have, with nothing else to fill our time but each other, sharing everything and nothing in our dashboard confessionals.

This feels a little like that.

He taps my fingers against his mouth, and I wait, knowing there's more. There's always more with Dax. The man is an iceberg. What's under the surface... For Dax, he's both what sinks the ship and the ship itself.

"What did you mean that I let you go with one word?"

A cringe spasms across my face. I could brush this off, try to smooth it over like I did before, but there's something about a road trip that makes me a little too honest. "All you said was"—I deepen my voice—"*Okay.*"

A ghost of a grin haunts the corners of his mouth. "That is not what I sound like." He turns to face me, dropping my hand against his chest to rearrange the sweatshirt he's using as a makeshift pillow. "What was I supposed to say?"

I shrug one shoulder. "I don't know," I say slowly. I'm too tired to fortify my walls, the truth slipping out unbidden. "I guess I thought you would fight me on it."

He twists my hair around his finger once, twice, studying my face. "I always knew you were going to leave."

He's not wrong, but there's something to the way he says it that hollows me out. He studies the city flying by outside the window for a long moment, and I hold my breath, half convinced this entire conversation is a lucid dream, all the answers I've spent three years holding my breath for.

"Would it have changed anything?" he asks, back to studying me instead of the highway flying by outside the window. "If I'd fought for you."

I loose my held breath, bobbing my head, not quite a nod, not quite a no. I trace the scar on my ring finger with my thumb, remembering the pact I made with my brothers, to not give up our dreams for love like our mom did, and how that summer three years ago, for the first time, I understood how she could have thought love was enough. How close I was to throwing all my plans to the wind when I was on the cusp of having it all—all to follow my heart, instead.

"I don't think so," I admit truthfully. "I don't think I actually wanted you to change my mind, I just—" I trace the faded logo on his shirt, trying to articulate my tangled emotions. "So much happened so quickly, so intensely, and to have it end so…like it was nothing…Our ending should've been something…*more*." It's not the right word, not even close, but it's the best I can come up with this far past my bedtime.

"Something epic," he says, supplying the perfect word effortlessly.

"Yeah," I murmur sadly.

Dax resumes combing my hair with his fingers, and I'm half asleep in a matter of a few shallow breaths. He must think I've drifted off—maybe I have, maybe none of this is real—when he murmurs, "We were something epic, weren't we?" His breath ruffles the hair at the crown of my head, and I shiver, burrowing deeper into him, his arms tightening around me. "Don't leave," he pleads against my brow. "I'm gonna fight."

[Excerpt from Sloane Donavan's Final Revelations interview transcript]

1998–1999: Really Fucking Fucked

CAIN: We recorded the *Ghost [in the Gallows]* EP in Barrett's closet.

JONAH: Must've done something right, because we managed to book a lot of shows. We toured around the Northeast and a bit of the East Coast. We didn't have any money, so we were in this moving van, three of us up front in the cab and one of us in the back with all the gear. We drove at night so the one in the back didn't die of heatstroke.

MARCUS: I think we toured for forty days and played shows for thirty-four of them. It was the only way we could afford the van.

BARRETT: You played wherever you booked, so that tour schedule made no fucking sense. Jersey one night, DC the next, then back up to Boston. *[grins]* Sometimes I miss those days, the open road, the van…

CAIN: Fuck that van.

JONAH: We almost missed our Long Island show because we broke down somewhere in Pennsylvania.

MARCUS: Thank fuck we didn't. That was the night Garage Door Records heard us play.

CAIN: They weren't a big record company, but they agreed to front the cost for the studio and to distribute our next record.

BARRETT: It wasn't a flashy deal, but it got us studio time and distribution. Of course we took it.

CAIN: We all skipped Thanksgiving and Christmas that year to write the album. We wanted to get into the studio first thing in the New Year. We finished the last song on New Year's Eve, around noon. We partied so hard I don't think my liver's been the same since.

MARCUS: We made no money off [*Sacrament*], but it didn't matter, because one of the interns at Garage Door shared our LP with their friends—and one of their friends? Was in Immaculate Conceptions.

CAIN: IC was one of *the* biggest names in hardcore at the time, and they were Ohio natives, so they were like gods to us.

JONAH: Immaculate Conceptions saw our set at RockFest and the next day invited us to open for them on their upcoming tour.

MARCUS: A *national* tour. [*grins*] It felt like everything was starting to happen for us. Like things were actually possible, y'know?

JONAH: But then...

CAIN: Marcus got sick.

MARCUS: Laryngitis.

BARRETT: We were on tour in the Midwest, and we tried to cancel shows, but Marcus insisted he was fine, could push through.

MARCUS: I was not fine, but I was young and arrogant enough to think I was invincible.

CAIN: He could barely speak. When he started coughing up blood, we canceled all our upcoming shows and headed home. We needed him better for the IC tour in a few months.

Jonah: We were driving back to Cleveland, only a few hours left of the drive, when Marcus broke down. Crying. He couldn't talk, but he didn't need to. We were all thinking the same thing. What if his voice didn't come back? What if we'd blown our chance at the IC tour because we were too stubborn to cancel a few shows at the Elks Lodge?

Barrett: I was driving. Marcus was crying. Jonah was stoned out of his gourd. I pulled over on the side of the road, let Cain out of the back of the van, and we all climbed on top of the cab. It was the middle of the night, and the sky was a bruised purple that we felt in our souls. We just sat there, watched the sun come up over this fallow field of nothingness. And then we all got back down and went home. I don't think we said a single word.

Cain: There wasn't really anything to say. If Marcus didn't get better, Final was over.

Marcus: I got better-*ish*.

Jonah: We waited until the last fucking minute to say something to the tour manager. Like, literally weeks before the tour was supposed to start. Which was a dick move to, like, literally everyone. But we were so scared we'd get kicked off the tour, that Final was over. We kept hoping a miracle would happen, and Marcus would be able to sing the way he could before.

Cain: That didn't happen.

BARRETT: I remember lying awake at night thinking, like, *We have to replace Marcus.* Do you know how fucked that is? Replacing the guy who wrote the songs? Really fucking fucked.
MARCUS: We needed a miracle.
BARRETT: [*begins humming "Hero" by Mariah Carey*]

CHAPTER TEN

I should've known better than to get my hopes up.

I woke up at an ungodly hour, buzzing with ideas about what to write—for Immaculate Conceptions. Running off no sleep and the barely palatable bargain coffee I regrettably bought in bulk, I put together three pitches for John. It's not what I'm supposed to be working on, but I'm inspired, feeling like myself again for the first time in far too long. The Final piece feels too big, and dipping my toe into IC may be just what I need to work up the courage to dive headfirst into Final. At least, that's how I'm going to pitch it to John.

The office is a ghost town. Most of the writing staff don't roll in until a bit later; only the accounting and executive teams are quietly milling about. As such, John hears my footsteps approaching, glancing up before I rap my knuckles against his open door.

Despite my not-at-all-manic practicing in the rearview mirror on my way to the office, I don't know what I'm going to say to him.

"Sloane, good—you got my email."

I did not.

Correctly interpreting my raised eyebrows, John smiles softly. "Or not. Grab Robb, will you?"

My stomach turns as watery as my morning coffee, and I nod

before heading in the direction of Robb's office in the back corner. I find her halfway there, mug of break room coffee in hand, her laptop bag hanging off one shoulder.

"Why is John calling us to his office?" I mutter under my breath, hooking my arm through hers and steering her in the new direction.

Robb blinks at me from behind her glasses, as if she hadn't been fully awake until that moment. "Oh, goody," she mumbles.

We file into John's office, sink into the whoopee cushion leather chairs, and wait for him to finish hunt-and-peck typing.

"Donavan," he says suddenly, turning his attention to us and pointing to me, as if saying my name weren't enough. "If you didn't get my email, I assume you already know?"

I glance uncertainly at Robb, whose eyes go wide.

"Know what?" I ask.

John frowns, as if he expected better of us. He turns his laptop around, and my stomach drops.

The Offbeat website is on his screen, an embedded YouTube video on the page: "Drop the Mike (Song) Vlog #42" The video's still is of Dax from last night, back arched as he held that note, mic pointed to the ceiling. It's a great fucking shot and I wish it and the article were mine.

How the *fuck* is Mike so fast from halfway across the country?

The need to justify myself, to prove myself, has the words tumbling out of me before I can think them through. "I...I was there—with Final. I have some pitches ready, could have you a draft by the end of the day," I promise wildly.

John's brows rise, and Robb's hand slides onto my knee, squeezing in silent warning. I shut up before I can dig myself deeper, not entirely sure what I've said wrong.

John peers over the top of the laptop screen, dragging the red dot in search of his desired timestamp. The still of Dax disappears, replaced by Mike Song, in what I know to be his office, a wall of framed vinyls behind his desk. The perfectly lit video shifts, a seemingly last-minute addition to his weekly vlog, Mike now bathed in moonlight.

John hits the play button, and my stomach is in knots.

"Last night, Final Revelations came out of the woodwork to perform with their predecessors Immaculate Conceptions. Now," Mike says, pushing his clear frames up higher on his nose, "we haven't had anything new from Final in years, and I'm delighted to report that a source close to the band exclusively confirmed they're back in the studio. I'd wager we'll have new Revelations by next summer—if their dueling frontmen, long rumored to clash behind the scenes, can put their egos aside long enough to finish the album."

The video cuts back to the previously recorded bit, and John hits the space bar to pause it. How is my former mentor still ruining my career from the other side of the country?

"A rumor he gave birth to and nurtures like a favorite child," Robb grumbles.

John turns the laptop back around, thank god. It's too early in the morning for Mike's smarmy mug. "Welp," he says with a pop of the *p*. "Cat's outta the bag."

When neither of us speaks, John leans in as if he'd just missed what we didn't say. "How is it that we have the story of the year, one of the biggest metal bands in our backyard, and Mike Song is the one breaking the news from San fucking Fran?"

"He has ghostwriters," I say on an exhale. "Someone must have been there."

John waves this away. "I don't care about the IC show. I care about *the album*."

Robb sighs heavily. "I mean, it takes a lot of people to make an album. Anyone could've let it slip. The studio, their friends who know—I think this is a good thing, actually."

John turns his owlish eyes on her, sitting back in his swivel chair and gesturing for her to continue. I stare at her with equally wide eyes, pleading. If she can spin this, I will kiss the ground she walks on for the rest of my life.

"This will only leave their fans clamoring for more information. Anyone can announce a new album, but not just anyone can get Final Revelations to give their first interview in eight years." She gestures to me like I'm some savant and not just stupidly lucky. "We should announce we have the article coming. Let people know where to go for all things Final."

My eyes prickle, and I blink rapidly, refusing to cry. So this is what it's like to have a mentor who fights for me instead of robbing me.

"And where are we at with the article?"

I stare at my ratty Chucks for a moment, composing myself before meeting their expectant gazes. "I'm working on it."

John raises his eyebrows. "And what does that mean?"

"We're trying to find the right angle," Robb supplies, giving me a reassuring nod despite having said my last draft read like a book report I didn't want to write.

"Is it that hard to find?" John asks with a humorless laugh. "This is Final Revelations we're talking about here. There's a million saucy angles—the rivalry between Dax and Marcus, the drama with their label, the Reverie Fest fiasco—"

"That's kind of the problem," I hedge, halfway abashed that I actually said that out loud and not just in my head like I'd meant to. But no going back now. "Every time I pick an angle, all I can see is everything I'm not getting to use that readers would eat up. How do you condense an entire career—most of which they've never spoken about publicly—into one article? I'm a fan, and as their fan, I would want everything—everything they're willing to share—and they're not holding back with me." Well, except maybe Dax, but I'm trying to dig myself out of this hole, not deeper.

John takes off his readers, twirling them between his thumb and forefinger as he swivels back and forth in his chair, thinking, probably enjoying the anxious silence far too much.

"Well, this is a first," he says at last, tossing his glasses onto the desk. "I brought you in here to scold you for getting scooped, and you're going to leave with a bigger feature and an extension."

I stare at him unblinking, convinced I've heard him incorrectly.

"You're right," he concedes with a sigh, like it pains him to admit it. "It would be a shame to not use everything—but I want you to get *everything*, Donavan. There's no room for friendship in journalism. I want every rumor, every bit of Final Revelations gossip addressed. I want articles to be written about this article it's so juicy. I'm going to push this back from the November feature to December and make this a two-parter, the second half out in January. Let's get their photo shoot scheduled ASAP, and we'll release a vlog after they headline the Halloween show, letting people know we have the exclusive. Mike Song can kick rocks."

Robb and I exchange a glance, her face equally as shocked as mine.

"Thank you," I manage.

"We'll go brainstorm—right now," Robb rushes out, her hand grasping my biceps and dragging me from my chair, the leather squeaking fartily. It's like she expects John to take back the offer if we linger too long, which, given how many promises he's made her and not followed through on, she isn't entirely off base.

Once we're safely behind the closed door of Robb's office—which I'm pretty sure is a repurposed closet—we stare at each other, open-mouthed and silently screaming. Robb stomps her feet and shakes her nonexistent hair, victory-punching the air. I wrap my arms around myself and try not to fall apart at the seams.

While I desperately needed this extension, making the article bigger only adds fuel to the fire of my imposter syndrome. "Please tell me I can do this," I say pathetically.

Robb ceases her celebratory dance, placing both hands on my shoulders, shaking me. "Sloane," she says, beaming. "You can do this." She enunciates each word slowly, giving them time to sink in.

"How do you know?"

After last night, my emotional walls haven't had time to refortify, and I don't have it in me to pretend I have it together. I feel five years old right now, the wound of my mom splitting still fresh, wondering if maybe it would've turned out differently if only I'd been better.

Robb fixes me with a sad smile, guiding me to sit in the worn chair. It's so cramped my knees hit the front of her desk when I plop down. She shimmies through the small gap between her desk and the wall, sinking into her fraying chair.

"I know you can do this, because—" She bends over, sliding open her file cabinet and rifling through it. She slaps a copy of *The Offbeat* down in front of me, flipping to a tabbed page. She looks at me meaningfully. I recognize the article. It's one of the first ones I "worked with" Mike on. When I don't say anything, she fishes another volume from her file cabinet, this one also tabbed, flipping it open to another one of my articles with Mike's name on it.

"You're not the only one who knows about Mike Song's ghostwriters."

I blink, and this time I'm not able to stop the tears before they fall. Wiping them off on my shoulder, I take a shaky breath, rubbing the scar on my finger to ground myself.

"Funny how his writing got a lot better two years ago. And then not so great again a few months ago, when you came to work for us." She ducks her head, forcing me to meet her gaze. "You can do this. You've already done it."

I nod, but all I can think is how I don't want to be that writer anymore. That was me writing as Mike, and yes, I was good at it, but I'm not proud of it. I'm writing as me now, and I want to be proud to have my name on this.

"Don't worry about Mike. He's a scourge upon the profession. He cannot scoop you, no matter how many 'sources close to the band' he has. No one else can get what you can get, and just think about how positively fuming he is about it."

That gets a watery laugh out of me. It does make me feel better, picturing Mike's face when we announce the exclusive, that I'm the one writing it, while he ferrets around for scraps about the band he burned a bridge with to make a name for himself, incorrectly predicting they'd be a flash in the pan and not one of the biggest bands of the decade.

I rake my hands through my hair, trying to muster a semblance of confidence. "Thank you," I say sincerely. "And I'm sorry. I know I've been floundering. I shouldn't have gone to the show last night—"

Robb waves this away. "Going to shows, networking—all of that is part of the job. They're letting you tag along, so *tag along*. Wherever they go, you go. You never know what you'll uncover just by being a fly on the wall."

I let out an involuntary gasp, nearly having forgotten in the midst of everything.

A Grinch-like smile curls the corners of Robb's mouth, her Monroe piercing twinkling in the yellow light. "What did you find out?"

"The album they're recording," I begin in a whisper, "is their seventh album."

Her brows pinch together, and she taps each of her fingers against her thumb as she counts, mouthing the names of each of Final Revelations' albums. *Sacrament, Covenant, Shadow Psalms, Prodigal Son, Purgatorium.* She counts again, and I wait for her to confirm what she already knows: that they've only released five albums. "What happened to number six?" she asks.

When I smirk, she matches it. Pushing back from her desk, she takes an eraser to her whiteboard, wiping it clean before picking up a dry-erase marker and uncapping it with enthusiasm.

⚡ CHAPTER ELEVEN ⚡

We spend the next hour brainstorming, recapping everything I've gotten from the four guys so far and plotting how best to structure the two-part article. By the time I leave for Dax's, I'm a weird mix of fortified and crumbling beneath the pressure of it all. A bigger article gives the content more room to breathe, but it also means an even bigger lift. Knowing how long their fans have waited for a new interview, it only makes the task more Herculean. I can't please everyone, but I want to do it justice, to give the fans the answers they crave *and* set the record straight for the guys. I just have to figure out how to make the truth more sensational than the lies told for the past eight years. I hope that after interviewing Dax, one of our ideas will naturally surface as the obvious direction for the article.

I type Dax's address, which is still scrawled on my forearm, into MapQuest before I leave the office, and I have to pull over twice to check it, frustration prickling my eyeballs when I have to turn around after missing my exit. Despite having lived in Cleveland for months, I only know how to get to a handful of places. I walk to the grocery store from my second-story apartment above the Vietnamese restaurant—the proximity to pho half the reason I signed the lease—and only know how to drive to work and a handful of concert venues.

By the time I reach his apartment, I'm only a few minutes late, but my emotions are frazzled. I take a few steadying breaths, trying to remember the last time I felt rested. Even with the two-week deadline extension, it will likely be a while until I know rest again.

I park—and then double back to move my car when I realize halfway down the block I'm in a tow zone—and make my way into Dax's building. The last time I was here was on our first "date," which was just me spending the afternoon with him, a rare day off on tour. He showed me all his favorite places around the city, and then I asked him to take me here. It was the first time we were ever truly alone together. We took full advantage of that.

The smell of cooking carries me down the modest hallway to Dax's corner apartment, and I realize the aroma is coming from his place. I probably should have asked to meet him somewhere else. I did all the other guys' interviews on a rickety picnic table outside the dive bar down the street from the studio. And while they were incredibly open with me about everything—well, everything except the album they hid—their demons aren't the ones that have been the butt of the joke for the past eight years. It makes sense to do this somewhere more private. I just hope our dance of one step forward, two steps back is at an end, and we can simply move forward.

I haven't allowed myself to think too hard about our conversation in the back of the car last night. It feels like a weight has lifted, finally having some clarity on how it all ended. It doesn't change anything, but it's nice to know his lack of fight wasn't for lack of caring. But there's still something to how he said *I always knew you were going to leave* that feels like *I always knew you were going to leave me* that I can't shake. The way he whispered into my hair, *Don't leave.* I'm not planning on going anywhere, and it was good to clear the air, but it doesn't change what we are *now*. I'm a reporter. He's my assignment. That's all we can be to each other right now.

I knock, my heart in my ass and my throat at the same time.

The door swings open, and my heart falls out of my body entirely. It's inconsiderate that he's so attractive. Black sweatpants hang low over his hips, and a thin, half-translucent white Henley teases the colorful tattoos beneath.

"Hey," he says. He's softer today, yesterday's melancholy no longer darkening his amber gaze, and the smile he gives me in greeting is easy, light.

"Hi," I say back, stepping inside as he holds the door open for me. I catch a whiff of his evergreen soap amidst whatever he's cooking. Toeing off my Chucks, I tuck them next to his assortment of black Vans before stowing my backpack under the small foyer table.

Following after him, I take in his apartment that feels more familiar than it should. I've only been here once before. The far wall is exposed brick, with floor-to-ceiling windows that provide a view of the waterfront. His bedroom is off to the right, the door closed. Thank god. As we pass through the living room to the open kitchen, I give the couch a wide berth. It knows a little too much about me. His place is exactly as I remember it, though slightly more lived-in. Walls that were once blank now sport gorgeous framed prints that I recognize as stills from Studio Ghibli films. Personal touches tastefully clutter every surface, as if he's finally given himself permission to take up space inside his own home.

I pause beside the island as he continues into the kitchen, grabbing two bowls from an open shelf. All I can think is how my mismatched Goodwill bowls would be embarrassing to display. His space is so clean, so adult, while mine is still furnished with the hodgepodge belongings I accumulated in college, most of them found on the side of the road.

Without asking if I'm hungry—I'm always hungry, but I tend to get so hyperfocused on work that I forget to feed myself until I'm well past hangry—he scoops a hefty portion of noodles into two bowls, and I plop myself onto one of the barstools with my hands out eagerly. He laughs quietly when he spies me, sliding the bowl into my waiting hands.

"Let me guess: You've only had a granola bar so far today."

I think as I chew, trying to separate the days that compose the marathon this week has been. "I ran out yesterday," I admit. My fridge and pantry are empty, and my laundry is in shambles.

Dax sets his bowl down, grabbing the wok and tonging more food into my bowl.

"Okay, okay," I say around a laugh, curling over my food before he can add another helping, shoving noodles into my mouth all the while.

He smiles softly before digging back in, and I study my food instead of him. We've eaten together before, at craft services and whatever late-night haunt was still open after midnight, but sharing a meal with him, in his home, a meal that he made... It's so domestic, so novel. I can't help but think how many things we never got to do that summer, how many of them we could do now. But this is business, not pleasure, and no matter how easy this feels, I can't think like that right now.

"Thank you," I say once I've finished, circling around the island to wash my bowl. He tries to take it from me, but I fend him off by sticking out my ass, stubbornly cleaning everything in his sink while he finishes eating.

"Thank you," he says when he loses the battle to clean his own empty bowl. As I place the cleaned dishes on the rack to dry, we meet each other's gazes. "Guess we gotta do this now, huh?"

I scrunch up my nose, nodding.

"Unless you want dessert?" he offers.

"I'm listening."

He laughs, his hand snaking under his shirt to scratch at the hair below his navel. I yank my gaze away. "Well, I don't have dessert," he laments. "But we could go get some," he says wistfully.

"Sit your ass on the couch, Nakamura," I call, already halfway to the foyer to retrieve my bag. He flops onto the cushions dramatically, and I desperately wish he had a dining room table or that I'd told him to sit at the bar, not the couch where, three years ago, he slowly peeled my clothes off and made me hear colors.

Settling onto the opposite end of the couch, I take a bit longer than necessary extracting my notebook, phone, and pens from my bag, waiting for the flush to recede from my cheeks.

"Okay," I say finally, meeting his gaze where he's watching me from across the couch, arm propped along the back, absentmindedly tracing his lips with the pad of his thumb. I'm not the only one remembering the last time we were on this couch together. I take a breath meant to steady me, but I'm straining at the seams, and it only frays my edges further.

"What do you want to know about me, stranger?" he asks, smirking.

I try to make words but my mouth refuses to do anything but curve into a smile. We sit there, smiling and gently laughing at the absurdity of this. I shake my head at the ceiling. "This is so much weirder than I anticipated."

He grins, his dimple on full display. Whatever force creates that dimple is tugging on my heartstrings in tandem. "It's a little weird," he agrees easily.

"It was your idea," I say petulantly under my breath, and his head falls back as he laughs.

My own laugh rattles around inside my hollow rib cage, sticking in my throat on the way out. I cough to cover it. "So, uh, with the other guys, I started with how they got into music."

When he doesn't say anything right away, I grow self-conscious. "It's cliché, I know, but it's a good warm-up question." Fuck, this is awkward. "Sorry," I mumble, shuffling through my notes.

Dax shakes his head, brows creasing in the middle. "Why are you apologizing?"

"I, well, this *is* how I started my other interviews and they went well, but despite that, I have no idea where I'm going with this article, to be honest, so I probably should have thought of a better approach rather than just"—I gesture limply—"doing the same thing." I sigh heavily, pinching the bridge of my nose. "Sorry, it...It's been a long day."

Dax scans my face, nodding. "Tell me."

I shake my head to clear it. "No, let's stay on task." I flip to a clean page in my notebook, but Dax slides it out of my hands, tossing it onto the coffee table without looking.

"Tell me."

He pins me with his gaze and I cave. It all comes spilling out of me—the Mike Song leak, the meeting with John, the article getting pushed back and made bigger all at once, my brainstorming session with Robb, my MapQuest directions that were definitely conspiring against me. I'm aware this is unprofessional, but there was nothing normal about this situation to begin with. "I don't know," I say heavily. "You may have made a mistake giving this to me."

His face screws up in confusion. "I didn't *give* you anything, Sloane. You earned it."

I make a noise halfway between a honk and a choke. "How? How have I earned this? I've got, like, two articles to my name."

His eyes bore into mine. "To your name, yeah."

I inhale sharply. "You know?"

He nods. "I'd know you anywhere, Sloane. Even when you're in a Mike Song–shaped trench coat. Besides, he doesn't know words that big."

A garbled laugh works its way out of me. "I can't believe you read his stuff."

Dax fidgets with his necklace, twisting the chain around the tip of his finger. "I don't, normally. But I subscribed"—his finger turns purple, and he untwists the chain—"two years ago."

He followed my career.

I can't help it. My chin wobbles, and tears well, blurring my vision.

"Hey," he calls softly. The cushion sinks as he moves closer, his hands cupping my cheeks as I blink, his thumbs wiping away the tears before they can fall.

"I'm sorry," I murmur, mortified. "This is so unprofessional."

Dax smiles crookedly. "I don't give a fuck about that."

I laugh wetly, and he continues to wipe away my tears with his thumbs, saying nothing, letting me get it all out. Once I'm confident my waterworks are done, I take a deep breath, finally meeting his gaze again. He smiles softly, and it's all a little too familiar. It shouldn't be. We haven't been *this* to each other in years.

As if realizing the same thing, he dabs the last of my tears with his sleeve before scooting a normal distance away on the couch.

I twist each of my seven earrings in turn to ground myself. "You're not gonna ask me why I did it?" I don't want to talk about it, but I want to talk about how we keep falling into old patterns even less.

He shakes his head. "Not unless you want to tell me."

This is how he gets me to tell him everything. He doesn't push, lets it be my choice, and the less I'm pushed, the more I want to pull someone closer. I twist my earrings one last time. "You know how when you're dreaming, and things don't totally make sense, but you go along with it anyway?"

Dax nods.

"It was like that," I say, speaking to my hands twisting in my lap. "I was doing it, y'know? I was so close to making it to *Rolling Stone*. I was going to shows every other night, writing them up, getting to cover bigger and better bands. Sure, my name wasn't on any of it yet, but I thought if I just stuck it out, got that referral from Mike, all my *Rolling Stone* dreams that I'd spent my whole life working toward would come true. But then I woke up, and...I tried to slip back into it, but all I could see was everything that didn't add up. All the promises he'd made, the excuses I made for doing what I was doing...Somewhere along the way, my dream had turned into a nightmare."

"Hey," he calls, ducking his head and forcing me to meet his gaze. "Fuck Mike Song."

I smile weakly. "Fuck Mike Song."

He nods in approval. "I didn't pick wrong," he reassures me. "And I can prove it," he begins softly. "How did you get into music journalism?"

I shake my head at him for turning my own question around on me. I brush my hair out of my face, trying to regain my composure despite feeling like an exposed nerve. "I'm supposed to be the one asking the questions here."

"Oh, now she wants to be professional," he mocks.

I make a noise of affront, laughing as I smack his arm with the back of my hand.

"Humor me," he pleads.

I sigh, sinking sideways into the couch. I have an interview-ready answer to this question, but it's not the real story. I don't even consider giving him the prepared answer for half a second.

"When I was sixteen," I begin. "I remember flying down back roads with Brooklyn, driving way too fast with my music way too loud, to get to a basement show for a band I'd never even heard of before that night. The band was heavy. B hated it. I loved it." My gaze goes hazy, my mind half in the past, still able to see it all so clearly. The dingy basement with its pale green walls, scuffed and fading. There was no stage for the band to stand on, every member eye level with the hundred or so people that had shown up to watch them. I can still feel the press of heat from that many bodies in a room with no windows. "After their last song, following an absolutely brutal breakdown, the lead singer opens his mouth, and the most beautiful melody comes out." I can't help but laugh, reliving the shock of hearing it in such quick succession to near-demonic vocals. "It was soft, slow. The crowd knew every word. I don't know how. I don't think they even had an EP out. Everyone in the room is scream-singing their hearts out, repeating the verse over and over. The band slowly fades out until it's a cappella. I look over at Brooklyn and she's crying. I realize *I'm* crying." I sniff, my eyes prickling with the force of the memory. "It's special, the way music can instantly connect you with a room full of strangers, sharing in a moment that will never be re-created quite the same way ever again. I didn't have words to describe it—that feeling—but I knew I wanted to spend the rest of my life chasing it, trying to find the words."

Dax smiles softly at me, and I glance away, feeling vulnerable. It's one of my favorite memories, which is why I rarely share it, not wanting anyone to paint over my childhood wonder with the jaded hues of adulthood. It's one of those once-in-a-lifetime moments where I thought, *Yes, this. This is the point of living.*

"That," he says quietly. "Is it really a question why I—why we'd—want you?"

I meet his gaze, still confused.

"You know how to tell a story, to turn the ephemeral into something eternal. You are rare, Sloane Donavan."

I want to sink into his praise like a warm bath. I want to prove him right. "Thank you." Mostly, I'm grateful to him for deftly hoisting me out of the emotional quicksand I'd fallen into and putting me back on my path. I've broken all my usual professional protocols, but maybe that's okay. I can't be Reporter Sloane with Dax, and I shouldn't try to be.

No one else can get what you can, Robb said. It's hard to let go of the ways my previous mentor crushed my spirit, but Dax has always been a safe space for me to do the things that scare me. I trust him, believe in him, and if he trusts and believes in me, then perhaps I can learn how to again.

Tucking my hair behind my ears, I retrieve my notebook from the coffee table. "But now"—I click my pen purposefully—"it's your turn."

[Excerpt from Sloane Donavan's Final Revelations interview transcript]

1999: The Beginning of the Beginning

Dax Nakamura, vocals: When you're a kid, you don't expect to find your life's purpose behind the dumpsters of a Mexican restaurant. I was, like, twelve or thirteen years old, and I'm pretty sure I had food poisoning, but the bathroom stalls were locked so I went out the emergency exit so I could puke, and I did, but that's not the point. There was this punk show happening in the gravel lot out back. I'd never seen anything like it. Bunch of big, scary-looking dudes with tattoos and metal in their faces, shoving each other around in a pit.

I was one of the only mixed kids at my school, and I didn't really fit anywhere. I did well in school—I had to—but I never fit in with the nerdy kids. Do you know how weird you have to be to not even be cool enough to be a nerd? Anyway, I was standing there in my puke-covered school uniform—navy polo and high-water khakis that I'd outgrown months ago—and I thought, *Oh. This is where the people who don't fit anywhere go.* It was the beginning of the end for me. Or the beginning of the beginning, I guess. Depending on how you look at it.

That was my first hardcore show. I was hooked. I saved up all my allowance and blew it on

CDs that I hid from my parents. I think in early interviews I said I stole the CDs because, I dunno, I thought that made me sound edgy. But I was, like, this scrawny fucking mixed kid. I wasn't stealing shit. Store owners watched me like a hawk. Anyway, I bought the CDs, and I didn't want to be a singer—the thought hadn't really crossed my mind yet at that point. Singing was just a thing my mom and sisters did around the house. But I wanted to know how those vocalists were *doing that* with their voices—the growls, the screams, the raspy edge. So, one day, I was in the shower and decided to go for it. [*fry screams, laughs*] Scared the absolute shit out of my mom. She thought I was being murdered.

    The summer before high school, I stopped playing piano and picked up guitar because it was more "metal." That was when I first started wanting to be in a band. Like, the guys I knew in bands were all really fucking weird, but because they were in bands, they were cool, y'know? I don't really know if I was obsessed with being cool so much as I just really wanted to belong somewhere, and a band felt like my best shot.

    I worked my way into the scene by going to shows. I lied to my parents, saying I was in a study group or something. I remember almost getting caught by my dad once. I'd been at a basement show, so I smelled like stale beer and cigarettes, but I'd stashed a change of clothes in our old tree house. My dad came to take out the garbage—we had one of those motion-sensor lights—and it lit me up, half-dressed in the middle of the yard. I think he assumed it was just some teenage shit he didn't want to know about and pretended not to see. But then my grades nose-dived, and they knew I wasn't going to a fucking study group. They grounded me for a month. I was so bored that I got really good at guitar, started writing my own stuff, with god-awful lyrics I'm glad are lost to time.

In a way, me being grounded helped me get into my first band. The guys were a lot older than me—in their early twenties or something, which, when you're fifteen, seems so old. But they'd had trouble keeping a guitarist, so they let me have a shot. I bounced around between a few bands after that, playing guitar, before I found one I kinda liked, but then the vocalist went off to college so I was like, fuck it. I can kinda sing? So I was in this melodic, whiny punk band for a bit. After that, I sang in every band I was in.

Then I joined this metal band. It was my first time screaming in a band and also the first time I wasn't playing guitar onstage—I felt so vulnerable. Everyone's just looking at you. All of you. No guitar to hide behind. And I was, like, well, this can't be worse than getting walked in on while screaming in the shower, so, I just let it rip.

Before, I would get kicked out of bands when someone better came along. After that, I wasn't getting kicked out of bands anymore. I was getting poached by bands. It was the first time I felt wanted. Like I belonged. It felt really fucking good.

CHAPTER TWELVE

"I haven't burst into tears in days," I say proudly.

Brooklyn snorts on the other end of the line. She doesn't know I'm not joking, or about that day where I embarrassingly cried in front of my mentor or how entirely unembarrassed I was crying in front of Dax. How it felt cathartic, actually, to share that with him. "Okay, but for real: How is the article coming?"

"Uh-huh," I say quietly, not wanting my voice to carry. From my position on the couch, I'm surrounded by printed-out transcripts of the guys' interviews, all of them highlighted and covered in scribbles as I try to piece it together in a way that will appease John's appetite for gossip, the guys' need for truth, and the fans' desire for both.

"That bad, huh? Did you finally get Dax's interview at least?" I can hear her opening and closing drawers. She's packing for her flight to Boston, where she'll visit family before road-tripping with the guys to see me next weekend. I hate that I'm jealous of a road trip that's *for me*, but I miss my friends so much. The network I'm slowly cultivating here is still too new to fill the void.

I'm grateful she's too busy packing to have Skyped me and thus see the guilty grimace that flashes across my face—or that I'm not at home. "Yep," I say under my breath.

"S, are you in a library or something?"

"No," I confess, waffling for a second about if I want to come clean or not, but god, I need to tell *someone*, and Brooklyn's the only person I trust to tell. "I'm at Dax's," I whisper.

The silence on the other end of the line is deafening. I can picture her in her dated LA apartment, messy bun of black hair that resents being contained, her bow mouth open in shock. All she gives me is a slight squeak of surprise and confusion.

"It's easier," I say defensively, still keeping my voice low. "If I need to fact-check something, I can just call into the next room."

"Uh-huh," B says, her voice more loaded than a baked potato. "I let all reporters camp out on my couch while they work. Especially when that reporter is *my ex*."

I purse my lips even though she can't see them. "Forgive me if I don't take your advice on ex protocols." I wasn't the only one who got swept up that summer. Only, what I thought was a summer fling for Brooklyn continued every time she and Asher were in the same city. As two touring musicians, it happens a couple times a year. Their situationship has more mileage than my car.

"That's done," Brooklyn says primly. Even without video, I can picture her fussily tucking a loose tendril of hair into her bun.

I snort, because I've heard that before.

"But more importantly, are *you* done?"

I glance toward the hallway, to Dax's mostly closed office door. The soft guitar melody I've heard off and on the past few days drifts over to me, and I doubt he can hear me, but I keep my voice low anyway. "It's not really an option right now."

Brooklyn blows a raspberry. "Boring. Dish."

"He's literally in the next room." I realize after the words are out of my mouth how telling they are. Because yes, there are a lot of things

I'd like to say to Brooklyn that I wouldn't want overheard, least of all by him, because they're all about him.

"Fine," Brooklyn says, undeterred. "I'll do the talking and you can just say yes or no."

I'm sweating. I know I can tell her anything, but I've spent the past few days trying not to assess what's going on between Dax and me head-on.

"Is he still unfairly hot?"

I laugh. "Yes. It's only gotten worse, I fear."

"Ugh, you poor thing," she groans, not sounding at all sympathetic to my plight. "Does he still stare at you every time you walk away?"

"I— How would I know?"

"Fair," she concedes. "But do you stare at him?"

I exhale heavily, cradling a pillow against my front. I feel like a cartoon character whose heart won't stop jumping out of her chest every time Dax comes around. "Yes."

"Do you wanna do more than stare at him?"

"I can't," I remind her.

"That's not what I asked."

That's the million-dollar question, isn't it? *Do I?* It's the trickiest part for me, deciphering if I'm interested in someone—or just the idea of them, an emotional-support daydream. How quickly I clam up when things move from theoretical to physical, everything so much safer in the confines of my carefully constructed fantasies where I'm completely in control. I spent years feeling like a bad feminist for not being more sexy, more empowered, *more*. It wasn't until two years ago when I discovered the word *demisexual* that I fully understood it, understood *myself*. I sat on my couch and cried, feeling seen in a way I never had before. There was a word for it—why I felt things so differently from my peers—and I wasn't alone in this experience. I'm not a prude, or a tease, or any of the other things I'd been called. I just need to trust the person I'm choosing to be vulnerable with.

Brooklyn begins humming the *Jeopardy!* theme song under her breath, letting me know she's still expecting an answer.

Before I can give one, Dax wanders into the living room, clearing a space on the couch for himself before plopping down and stretching his legs out across my lap. When he realizes I'm on the phone, his eyes widen and he makes to get up and leave, but I place a hand on his knee, keeping him there. *Brooklyn*, I mouth silently.

He nods in understanding, settling back on the couch. He tucks one arm under his head, his shirt riding up, exposing a strip of skin above his waistband. If I didn't already have an answer to Brooklyn's question, I do now. I wrench my attention from the dusting of hair below his navel before my eyes can trace the path to what his sweatpants barely manage to conceal.

"Yes," I say hoarsely when Brooklyn finishes humming her tune. "Call me when you land, bye!" I say over her screech, hanging up. We can dissect what I just admitted when she's here next weekend.

"Sorry. Did I interrupt?" he asks when I toss my phone onto the coffee table.

I shake my head. "No, we were done."

I shift sideways on the couch, tangling my legs with his, even though I know I shouldn't. It's what I've told myself every day for the past four days that I've been working out of his living room. I tried writing at my place the day after I interviewed Dax, but I ended up calling and texting him so much to confirm or clarify certain points that he told me to just come over—and he promised to feed me. How was I supposed to refuse? After the second day, I stopped asking if I could come back and just told him when I'd be there the next day.

We've fallen into a rhythm of sorts. I come over midmorning with coffees from the shop down the street. He makes breakfast while I spread out all over his living room. He drops my plate on whatever available surface there is before retreating to his office. He spends his mornings writing, melodies drifting down the hall to me as I attempt to work. Come midafternoon, he leaves to rehearse with the guys for next weekend's Halloween show. He returns and either cooks or we eat leftovers or get takeout from down the street.

I don't know what it means, us cohabitating like this, but it's easy, natural. I wish I could say the same about my progress on the article. I could relent and write it the salacious way Robb and John want, but I don't want to be that writer anymore. I can't be. It was one thing when I was writing as Mike Song, but now... My name—my integrity—means too much to me. So, instead of writing, I spend most of my days organizing and reorganizing my notes as my deadline creeps ever closer. The only time I feel like I have a direction for the article is when Dax wanders in, worming his way between my research, tangling our limbs together, and whispers, "Tell me a story."

He's given me so many of his over the past few days that it's only fair to give him some of mine, too. I just wish I could figure out how to convert the simple magic of our couch talks into an article. Every time I try to translate the guys' stories, my own voice gets in the way—or rather, my lack of one. Swapping stories with Dax, I'm beginning to find it again.

We spent weeks doing this, hours on the road with nothing to do but talk. We shared so much that summer, but there are still so many nooks and crannies of each other we've yet to uncover. Big things, like him reconciling with his dad and my youngest brother coming out as bi, and small things, like the smell of ketchup makes him nauseous and he thinks I'm a psychopath for eating pizza slices crust first.

Today, with it top of mind after my phone call with B, I tell him about me discovering the term *demisexual*, and he asks me to explain it to him. I do, and he asks what he could do differently next time. *Next time*, he says, like it's not only a possibility, but an inevitability.

I think back to that summer, how I kept running away from him, scared he'd want things to move more quickly than I was comfortable with, how he apologized without even knowing what he'd done wrong, because I hadn't explained what I needed from him, how he was the first person to make me feel comfortable enough to ask for it. He let me set the pace after that, put all the power in my hands. In the end, giving him everything didn't feel like giving anything up at all. I tell him he was perfect.

He lightens the mood by telling me about the time he and his sisters attempted to make their own zip line with a coat hanger. I convince myself this break from working is necessary, that I'm doing this for the article, relearning how to tell stories again. I'm doing this for us. Not *us*, but for Sloane and for Dax, not Sloane *and* Dax. We can't be that right now, I remind myself not for the first time.

But god, I wish we could be.

At first, I wondered if us having so much still to learn about each other meant that what we'd shared wasn't as deep as I thought, but I'm beginning to understand we went as far as we could that summer. In the intervening years, we've grown up, discovered new depths in ourselves. We have the capacity to hold so much more now, and I'm greedy for every drop of him.

Sinking down, I rest my cheek against the back of the couch, peering over at Dax doing the same from the opposite end.

"Tell me a story," he murmurs.

"Another one?" I laugh.

He grins, nodding as his ink-stained hands trace the curve of my ankle.

I think he might be greedy for me, too.

[Excerpt from Sloane Donavan's Final Revelations interview transcript]

1999: To Dax or Not to Dax

JONAH: We had no fucking clue what we were gonna do.

BARRETT: Wes [from Immaculate Conceptions] and I had gotten really tight, and I felt like shit about our situation—Marcus not being fully better—and I had to come clean: Final Revelations needed to drop out of the tour. Wes wouldn't let us quit. He drove up from Columbus, said his cousin was in a band, and maybe their vocalist could fill in for Marcus on tour. None of us really liked the idea, but it was kinda our only option. We'd let some other guy do the bulk of the vocals, Marcus could do backup and play guitar, and Final Revelations wouldn't lose the momentum we'd worked so hard for.

CAIN: I didn't think it would work. Marcus has a good voice, and he was pretty. Girls actually came to our shows. Girls didn't go to lots of hardcore shows back then. I didn't think anyone could fill his shoes, but I humored everybody and went to check out this new guy.

DAX: I had no idea that show was an audition.

BARRETT: I laughed my ass off when Dax got on stage. I knew the kid. He skipped school to hang out at my house a lot. We kinda forgot he was a kid because it just felt like he'd always been around, and he didn't act like a kid. Y'know how kids are usually overeager and try too hard to prove themselves? *Look what I can do!* Dax wasn't like that. He was quiet. He just… listened. I knew he was in some pop-punk band, but I'd never really seen him perform because he was playing at The Lot and all the starter-band venues and we were playing bigger places at that point.

CAIN: So we roll up to the dive bar all-ages night and head down to the basement—and it's packed. It's so hot in there you can practically see the sweat dripping down the walls.

JONAH: I'd seen Dax sing before—with his other band. He had a good voice, but we were a metal band, so I was like, *This guy?* Actually, I think I said, "This kid?" because that's what Dax was, even if he didn't totally look like a kid because he's fucking giant. [*laughs*] He didn't have any tattoos yet, because his dad wouldn't let him. Like, he was a *baby*.

DAX: I remember losing one of my gauges right before I went out, and not wanting to go on stage with one butthole ear, I shoved a soda pop cap in my ear.

BARRETT: I may have laughed when Dax came out—but I quickly shut the fuck up.

JONAH: I remember thinking, *Wes's cousin is going to be so pissed at us for poaching their guy.* I think I'm the only one who knew immediately that Dax wasn't going to be just a fill-in. Marcus was good—*is good*—but Dax has that… "star power" sounds so dorky but that's what it is. You can't *not* watch him.

CAIN: I'd never seen anyone that young be so good, so confident.

Dax: I had no idea what I was doing.

Barrett: After the set, we—Jonah, Cain, Marcus, and me—looked at each other, nodded, and that was it. It wasn't really a question. It was either drop out of the tour or... Dax.

Dax: I'd heard of Final Revelations. Everybody had. Anybody local that was semi-making it? You were both rooting for them and deeply jealous of them. But I was still in high school, so I figured my time would come later, once I found a band I actually wanted to stick with. I was almost always in two bands at once. I liked the more melodic stuff, but I also liked the heavier bands. I wanted to do both, but no one was really doing both *in one band* back then—not yet. Final [Revelations] was pretty heavy in their earlier days, but there was something to how Marcus wrote, the way he structured the songs—I felt like we got each other in a way that ten, twenty, thirty years down the line, people would cite him as paving the way for my future band. I didn't dream we would end up in the same band. So, when they asked me to fill in? I went to school the next day, cleaned out my locker, and went to rehearsal.

CHAPTER THIRTEEN

There's an arm on my chest and it's not mine.

My eyes fly open, taking in Dax's apartment, the wall of warmth at my back.

I fell asleep.

I fell asleep *with Dax*.

I close my eyes, praying that when I open them again, I'll realize this was a dream. Reopening them, I shift, peering over my shoulder.

I'm not dreaming. Dax is still very much behind me.

"Not yet," Dax murmurs into my hair. His arms tighten around me, pulling me closer. I squirm, rolling over to face him so my ass is no longer aligned with his crotch, but I'm not sure this is any less dangerous.

Golden light spills into the living room, announcing that we've slept for a few hours, passing out after our latest round of Tell Me a Story.

"Stop squirming," Dax chastises gently, his voice scratchy with sleep.

I give one last squirm to annoy him, and he cracks an eye open, his lashes casting long shadows over his cheekbones. His hand at my side tickles my rib cage, and I squeak at the contact.

"Five more minutes," he pleads. Pulling me tighter against his chest, he nuzzles his face into my neck, throwing one long leg over me. I curse that I still haven't done laundry, meaning I'm wearing a body-con dress with a cropped ElectricOh! band tee on top. The brush of his jeans over my stockinged thighs is erotic. Something more than body heat has my skin flushing warm.

Lying next to him in the back of Barrett's SUV was one thing, four other people within arm's reach. But napping on the couch with Dax, entirely alone in his apartment... We've never done this before, not even when we were a couple. Our moments alone were all stolen, measured in seconds, not hours. What a luxury it is to wake up in Dax Nakamura's arms.

It's a luxury I cannot afford.

"Dax," I murmur. I've practically lived at his apartment all week. Working in the same space I can rationalize. Cuddling on the couch, however... That's blurring a line. A line I desperately need to stay in place. The devil on my shoulder—that feels a lot like Brooklyn humming the *Jeopardy!* theme song two days ago—waits for me to make a move, to stop this.

I don't.

Dax extricates himself from my neck, the stubble on his jaw rough against the sensitive skin there. But Dax's face next to my face, sharing the same pillow, is worse. He gently brushes my hair back, gathering all of it in his fist before twisting it out of the way. A stray strand tickles my cheek, and he tucks it behind my ear. His finger traces along my jaw down to my chin, pinching it between his thumb and forefinger the way he used to before tilting my mouth up to his.

"I should go," I say, despite making no moves to do so.

"Mmm," he hums thoughtfully, also not moving.

His thumb brushes over my bottom lip, his attention wholly on the freckle he claimed as his favorite three years ago, the one at the corner of my mouth. "Dax," I warn gently. "We can't."

"I'm not doing anything," he says innocently.

I make a noise of disbelief. "Then why are you looking at me like that?"

His gaze flicks up to meet mine. "You know why."

I squirm beneath the heat of his gaze, looking away.

He shifts, hovering over me slightly before tucking his face into the crook of my shoulder, his breath warm against my skin as he confesses, "I want to kiss you so fucking bad right now."

A strangled noise escapes me. "We can't." I meant it to come out firm, but it's more of a whine.

"For what it's worth," he muses, the tip of his nose tracing down the curve of my neck, his mouth a whisper against my gooseflesh skin. "I'm one hundred percent positive *AP* doesn't have my place bugged."

I roll my eyes, grinning despite myself. "I know that. That's not the problem. I mean...it is, but it's not just that."

"Then what is it?" His hand trails along my shoulder, my arms, the curve of my hip, tracing all my edges, fraying them.

My mouth is as dry as a desert, every fiber of my being restructuring so it's no longer oxygen that sustains me but his gently wandering hands.

"We're working together," I begin shakily. If he stops touching me, I'll combust. If he keeps touching me, I'll combust. Forming coherent thought is a struggle. "Tomorrow, we have the photo shoot," I remind him. His fingers trail up my leg, his thumb arcing out so he can grab a handful of my upper thigh, a groan of longing echoing deep in his chest. I swallow thickly, pushing past the lump in my throat. "And then there's the Halloween show—" His hands continue their slow exploration, and I know he'd stop if I told him to, that he's only pushing his luck because I'm letting him. "If I kiss you now"—I force the words out, because a few more moments of this delicious torture and I won't remember why they're important—"I won't be able to pretend like I didn't. If I kiss you now, I won't be able to stop kissing you. And that's a problem."

Dax's attention, which was following his wandering hands, snaps to mine. The hand grazing my hip turns into a grip, rolling me onto my back as he comes to hover over me fully. Ducking his face down until his mouth grazes the shell of my ear, he murmurs, "So then don't kiss me." He takes my earlobe between his teeth, tugging gently.

"What?" I say around the hitch in my breath.

He smiles against my neck, and goddamn if that isn't as sexy as his touch. His lips brush over my pulse point, his breath raising goose bumps everywhere it ghosts across my skin. Kissing—but not kissing. He pulls back, studying me with heavy-lidded eyes, asking if this is okay.

We shouldn't. We should wait until after the article is done, when this can be aboveboard. It's like someone turns the volume down on my logic until the knob clicks to Off. I haven't been touched in so long, haven't found anyone I wanted this with in years—three, to be exact. Surely I've earned a hall pass. Just this once.

My head sags against the pillow as I give in. "Do your worst, Nakamura."

Challenge lights his eyes and I flush as his attention returns to my neck.

When Dax touches me, my skin sings. I can't create melodies the way my friends can, the way he can, but I can feel them, deep in my bones. Dax is the ache of a Fleetwood Mac song, two exes, one microphone, a lost future on their shared breath. Dax is the hope of a fledgling band, their voice breaking with the want of it all, the notes coming out wrong, the imperfections reaching out across the void we're all screaming into, perfectly imperfect. Dax is the worn-away paint on the buttons of your CD player, where you pressed Rewind over and over to hear that line again, the one that made you feel seen in a way no one else ever has before.

He moves torturously slow, not-kissing his way down my arm, the warm drag of his mouth and the rough scrape of his teeth so at odds with the cool press of his septum piercing. Sinking back onto the balls of his feet, he kisses the pad of my thumb, my pinkie, my index finger, my ring finger, pausing when he gets to my middle finger, meeting my gaze when I show it to him. He grins drunkenly, nibbling it affectionately before releasing my wrist. It drops, limp, against the top of his thigh.

The words rush out of me. "Can I touch you?"

"If you think you'll be able to stop," he says with a smirk. At the same time, his hand slips around the back of my thigh, hitching it up around his waist.

I make an unintelligible noise, forgetting entirely what I'd just asked.

Dax guides my limp hand to rest against his side. Touching him feels both new and old, forbidden and inevitable. "Always, Sloane," he answers for real this time.

"That's a broad statement," I say, amazed I'm still forming words, my entire body pulsing like a bomb about to detonate.

"Always," he repeats without hesitation, meeting my gaze with an intensity like he's saying one thing but vowing another.

Before I can overanalyze it, my mind goes blank as he resumes meticulously reclaiming my body. He doesn't know I never stopped being his.

Dax doesn't break eye contact as he continues his slow mapping of my body, kissing along my other arm, from my shoulder to the crook of my elbow, nipping at the pulse point in my wrist. This time, he interlaces our fingers before working his way back down. He nuzzles the frayed hem of my T-shirt but doesn't explore further, which is a shame because this dress makes my boobs seem almost impressive.

His hand not intertwined with mine grabs my hip with the exact pressure I like, not too light to be ticklish, just shy of too rough. His stubble snags on the hem of my dress, and I hold my breath in anticipation of the scrape of it against my inner thigh. He stills.

"Don't stop," I plead.

He's groaning before his mouth is even on me, lips parting as his canines scrape across my stockinged thigh, not quite hard enough to rip them. He pulls back a fraction, his movements trackable by the heat of his breath coasting higher on my leg, my dress now less of a dress and more of an overlong tank top for how high it's ridden up. He rests his head against my pelvis, his shaky exhale taut, like he's warring with himself. His nose nudges along the core of me, over the damp fabric of my tights. When his mouth comes over me entirely, his hand at my hip is the only thing keeping me from bucking off the cushion.

"Dax," I rasp, need curling my fingers into his shoulder.

He pulls back, pressing his face into my thigh, taking one, two, three deep breaths, his eyes shut tight. "I know, baby," he breathes. "I know."

I don't know what he knows—how good it feels, or how we shouldn't be doing this—I just know all thoughts fly from my head at the sound of the endearment sighing past his lips.

His mouth traces a line to my knee, where he presses his forehead against it, as if he's the one falling apart right now and not me.

"I need to tell you something."

[Excerpt from Sloane Donavan's Final Revelations interview transcript]

1999: The Petty-Little-Bitch Tour

Marcus: We started rehearsing with Dax, and I knew my place in Final Revelations was in jeopardy. We needed him to get through the tour, but I made sure he knew—that everybody knew—he was only temporary. A fill-in.

Cain: Marcus was an absolute dick to Dax.

Barrett: [*laughs*] Dax didn't care that Marcus was marking his territory. He was just so fucking happy to be there.

Jonah: That only pissed off Marcus more.

Marcus: I wasn't *that* bad...Okay, maybe I was.

Dax: I had no intention of just being a fill-in. For the first time in my life, I was all in on a band. Marcus being a brat about me being there when I was doing them a favor? Just made my job of convincing them to keep me even easier. [*grins*] I can be a good boy when I need to be.

Cain: The rest of the guys, we all have brothers. Marcus and Dax don't. Dax was like the annoying little brother who worships his older brother, tagging along behind him, and Marcus had no idea what to do with that. It was really fucking funny watching the two of them figure out how to share a stage.

Barrett: [*laughs*] Marcus wasn't used to standing stage right and would wander into the middle, but Dax didn't care. He was like a Tasmanian devil, running all over the fucking place, jumping off risers and amps and never missing a note. The guy's lungs were—are—insane.

JONAH: Marcus couldn't really scream anymore, but he wasn't content with just playing guitar, so a few shows into tour, he came to us with the idea of adding in some melodic backing vocals.

CAIN: It was clearly a ploy at getting more control, reminding everyone who the real frontman was, but—

BARRETT: Dax and Marcus battling to be frontman was the best thing that ever happened to Final Revelations. Their tension was impossible to look away from. They gave every line, every note, their all.

JONAH: Then someone— [*coughs*]
BARRETT: [*coughs*]
CAIN: [*coughs*]
MARCUS: [*coughs*]
DAX: [*grins*]

JONAH: Someone put our album on Napster, and suddenly, kids from all over the world could download our album. We put up a shitty camcorder recording of our set on our website, and as tour went on, the audience learned Marcus's melodies—

CAIN: People could sing along to our songs for the first time ever.

BARRETT: That was really fucking cool.

MARCUS: I basically guaranteed that Dax had to formally join the band, because now people expected the melodies. Our songs required two vocalists. Really played myself with that one.

DAX: [*singsong*] Thank you, Marcus.

MARCUS: Sometimes, being a petty little bitch makes your band better, y'know?

CHAPTER FOURTEEN

"Right now?!"

When Dax meets my gaze again, I know our reprieve from being responsible is over. The heady lust that scorched through my inhibitions turns to ice water, shocking me back to my senses. Everything I've been ignoring froths to the surface. My deadline, my career that I was about to fling the same way as my underwear—

Dax shifts so he's sitting beside me, and I draw my knees to my chest so I can do the same, tugging the hem of my dress back down. I've never done a walk of shame, but I imagine it would feel something like this—and we didn't even do anything. But it feels like we did.

Dax runs a hand over his face, staring at the wall when he speaks. "It's the Final album."

I wait for him to say more. He doesn't. "What about it?"

His attention cuts to me, shoulders curled inward. "It's the *final* album," he says again.

This time, I understand what he means. Technically. But it doesn't— It couldn't— *Why?* "What?" I splutter. Shock, rage, grief, and confusion fight for dominance.

"I wanted to tell you from the start, but... I was overruled. It's why we decided it was time to do another interview—one last interview," he amends, studying his hands, not looking at me. "The guys didn't want the article to read like an obituary, so we didn't tell you. And it's one thing to keep a secret from my ex, from a journalist, but you're not just some ex, some random journalist. I can't lie to you if we're—" He gestures to the couch, the memory of what we did—almost did—a palpable thing. We crossed an invisible line just now, one that I don't know we can redraw. "This changes things."

He meets my gaze at last and I look away. It's my turn to stare at the wall, unsure how to even begin digesting everything he's just said.

"Sloane," he calls softly, but it only makes my eyes prickle. "Say something, please."

I rub the scar on my ring finger, trying to ground myself. As shock, rage, grief, and confusion fight it out, embarrassment sneaks in and wins. It makes complete sense. Why they decided to do the article, why they'd pick me, someone whose eyes they could pull the wool over. I've been fighting so hard to protect them with this article, and to know they've been lying to me, withholding information much bigger than a secret album...Betrayal stings my eyes.

"You're right," I say numbly, my voice sounding a thousand miles away, a thousand leagues underneath the crush of conflicting emotions inside me. "This does change things."

Hurt flashes across his face, and I wish I hadn't seen it, because underneath my own hurt, I know this is a huge decision for him—for all of them—to have made, but I'm too blindsided to coddle him right now. They've had god knows how long to sit with this news. I've had less than a minute.

I need to think. Pushing off the couch, I begin gathering my things, trying to will my hands to stop shaking.

"Sloane, please."

I don't bother being gentle with my papers or my notebooks,

shoving them unceremoniously into my bag. What's the point? It's not like I have any clue where I'm going with this article anyway.

He places a tentative hand on my arm, the same one he so lovingly reclaimed earlier. "Please don't leave."

I blink, and we're in the back of Barrett's SUV. *Don't leave. I'm gonna fight.*

"Why?" I ask, slipping out from under his touch. *"Fuck."* I pull my hand back with a wince as my thick notebook cover splits my skin. I stick my middle finger in my mouth, the tang of blood coating my tongue.

The instant I take my finger out of my mouth to inspect the damage, it wells with blood again.

Dax is halfway to his bedroom when he pauses. "Please don't leave."

The fight is already ebbing from my body, but it leaves a hollowness in its wake. I nod in confirmation, and he slips out of the room for a moment, the only sounds my racing heart and the opening of bathroom cabinets. Dropping my bag to the floor, I sink onto the couch.

Dax reappears, sinking down in front of me and easing my finger from my mouth. Carefully, he smears antibacterial ointment on the cut that claimed a chunk of my cuticle before wrapping it with a bandage.

Once he's done, we stare at each other for a long time, breathing heavily, swallowing thickly. There's so much to say, but I have no idea where to start. I don't know why I'm so upset. It's not like it's my career that's ending. Except... if this gets out before my article, it might be.

"How could you—" I inhale shakily. "But you *are* Final Revelations."

I swear the color leeches from his face, his gaze casting downward and away.

"Why?" I ask again.

He sinks back against the couch cushions, toying with the chain around his neck. "We've been at this for over a decade," he says hollowly. "Touring almost nonstop, writing an album as fast as we could so we could get back on tour. Until the past few years. We slowed down a bit, and..." He runs his finger along the chain, his gaze unfocused as he thinks. "Cain got engaged and had a baby. Marcus has had time for his solo project. Barrett's doing other stuff. Jonah moved in with his girl. Things are finally good with my family. Mariah just graduated—she's the baby and the favorite... Well, Breanna's pregnant, so maybe she's the favorite now? I'm so excited to be an embarrassing uncle," he says with a look so sweet my teeth ache. "Daisha's doing something new every week, but she's the other middle child after me, so she gets away with everything. We have dinner at our parents' every other Sunday, and—" He shrugs. "It's nice, being home—having one again."

He's rambling, which is so unlike him, and my anger softens, knowing how much work it took for him to get to this place.

He leans forward, propping his elbows on his knees. "We've done it, y'know? I started when I was seventeen, and I'm turning twenty-nine next week. I started out singing and writing about shit I'd never experienced, then went out and had a bunch of experiences—some good, some bad, some I regret but can't change. And that gave me a lot to fucking unpack, and I finally had the time to." He exhales heavily. "I was really fucked up for a really long time, but I'm not *that* anymore—or I am, I always will be, it's me, but I don't want to keep living in that headspace. I've written a lot of angry music about all the ways I fucked up. I needed it once... But I don't anymore. But I don't want to change Final, either. None of us do. We made something great, something we all needed back then, something that we're really fucking proud of, but it's time for us to do something else. Maybe we'll come back to it—I don't know. But none of us want to be *just* Final Revelations anymore. We want lives, partners, families, to unpack our fucking suitcases. And we did that for the past two years, and..." He nods slowly. "We wanna keep doing it, but last time we were on tour, we weren't doing it like it was the last time, because we didn't think it would be. It didn't feel right to go out that way. So, this is it. We're throwing everything we've got left at this album, this tour. We wanna go out right."

I nod slowly. "Thank you—for telling me, for explaining." I push to my feet, easing the strap of my backpack over my shoulder.

"Sloane," he pleads, standing. He's between me and the door. "Don't leave."

"I need to think, Dax," I say wearily. "And I can't do that if we're—" I gesture to the couch.

His phone on the coffee table buzzes, and we both stare at it as it goes to voicemail, then resumes buzzing.

I glance at the clock. "You're late for rehearsal."

"*Fuck.*" He snatches up his phone, tapping out a message before tossing it back on the coffee table. "It doesn't matter—"

"Go to practice," I say definitively. "We'll talk tomorrow. *Don't* be late for the shoot."

"I won't be." He places his hands on my shoulders, massaging them comfortingly. "I'm sorry. I should've known."

"Known what?"

One of his hands drifts to the back of my neck, his thumb brushing along my pulse point. "That if you were in my life, I would be trying to get you back. That it was pointless not to tell you from the jump."

I hate that the lopsided grin he gives me makes me soften. I hate that he's not even giving me a minute to breathe. He went from not-kissing me on the couch to announcing a career implosion, to declaring his intentions all in the span of a few minutes. I hate that I'm confused and yet completely clear about him, all at once. "I cannot fucking stand you," I mutter.

His smile grows until his dimple is winking at me. "I know," he says fondly. "Me, too."

I duck my face to hide my disappointment. *That's not your line*, I want to tell him.

Suddenly, my feelings aren't so clear. How can he say he's ready for our reunion tour when he doesn't even remember our greatest hits?

When he pulls me in for a hug, I wrap my arms around his middle, rubbing the scar on my ring finger all the while.

I let my focus slip for a moment, but not anymore.

[Excerpt from Sloane Donavan's Final Revelations interview transcript]

1999: Bad Decisions

DAX: I remember the last week [of the IC tour], all the guys talking about how ready they were to be home, and it hit me: *I don't think I have a home anymore*. Before tour, I quit school so I could rehearse—I had a lot of songs to learn and not a lot of time to do it. But after a week of missing classes, the school called my parents. There was a big fight that culminated in my dad kicking me out. I was leaving to go on tour, so I didn't really care—I mean, I *did*, but I told myself I didn't. I crashed at Barrett's, which meant all I had to do to get to rehearsal was walk downstairs. But then, after tour... I don't know if Barrett knew I had nowhere to go, but while we were all loading out the van, Barrett put my duffle in his guest room, and we never really talked about it.

BARRETT: I knew something was going on with the kid—I mean, the whole time we were on the road, I don't think he called home once.

DAX: I wanted to. I probably could've called my sisters—my older sister had a phone in her room, but all we had was the one landline, and I was too scared of my parents being the ones who picked up. I remember being insecure that I didn't have anyone to call. Like, how fucked up is that? I wasn't worried about losing my relationship with my entire family who I'd always been close to. I was worried how other people would perceive it. Or...I dunno, if family could cut me off, what were the odds this band wouldn't, too? And then I'd have nothing, nowhere to go.

Jonah: I was the youngest after Dax, so I watched out for him on that first tour. He was pretty tame. He's always been quiet, which is why I think he was able to hide it so well. Or we just stopped looking. I don't know. Shit.

Barrett: We all kept an eye out for him at first, but he was a good kid. He'd drink a few beers with us after the show, but never before a set. He didn't really party. I think he wanted to be in the band so badly he wouldn't do anything that would jeopardize it. It wasn't 'til after the IC tour that he really started getting into shit.

Cain: We were setting up the keg for the Halloween rager Barrett was throwing when Dax said he had to go and we were like, *Why?* Dax never really went anywhere or did anything outside of the band and his job at the mall.

Jonah: He was going to get a tattoo.

Barrett: At first, we were like, *Right now?* Then we realized: *Ho-ly shit. He's old enough to get a tattoo.*

Cain: Our lil boy was a man now.

Marcus: We'd been together all day and he hadn't said shit about it being his motherfucking eighteenth birthday.

JONAH: The party at Barrett's house still happened, but Barrett wasn't there. We all missed it so we could sit with Dax while he was getting inked.

CAIN: The ugliest fucking tattoo you've ever seen.

BARRETT: [*uncontrollable laughter*]

MARCUS: He covered it up not too long after.

JONAH: Labels were starting to court us, and we were all kinda caught up in the promise of things happening, and I remember sitting in that tattoo shop and feeling so shitty that I didn't even know when Dax's birthday was. Like, we'd almost missed it. He was going to *let* us miss it. And I thought that was maybe one of the saddest things I'd ever heard. That was the first time I thought maybe Dax wasn't okay.

DAX: I dunno. I tried not to draw attention to the fact that I was so young. I was really insecure about that—how much less life I'd lived than them. I'd been singing Marcus's songs for months and feeling like such a poser. I hadn't experienced most of the things I was singing about. I was trying to grow up at warp speed. If I got enough piercings, enough tattoos, no one would see I was a quasi-homeless high school dropout who was still deeply afraid of being told he didn't fit in. That was the start of me making a series of bad decisions.

CHAPTER FIFTEEN

I'm still mad the following morning.

I recognize that part of my anger is grief. Selfishly, they're one of my favorite bands, and the thought of never getting another album after this is gutting. Annoyingly, I also understand their reasons for wanting to move on, to go out on a high rather than continue to create when their hearts are no longer in it. I respect it, but I'm not quite over it yet.

I'm mad at them for not telling me. I get why they didn't tell me. I wish they hadn't told me, the pressure to get this article right tripling, after already being doubled by John making it a two-parter.

I feel better after sleeping on it, but the conflicting emotions are still there, dulled from a deafening roar to an ever-present unease, roiling menacingly beneath the surface. The only thing holding me together are my objectives:

- Get through this shoot without anyone catching even a whiff of history between Dax and me.
- Wrest the unreleased album out of Dax.
- Draft this damned article before anything else leaks.

All of which I doubled down on when Mike Song teased "shocking news" in his latest vlog that I hate-watched this morning. It could have nothing to do with Final Revelations, but I'm paranoid.

Robb asked me about the unreleased album nearly in the same breath as she said good morning, and even though it was already on my list, I can't ignore the mosh pit of nerves in my stomach at the mere idea of listening to it. There's a high probability that there are songs about me—either our relationship or our breakup—and I don't know which one scares me more. I may have been letting Dax off the hook a bit too much by not following up about it, because I don't know that I'm ready to face it yet.

I'd be madder at all of them for keeping so many secrets if my life hadn't been simpler without them. I've got enough on my plate as is.

Like making sure Dax is on time for this shoot.

I check my phone anxiously. The rest of the guys rolled in a few minutes ago, Barrett dropping a massive carafe of coffee and donuts in the break room for everyone. Dax isn't late—*yet*—but having everyone else here already makes it feel like he is.

My stomach swoops with relief when the front doors open and he slips in, double-fisting coffee, with one minute to spare.

He curls his long frame over the front desk, checking in with our sweet elderly receptionist, who—I can tell from halfway down the hall—is blushing. I can't blame her. He's so *on* right now, his stage aura permeating all the way to where I stand between the break room and line of cubicles, one eye on the rest of the band chatting with my coworkers, the other on Dax's nerve-rackingly punctual arrival.

"Finally," I mutter, waving to the guys before going to fetch Dax and spare Dolores.

When he spies me approaching, he straightens, saying something to Dolores that I can't hear, but I can see the wink he gives her.

"Stop flirting with my receptionist," I grouse as he approaches.

"Why?" he says with a backward glance at Dolores, who is still watching him. He waggles his fingers in a wave over his shoulder. She flushes deeper before becoming suddenly very interested in her day planner. "You got dibs?"

I glare at him, clenching my teeth together to fight a smile.

"Good morning to you, too, by the way." He extends the second coffee in his hands to me.

"Barrett already brought coffee for everyone," I say, words clipped, accepting the coffee anyway. "And donuts."

"But you prefer muffins," he counters, extracting a pastry bag from the pocket of his hoodie.

I accept it begrudgingly, because damn it, I *do* prefer muffins.

"You look good," he says under his breath, and I want to throttle him.

"Shh," I hiss. "I'm still pissed at you—"

"Oh, trust me. I'm aware."

"And if anyone hears you—"

"They'll think I have eyes?"

A small grunt of frustration escapes me, and I turn on my heel, nearly running bodily into John, whose office we stupidly had this conversation outside of. I pray his door was closed and our voices didn't carry, never mind the glass wall that would've meant he saw everything.

"Morning!" John says cheerily. Having Final Revelations in the office is the editor equivalent of being a kid in a candy store.

"Morning," Dax says congenially, shaking John's proffered hand.

"Excited for the Halloween show," John says in his weird way that's not a question but you still feel obligated to answer. He hasn't written in years, but it's said he was an absolute shark.

"Of course," Dax answers around his straw, clearly taken aback by John's... *John-ness*.

"And the new album," John plows on, either oblivious or invigorated by catching Dax off guard. "Good odds on new stuff making the set list this weekend?"

Dax cuts a furtive look to me for a second, clearly unused to not being the one in charge. Unbridled glee lights up my insides like a holiday tree-lighting ceremony. "We'll see," he manages.

John smiles broadly, a twinkle in his eye, Dax failing to realize that an evasive answer is like catnip to a journalist. "Uh-huh," John says, seemingly dropping it, but I know he's only tucking it away for later. Taking a large bite of donut, John checks the time on his watch.

"I'll take them over now," I announce. I might be floundering with my article, but I can keep this shoot on schedule. And as amusing as watching Dax be wrong-footed was, I fear leaving the two of them in conversation any longer.

I gesture to the guys in the break room, letting them know it's time to move, and they scramble to gather their things. Cain shoves a whole donut in his mouth to free up his hands. He laughs, powdered sugar flying everywhere, and Robb follows after him, brushing it off him as they file out of the room.

"Robb can take them over," John says decidedly. Robb has the good grace to only look bewildered for half a moment before recovering, motioning for the guys to follow her. "Sloane and I will catch up—after we catch up," John says to me, grinning with pride at his play on words.

I match his expression, but it feels like carving it out of granite. I wish we'd chosen a different location for the shoot. A collective of artists operate out of the other side of our warehouse, and John offered the space to Isaac—the only photographer Final has worked with in years. It made sense, since we need to film the short video announcing the upcoming article—take that, Mike Song—but I'm now realizing John offering it wasn't pure charity but a way of keeping an eye on things. I can't blame him for it. This is a big piece, but the mounting pressure only makes me clam up more.

"All good?" John asks, a hand at my elbow, guiding me into his office.

"Yeah. Why?" I hate how defensive I sound, mentally a million other places, trying to deduce what prompted this.

John sinks into his chair, studying me over his glasses. "I sensed some tension—with Nakamura."

He couldn't *possibly* know. Instinct kicks in, and I bluff harder than the time my brothers and I accidentally slap shot a hockey puck through the basement window. "Well." I laugh. "You know frontmen and their egos."

John nods, his gaze a little too piercing. "Is that all?"

I open my mouth to speak, unsure how to lie my way out of this when I don't even know what we're talking about. "Sir?"

John tosses his reading glasses on the desk. "Sometimes"—he clears his throat—"with the female writing staff, the talent can be..." John gestures vaguely. "Inappropriate."

Oh. My cheeks flush. "No," I rush out. "They're all perfect gentlemen." While they'd all laugh their asses off at being called "gentlemen," there's a reason they've never been the subject of that kind of rumor, unlike some of their counterparts.

"Glad to hear it," John says, relieved. "Y'know," he says thoughtfully, punctuating the air with his finger. "Actors often give their best performances when working opposite someone they can't stand. I think this bodes well for you. How's the article coming?"

"Good," I lie. "Great," I amend. With vocabulary like that, no wonder the article's been a struggle.

"Great," John echoes distractedly, checking the caller ID on his buzzing phone. He sends it to voicemail. "Sorry I've been so hands-off." That makes one of us. "I gotta get through the Halloween show this weekend, but after that—" He flashes me a grin. "You have my full attention."

"Sounds great." If fissure lines appeared on my face from the force of my faked smile, I wouldn't be surprised.

"Monday," he decides, pulling a date out of his ass. "Let's meet and go over everything. I want a full progress report."

I can tell him right now the progress is zero, but I continue smiling and nodding. "Monday," I confirm.

His phone buzzes again, and he sighs. "I have to take this—"

I'm out of the room as fast as I can without running.

Fuck fuck fuck fuck fuck fuck, I swear internally all the way to the door that connects our side of the warehouse to the other sections.

I let myself into the art studio, momentarily forgetting my completely self-created problem by getting swept up in a guy and not in the massive career opportunity at my feet.

The windows, which normally lend ample natural light, have been draped with olive-green fabric, casting a yellow-green glow over the space. They've set up a couch in front of the wall that's still tagged in graffiti from when the warehouse was abandoned. It's both eerie and incredibly cool.

Isaac's face is buried behind his camera as he takes a few test shots while a hair-and-makeup artist fusses over the guys' appearances, polishing them up.

I wait until Isaac's done studying the screen on the back of his camera before wandering over.

"Hey," I call.

He glances up briefly, tapping a few buttons to adjust his settings. "Hey, Sloane. Almost ready for you."

I nod, nerves churning my stomach. I'm not an on-video type of journalist. I should probably learn, but this is a first for me. At least it's Isaac, who's been in and out of the recording studio as much as I have, documenting the album, so I'm glad it's someone I know. He's a childhood friend of Jonah's and has been working with the guys since forever, but it's not just favoritism that's kept him as their primary photographer. His work is beautiful. I can barely take one decent selfie, and this guy has hundreds of artistic shots of musicians in dimly lit rooms with strobing colors, all taken whilst running around a stage.

"Make me look good?" I ask, trying to quell the quaking in my voice.

Isaac flashes me a grin before going back to his camera, too engrossed in his work to coddle me.

"You always look good."

I jump, not having heard Dax approach. Spinning around to face him, I spy John in the corner, chatting with Robb. No doubt about what a shame it is that this undoubtedly gorgeous shoot won't have a juicy article to go with it. I glare up at Dax, and it's either a trick of the dim lighting or the makeup artist put the barest hint of eyeliner on him. I want to kiss her for it and curse her for making him even more alluring. "Not here," I hiss.

"Just stating facts," he says innocently. "You look extra good today."

Right back at you is on the tip of my tongue, but I reel it in. He's shed his hoodie from earlier, effortlessly stylish in a series of faded blacks that don't match. I wish I could've worn my usual uniform of jeans and a band tee. I finally did laundry last night—except I fell asleep with all my clothes in the wash and didn't have time for a dry cycle this morning. So I'm wearing pieces I don't normally wear: belted plaid pants and a half-unraveled sweater over a black turtleneck I swear I've had since I was twelve. It's very 1990s Winona Ryder—the ruler against which I measure any outfit to determine its coolness. Brooklyn helped me put it together after I panic-called her at eight a.m., near tears because I had nothing to wear and I had to be on video in an hour.

"John saw us bickering outside his office. He thinks we hate each other, and I'm not going to dissuade him of that belief, lest he get any other ideas, ones a bit too close to the truth?" I raise my brows.

Dax pinches the bridge of his nose, and I mentally thank him for having resting bitch face and mannerisms of near-constant annoyance. He's selling this narrative without even trying. "Us hating each other is more professional than us actually liking each other?"

"Yes," I confirm. "John was concerned I might be getting unwelcome advances, much less—" I catch myself at the last second, but Dax's face lights up.

"Welcome ones?" he says under his breath, gaze heavy lidded.

I glare up at him, and it's only half to keep up our ruse. "I cannot fucking stand you."

A laugh rumbles in his chest, his lips pressing into a thin line to conceal a grin. "I know, baby. Me, too."

I narrow my gaze, crossing my arms in frustration. He keeps saying that, like it means something, like he changed the steps to our old dance without telling me, leaving me tripping over my feet. *Baby.* I can excuse it slipping out when he's seconds from going down on me, but here? Calling me baby before noon? Unacceptable.

"I'm still mad."

"Did you have breakfast?"

My nostrils flare as I inhale sharply. "That is *not* why I'm mad,"

I chastise him before storming off to eat the muffin he brought me, hoping the stomp of my Docs against the warehouse floor conceals the growling of my stomach.

I do feel slightly better after inhaling the muffin in four large bites, but I'll take that secret to my grave. But now, a ball of dough is caught in the swirling tornado of nerves in my stomach like the cow in *Twister*.

Isaac motions me over, and I wipe my sweaty palms on my pants. I just have to get through this video, and then I can disappear while they do the rest of the shoot. By comparison, working on my article sounds like the most fun thing in the world.

I weave through the small crowd of my coworkers that have wandered in to rubberneck at the spectacle, and I pause next to Barrett, who lingers behind the cameras and monitors. He gestures me forward, and I glance up at him in surprise. "You're not...?"

He shakes his head, swallowing a bite of donut. In my periphery, I spy the makeup artist glaring at the fleck of glaze that falls on his shirt. "Just you, Tweedledum, and Tweedledee for this."

I huff. "How'd you get out of it?"

Barrett nods gravely. "Well, so, like, ten years ago, I made sure we had a good-enough-looking frontman that no one would require my ugly mug to do promo. There's five of us but only one of you, Boston, so you're kinda stuck."

Immediately proving his point, Isaac calls for me. It could be my own panic setting in, but I swear the room quiets, everyone at the periphery pressing in like the crowd at a concert when the lights flicker, announcing the start of the show. Only, unlike Dax and Marcus, whom Isaac is settling me between on the weathered couch, I chose a career that did not require me to be on stage, because I am very, very uncomfortable being on one.

I wipe my hands on my pants once more. Not only is the bright light Isaac switched on for this part of the shoot stiflingly warm, but it guarantees he'll be able to catch every facet of my discomfort on his high-definition camera. I wish we could go back to the dim yellow-green lighting from earlier, but I know that would leave us half in darkness, which is not the vibe for this segment. I'd feel much better with some shadows to hide behind. I'm acutely aware of every single pair of my coworkers' eyes watching from the sidelines, even if they're impossible to make out with a spotlight trained directly on me.

At Isaac's direction, Dax scoots closer to me, his thigh pressing against mine. I swallow thickly, trying to ground myself in the touch, but all I can think is how if we touch at all in front of my coworkers, somehow they'll know.

"You alright?" Marcus asks, slapping a hand over my knee.

I tear my attention from the crowd of faceless onlookers to meet his gaze, feeling like a wild rabbit caught in a bear trap.

He glances around me to Dax, giving him an infinitesimal shake of his head.

"Can everyone nonessential fuck off, please?" Dax calls, scratching his eyebrow with the back of his knuckle as if bored, commanding the entire room while barely raising his voice.

I cannot believe he just told my boss to fuck off. More than that, I can't believe John listened and is now filing everyone out, completely nonplussed about it.

I'm infinitely grateful he's using his diva frontman powers for good. As the door clicks shut behind John, I exhale deeply, loosing the breath I didn't realize I was holding.

"Okay," Isaac calls, taking a few test shots and analyzing them. "Marcus, lean back, same as Dax. Sloane, stay leaning forward. You can leave your arms on your knees or whatever feels most natural."

"Nothing about this feels natural," I grumble.

A ripple of laughter goes through the remaining people in the room, and I'm relieved to see it's all people I know, save for the hair-and-makeup artist.

Isaac slips behind the tripod that holds the video camera. "Okay—"

"Wait!" the makeup artist calls, jogging over. She rearranges my hair for me and tweaks the way my sweater falls. When she grabs my chin to study my makeup, I blink, fully seeing her for the first time. Her skin tone is cooler than Dax's, but there's no mistaking the resemblance. I turn to look at Dax, and he startles to awareness.

"Oh yeah. Sloane—" He gestures to me and then to the girl crouched before me. "Daisha, my younger sister."

"*Second* youngest," she clarifies. "Nice to finally meet you."

"You, too," I intone automatically. His family's genetics are unfair.

She swipes a brush across my nose and cheeks before nodding satisfactorily. "You look perfect. Dax didn't do you justice," she says with a purse of her lips to her brother, who huffs the universal sibling laugh of affectionate button pushing.

Dax has talked to his family about me? And in what context? Before the shock of that revelation can fully sink in, Daisha is stepping back, surveying her handiwork.

"All good," she calls to Isaac, whipping her braids over her shoulder as she retreats back to the sidelines.

"Ready?" Isaac calls.

Not really, but I won't lie—there's nothing like a compliment from a fellow woman to make you feel like Wonder Woman. Between Daisha's primping and Dax kicking everyone out, I don't feel so much like a zoo animal now. How any of them get on stage every night without quaking in their Vans, I'll never understand.

Isaac nods to me, holding up three fingers.

On two, Dax's hand slips between my shirt and my sweater, the warmth of his hand on my back melting the tension from my bones, my shoulders relaxing away from my ears. He's touched me a million times before in a million different contexts, but right now, he's grounding me. I get it now, why he wanted me to do the article. New, scary things seem possible with him by my side, at my back, believing in me, making a safe space for me to be brave.

On one, I smile genuinely. I have to do this, but more importantly, I *get* to do this. I'm scared as fuck, uncertain as fuck, but I know no one in this room is going to let me fail.

It takes me a few tries, but I finally manage to get through my laughably short script without stumbling over my words.

"One more, just in case," Isaac says, holding up his hand to count it down. It feels infinitely more doable now, knowing I've done it once.

Dax rubs his hand across my back before letting it fall to my side, giving my hip a reassuring squeeze, the ghost of his handprint still between my shoulder blades. I find Barrett behind the camera and smile, delivering the line to him when Isaac's fingers drop from three to two to one, pointing at me to start.

"Hi, guys! Sloane Donavan from *Alternative Press* here with Dax and Marcus of Final Revelations to let you know that we have an exclusive *two-part* interview with these guys dropping next month. In it, we talk about their new album, the upcoming tour, and the future of Final Revelations."

I can write hundreds of words no problem, but saying fifty words in a row without stuttering? It feels like my greatest accomplishment to date.

"Okay," Isaac says cheerfully. "I think we got it."

I launch myself off the couch so fast that everyone laughs.

"Take five," Isaac says around a low chuckle.

Barrett hands me a water bottle, which I chug immediately, not realizing how parched I was. He makes himself scarce before I can thank him. I'm about to follow after him when I realize why he slipped off.

Dax slots into place beside me, everything we haven't said hanging in the air between us. "Thank you," I say genuinely, jerking my head back toward set. He smiles softly at me, and I know what he wants to ask, now that we're mostly alone. "I'm not mad anymore, but I need to focus, and to do that, I need some space. So," I say with a heavy exhale. "I'm going to work out of my apartment from now on."

He nods in understanding, brushing my hair back from my face. His fingers catch on the hinge of my jaw, and I lean into his touch, his palm cupping my cheek.

"We're okay?" he asks.

"We're okay," I confirm.

"And you're sure you can't focus better on my couch?" he asks with an adorable scrunch of his face, his thumb stroking my cheek.

A laugh gusts out of me, and I shift out of his touch. "I'm one hundred percent positive I can't. You're very distracting, Nakamura."

He smirks at that. A laugh rings out, and we turn to watch Daisha fussing over a reluctant Barrett. "Wanna meet my sister—properly?"

"And how would you introduce me?" I ask, arching a brow. "As your ex?" A muscle in Dax's jaw twitches in displeasure. "As your reporter?"

Dax grunts in understanding.

"I'd love to meet your family," I say sincerely. "*Properly*. But not while we're—" I gesture between us. There's no word for what we are, this unnamable in-between thing that's not quite a thing. "But right now, I need to focus. I'll never be able to look them in the eye if I botch this article."

Dax shakes his head. "You're not going to."

"Y'know what would help?" I hedge, fluttering my lashes at him. "If you brought me that unreleased album..."

A series of emotions flash across his face in such quick succession that I can't get a read on them. "Right." He nods.

Dread fills me to the brim. If that's his reaction...

What the fuck is on that album?

[Excerpt from Sloane Donavan's Final Revelations interview transcript]

2000: Beautifully Insane

BARRETT: Everybody wanted to sign us after that tour.

CAIN: Well, not the major labels. What we were doing was not cool on that level yet. But the big indies were interested. We were getting offered royalties on album sales for the first time ever. We were like, *Wait, we're gonna make money?*

DAX: I remember being in Barrett's basement, writing songs for the second record, and Marcus asked my opinion on something vocally and I was like, *Oh, I guess I'm officially in the band.*

MARCUS: I wanted our band to be successful more than *I* wanted to be successful. And to do that, we needed Dax.

DAX: I got writing credit on that album, but it was mostly Marcus. I tried writing a few things on my own but didn't think they were good enough, so I focused on making Marcus's stuff stronger. I was so drained after each writing session because I felt like I was cosplaying as someone who'd lived this gritty, existentially questioning existence and not a middle-class kid from the burbs.

MARCUS: I don't think any of us realized how smart Dax was until we started writing that album. He would take my half-formed ideas and be like, *Oh, this is like Sisyphus*, and dress up my lyrical whining in metaphor until it felt like this sweeping but devastating epic tale.

JONAH: Our songs on that second album were ten times better than anything we'd ever written before.

BARRETT: I would sit back and let them flip-flop between bickering and getting high on their own genius, like, *Let me know when you need me to drum something*.

CAIN: I felt smarter just being in a room with Dax and Marcus. I always wanted to be in a band, and of course I wanted to do well, but... That was the first time I thought we actually stood a chance, that I let myself really want it.

MARCUS: Wanting things is dangerous.

JONAH: And we all really fucking wanted it.

DAX: We'd heard the rumors about Dropkick Records, but they offered us the most money, and every band on their docket was doing well. We wanted a piece of that. They were *the* label in the hardcore scene. In hindsight—

MARCUS: I don't know if I'd do it any differently. Like, no one else was pushing what we were doing at the time.

JONAH: Legally, I don't know how much we can say.

BARRETT: Dropkick was a bunch of predatory motherfuckers who knew rock was about to have a moment again, and they gobbled everybody up and then fucked 'em all.

DAX: I mean, we didn't know we'd signed a deal with the devil—not at first. We recorded *Covenant*, which we were so proud of, and they booked us as the supporting band on a national tour—our first time not being bottom of the bill. We had sick fucking merch. An actual *tour van*—not a sleeper bus or anything fancy, but it was a step up from the moving van, so we felt like kings.

Jonah: Ahead of our fall tour, we got invited to play Punkapalooza.

Cain: Punkapalooza was a grind. So many cities, crisscrossing the US in the span of, like, two months. But if you were in a hardcore band, that was *the* summer festival to book. If you were a small band like us, that festival could be the thing to break you out—or break you.

Barrett: We made Dax and Marcus work the merch booth because they were the prettiest.

Dax: [*shrugs*] I didn't mind being pimped out if it meant people actually showed up to our set.

Jonah: [*laughs*] Girls would walk by the merch booth, do a double take, and then double back to buy merch for a band they didn't even know just to talk to Marcus and Dax.

Marcus: I flirted with everyone who came to the booth—guys, girls, I didn't care. I knew if we could get them to show up to our set, we could turn them into fans. We were often playing at the same time as much bigger bands, so getting people to pick *us* to watch was an uphill battle and we fought it, in the blistering fucking heat, every single day of that tour.

CAIN: Marcus was such a little slut.

BARRETT: Marcus can charm anyone. He could feed you shit and you'd thank him for the sundae.

CAIN: Dax is Marcus's opposite, so they were a good duo in the merch booth. Where Marcus was charismatic, Dax was quiet, but he's got these, like, *eyes*. That sounds dumb, but if you've ever met him or seen a video of him, you know what I mean. You know there's shit going on inside that brain of his, and everybody wanted to be the one who "got" him.

MARCUS: Dax's stage presence evolved that tour. Before he was this chaotic gremlin running around, like he thought more movement made him more interesting to watch?

DAX: I moved around a lot the first tour because I was shaking with nerves. If I didn't stop moving, no one would know.

MARCUS: The first Punkapalooza set, we were on one of the smaller supporting stages so Dax couldn't move around as much and it was, like, all that energy still had to go somewhere, and it just emanated off him. We all fed off of it—especially the crowd. There weren't a ton of people there to watch us, but I didn't even care, because the people that were there? Were *so* into it. It was easily the best set we'd done to date.

JONAH: Dax is stupid tall and kinda slouches around most of the time, but when he's on stage, he becomes this whole other guy. Wolfish, the way he prowls around. He really came into his own as a frontman that tour.

DAX: I was playing a character. It felt...safer than being myself. Like, if they hate me, well, it's not *really* me. It freed me to act in ways I don't normally. Well, that and I, uh, was not sober most of the time, so my inhibitions were nonexistent.

BARRETT: The way Dax works a mic stand...Every girl in the audience wanted to *bibbidi-bobbidi-boo* themselves into being a mic stand.

MARCUS: We were selling out of merch so fast we almost couldn't get more fast enough. Dropkick was sending boxes of CDs ahead of us every few cities. It was...insane. Beautifully insane.

CAIN: We started the summer on the smallest side stage. We ended it on the big one.

CHAPTER SIXTEEN

Ah, fuck. I'm crying again.

As the van pulls into the no-parking zone outside my apartment, the familiar prickle starts behind my eyes. The side door of the sleeper van slides open before it's fully parked, and my best friends since my awkward preteen years pile out of it.

Tyler reaches me first, because of course he does. His puppy energy cannot be contained, and he immediately gloms onto me in what I think is meant to be a hug but is more like a koala clinging to a tree (me). Brooklyn and Charlie are next, and that's when the tears really begin to fall. Charlie, who I've known since diapers and every single day of my life since, who I should definitely call more often. Brooklyn, who couldn't be less like me but is somehow my other half. Drew bounds out of the passenger seat, wrapping his long arms around us all. Finally parked, Reid slides out of the driver's seat, moseying over to reluctantly join our exuberant reunion.

"Are you crying?" he asks, mortified on my behalf.

"I know." I sniffle. "It's disgusting."

"She *does* like us," Drew declares triumphantly.

"Shut up," I say around the lump in my throat, laughing.

"We missed you, too," Charlie says. I think he's rubbing my back comfortingly, but I'm not entirely sure whose limbs are whose in this six-person bear hug. If I weren't already crying, this hug would've squeezed it out of me, my insides as gooey as a marshmallow. I can't wipe the dopey grin off my face. This lot is terrible for my reputation as being cool and unbothered.

"Okay," I say, shaking my hair out of my face as Brooklyn wipes away my tears. "Let's unload before Mr. Fluff and Fold gets mad at us." I'm still scarred from him chastising me the day I moved in, even though our mutual landlord said I could park in the loading zone. Glancing over my shoulder to the laundromat, I can already feel him eyeballing our illegally parked van, its doors flung open wide in my friends' haste to greet me.

Surely he's impressed by how efficiently we unload. If the whole alt-band-stardom thing doesn't work out for Post Humorous, they'd have a killer career as movers. The Tetris of their tiny van trunk is a work of art.

Reid disappears to find somewhere to park the van, and I grab his stuff, trailing behind my friends as they bitch the entire three flights of stairs up to my place.

"What is this, a Mayan temple?" Tyler screeches from the front of the line.

"Knew I shouldn't have skipped leg day," Drew moans.

"Carry me, Sloane," Brooklyn whines.

"For fuck's sake," I say, pushing past them once we reach the landing to unlock my door. "I'm renaming the group chat from Buncha Punks to Buncha Divas."

"Accurate," Charlie murmurs under his breath with a secret smile just for me, easing Reid's bag from my grasp as he passes by.

My apartment isn't fancy. It always smells faintly of pho broth, which I consider a feature, not a bug. Most of my furnishings are roadside finds that I pilfered in college. None of it looks like me, each piece selected because it felt like something my friends would pick, and thus they're always with me, even when we're on opposite sides of the country. My multicolored fabric desk at the bay window is Brooklyn. The crystal floor lamp that casts rainbows on my walls every morning is Tyler. The worn trunk that I use as a coffee table is Charlie. The industrial barstools are Reid. And the slightly shabby, chaotically patterned but incredibly comfortable couch is Drew.

"First order of business," Tyler calls, uncharacteristically solemn.

I still as all their gazes fall on me. "What?"

"You and Dax—"

"Y'all fucking again or what?"

"Jesus," Brooklyn says, chastising them. "Let the girl breathe." Then, to me, "But seriously. Dish."

Never mind. They're all the garbage can. Every single one of them.

"Leave it to y'all to make sure we fail the Bechdel test not five minutes in," Reid grumbles from the doorway.

"Says the guy who started the bet," Tyler counters with a pointed arch of his brows.

Reid smirks, sinking onto the couch and sticking a joint in his mouth. He pauses with the lighter held to the tip, and I motion for him to go ahead, walking over to open the bay windows.

"And what bet would that be?" I say prudishly.

"What base you two got up to in your—" Drew strikes a Marilyn Monroe pose: knees bent, one hand in his hair, the other holding down his imaginary white dress. "Interviews," he finishes with a dramatic toss of his head, voice breathy.

"Haven't even stepped up to the plate," I say matter-of-factly.

"What?" Drew and Tyler scream in tandem. With a groan, they

pull out their wallets and throw bills at Charlie, who extends his hand for me to high-five.

"Et tu, Brute?" I say as Brooklyn fishes five dollars from her purse.

"It was wishful thinking." She sighs, hoisting her bag and kicking the door to my bedroom open to stake her claim.

"Shit," Tyler says under his breath, lunging for his own bag. He and Charlie collide in my bedroom doorway, fighting to claim the third spot on my bed.

When I last toured with them, Post Humorous's budget was modest at best. We slept in the van most nights, but when we did splurge on a hotel room, we squeezed the six of us into one room, three to a bed. To this day, whenever I have trouble sleeping, I stack pillows on either side of me and convince myself we're all puppy-piled together tour-style.

Tyler's lanky frame works in his favor, edging out Charlie's broad shoulders. Tyler slips past, starfishing on my bed. "Dibs!"

Reid kicks off his shoes and stretches out on the couch pointedly.

Drew tackles him immediately, and the way Reid manages to headlock Drew whilst smoking is honestly impressive. Charlie joins the fray, the three of them trying to shove each other off the couch, despite the fact that it's midafternoon and no one will be going to sleep for a long while yet.

"Don't break my couch," I call, the fondness in my voice outweighing the authoritative tone I was going for. It always felt a little fated that as my four brothers grew up and went off to college, I collected more guy friends until I had four, the balance always maintained.

A knock sounds at the door, and I furrow my brow, wandering over. My confusion doubles when I peer through the peephole. Unlocking the dead bolt, I swing the door open.

"Hi," I say in shock.

Dax's greeting sticks in his throat as his attention catches over my shoulder. Following his gaze, I spy the latest development of the guys' battle for couch supremacy. Charlie has Reid's upper body in a lock, but Reid has Drew's legs pinned over his head, and Drew is grasping at Charlie.

Turning back to Dax, I smile blandly, like this is completely normal, because for me, this is the most normal I've felt in months. Years, really. But still, I find myself blinking twice, pointedly. *Save me*, I mouth.

Dax's face lights up. I mouthed the same thing to him three years ago when I was stuck being mansplained to ad nauseam by some drummer. Dax and I had barely spoken to each other before, but he swooped in with some excuse about someone looking for me. We talked and walked around the city for hours after that, and somehow I ended up with his sweatshirt, which I still have to this day and may or may not be wearing... right now.

"Speak of the devil," Tyler calls cheerfully as he reenters the room, spotting Dax.

Dax's brows draw together in an unspoken question as he meets my gaze.

"Ignore him," I say with a saccharine smile.

Realizing we have company, Drew, Charlie, and Reid break apart, bounding off the couch to greet Dax like the fangirls they are.

Brooklyn enters the room, closing the still-open front door as the guys corral Dax into my kitchen. "Long time no see, Nakamura," she calls coolly.

Dax grins, abashed. "Good to see you, too, B."

Brooklyn bristles slightly. We're the only ones who call her B, but Dax has heard me call her it enough that it must have infiltrated. I duck my head to hide my smile. It's been a really long time since I've had all of my favorite people in one place, and it feels really, really fucking good, like a hole I hadn't known I had filling back up.

Dax extricates himself from the guys, the dimpled grin on his face filling me all the way up to the brim.

"What are you doing here?" I ask under my breath. We haven't spoken since the shoot two days ago, which I thought would clear my head, but instead I just spent the past two days thinking about how much I hate him for giving me the space I asked for.

Dax holds up a clear CD case, and my eyes go wide.

"Nixed?" I ask, reading his sloppy Sharpie scrawl on the reflective surface.

"That's what we call it. Just—" He wiggles it between his fingers. He's nervous. "Text me once you've listened to it, and...try not to judge me too hard. I was in a bad place."

I reach for it, feeling like I'm moving in slow motion. Pinching the case between my fingers, I meet his gaze for a moment that feels like a lifetime. What is on this fucking CD? And am I ready to find out? I'm only now recovering from the shock of them retiring—a secret I have to keep from my friends, though it's seconds from bursting out of me.

Movement in my periphery catches my attention, and I fix my gaze over Dax's shoulder, to where Drew is making kissy faces and Tyler is fanning himself like a damsel. I hate them so much.

Dax begins to follow my gaze, and my hand shoots out of its own accord, clamping down on his biceps. "Thank you so much!" I say, my voice far too loud. Once I'm sure the guys are done, I spin Dax around and begin shuffling him toward the door. "I'll listen to this later—once these goons are gone, and, uh, yeah. I'll text you." I paste a smile on my face, and Dax smiles in bewilderment, gaze bouncing to everyone in the room in turn.

"Good to see you all," he calls bemusedly, one hand on the doorknob.

When he doesn't turn it, I place my hand atop his and squeeze, twisting the knob. "So good," I confirm. "Bye!"

He allows me to hurry him over the threshold as my friends shout their goodbyes and well wishes for Final's set at the Halloween show tomorrow night. Before I can close the door, he turns, bracing his arm on the doorframe. My body flushes as his gaze roams hungrily over me. I've never felt sexier in sweatpants in my entire life.

"See you tomorrow night?" he says quietly, just for me.

"Don't forget," I murmur. "We're supposed to hate each other."

"I remember," he promises. "We're not friends and we're definitely"—he leans in, his lips coasting over my cheekbone, pressing a kiss to the space between my jaw and my ear—"not kissing."

I move my head in an approximation of a nod, my tongue too tied up in lust to form coherent speech, the memory of all our not-kissing heating my skin. I shoo him out of the doorway. A moment longer and I'll be melting into a puddle at his feet.

He smirks, pushing off the frame, his gaze raking over me one last time before heading for the stairwell. I can hear him laughing even after I close the door.

"I hate every single one of you," I tell my friends, tossing the CD onto my mail pile by the door.

"Love you, too," they call in unison.

Miracle of all miracles, I make it through the rest of the night without my friends eternally mortifying me—their favorite pastime.

I'm both drained and refilled by the time I crawl into bed with Brooklyn. Tyler ended up passing out on the couch with Charlie, though how either of them is sleeping with the other's feet in their face, I have no idea. I'm more familiar with what those feet smell like than I care to be.

In true rhythm-section fashion, Reid's stoned-oblivion snoring keeps perfect time from his sleeping bag on the floor. Also on brand is Drew's occasional upstaging by talking nonsense in his sleep.

Brooklyn hums Céline Dion's "It's All Coming Back to Me Now" under her breath as we settle into bed, the song still ringing in my ears from our impromptu—but no less overeager—postdinner power-ballads-of-the-'90s sing-along session.

I wiggle until comfortable, which, for me, is no fewer than three flops from side to side.

"Comfy?" Brooklyn teases me.

"Quite." My voice is more hoarse than usual from scream-singing diva classics off-key, this group the only group I'll ever sing in front of. Thankfully, Charlie is as tone-deaf as I am, but at least he has a drummer's rhythm. I couldn't carry a tune in a bucket with a lid on it.

"What did Dax bring you?"

"Unreleased album—the one before the one they're recording now." I press a finger over my lips. They could sue me for telling her this, but I decide best-friend privilege supersedes my NDA, and I know I can trust her to keep quiet until after the article comes out.

Her eyes widen, and she whips the blanket over our heads, cocooning us. *"What?"*

I catch her up, her eyes saucers by the end. "Holy fuck," she murmurs. "No wonder the article's been impossible to write."

I avert my gaze, her validation lifting a weight off my shoulders. "Yeah." I sigh.

Her hand wraps around my wrist, halting my anxious toying with the stray thread on my pillow. "You'll figure it out. You always do."

I nod, my throat too clogged with emotion to speak. I've missed her so much.

"But you owe me five dollars," she says saucily.

"What?" I laugh. "Why?"

"Because you and Dax might not be canoodling, but what y'all are doing is way more serious."

It's my eyes' turn to bug out.

She wiggles her head side to side like no explanation should be necessary. "You're totally dating, just without the sexy stuff. Though," she adds pensively, "y'all staring at each other in the kitchen was so hot I felt like I should excuse myself."

"Stop," I say around a laugh, nudging her shin with my toe.

"So," she says, plowing on unperturbed. "To answer my own question from last week: Yes, he still stares at you like he wants to devour you."

I hide my face in my pillow, cheeks burning. Peeking one eye over at her, I mumble, "There may have been *some* canoodling."

"Sloane Marie Donavan," she whisper-screams, slapping the mattress between each word. *"What?!"*

"We accidentally took a nap together," I say as quietly as I can, though the guys' symphony of snores and deep breathing tell me they're all zonked.

"Naturally," Brooklyn breathes, her voice laced with barely repressed glee.

"And when we woke up…" I can't conceal the grin that stretches across my face, cheeks burning. "He told me he wanted to kiss me, but I told him I couldn't kiss him or I wouldn't be able to pretend like I hadn't, and that I wouldn't be able to stop if we started—"

Brooklyn lets out a closed-mouth squeal, kicking her feet under the covers. "S! You dirty dog."

"And then he says, 'So don't kiss me' and proceeds to, like, get his mouth on me. Kissing but not kissing?"

Brooklyn lets out a groan like she's being tortured. "And?!"

I shrug. "Then nothing," I say anticlimactically. "We can't."

She kicks her feet like a toddler having a tantrum. "You're a stronger woman than me. I would've folded like a chair. You should let him fold you like a chair," she declares decidedly. "And then give me the five dollars you owe me, you canoodling canoodler."

I choke on my own tongue, and she cackles as if she can read my mind, how badly I do want it, want him, how he feels like the only thing I've gotten right in years. And I can't have him. Not yet, anyway. But my head and my heart and my other parts are at odds, my ever-in-control logical side floundering.

I don't know how much longer I can hold out.

Brooklyn's mouth twists off to the side, her laughter giving way to something more pensive. "I know you don't like being told what to do and will just do the opposite if I try, and I know it's complicated right now with the article and everything, but...please don't get in your own way about this. I really like him for you."

I emotionally steel myself, because I know she's not done. When Brooklyn gets in her feels, she gets *in them*. It doesn't help that she has help from the holy trinity right now: Jose, Mary Jane, and Céline Dion.

"When I first met you guys, I thought you'd be the one in the group I was the least close to. We were so different." We both laugh softly. We still are so different. "But then, once you decided you liked me, this whole other side of you came out, and I realized you're not a total wet blanket."

I scoff in mock offense, kicking her shin lightly. "Just because I don't like being the center of the attention—"

She plows on as if she didn't hear me, the giggle in her voice giving away that she did. "You're funny, and mischievous, and really fucking clever. And I thought, *Holy shit*." Her teasing lilt gives way to something throat-cloggingly sincere. "I'm so lucky to truly know you. You don't show your true self to many people, and I—" She shakes her head. "That summer, I thought the thing with Dax was done the first time you bolted after he kissed you. But he kept showing up, and I watched as you opened up in a way I'd only ever seen you do with me, or the guys, or your brothers, that secret side of you that only comes out in your writing. And I was like, *Oh*. This is big. Something more than just a summer fling. And maybe the timing wasn't quite right, but I don't think the two of you are done yet."

I nod, wrapping my hand around Brooklyn's and squeezing it in thanks in lieu of a response. My throat is too tight to form words, but if I could, I'd say, *I don't think we're done yet either.* And if I were feeling especially brave and honest, *It all feels a little too good, too easy to be true*, and *I don't trust it.*

[Excerpt from Sloane Donavan's Final Revelations interview transcript]

2001: No One Has Time for Your Fucking Feelings

MARCUS: For the record...I don't hate Dax. I love him, but I'm not *in love* with him, despite what every epic slow-burn, enemies-to-lovers fan fiction about us might suggest. We weren't enemies, but I was definitely a dick to Dax in the beginning.

DAX: Was he? I...don't remember most of 2001, to be honest with you.

CAIN: Marcus is good at what he does because he's worked really fucking hard at it. Dax is good without really even trying. He's one of those rare talents that you're lucky to have but also you kinda hate him a bit, even though it's not his fault.

JONAH: Fuck, 2001. I was sober and barely remember it, it was such a whirlwind.

BARRETT: Jonah's California sober, okay? Don't let him act like he rawdogged 2001. None of us did. We'd been touring almost nonstop trying to break out, and now that we had, what're ya gonna do? Stop? No! We were exhausted, but we kept going—most of us with some vices in tow.

CAIN: The year that made us was also the year that almost broke us.

MARCUS: Our second album, *Covenant*, went gold. We were on our first headlining tour. Everything seemed to be coming up Final, and then—

JONAH: I was in school to be an accountant before Final blew up. I'd had suspicions that [our label] Dropkick was being shady. Our royalty checks were always late and super small. It didn't make sense... We were one of the biggest bands on the scene and completely broke.

DAX: The way we performed the songs off *Sacrament*—the record Final put out before I joined—was completely different from the album, and our fans had been asking us to record the new version. We were one album into a three-album deal with Dropkick—who were screwing us. So, to get us out of our deal one album cycle faster, I suggested rerecording it.

BARRETT: And Marcus took that personally.

CAIN: In Marcus's defense, that album was his baby, and the idea of rerecording the album with Dax as lead vocalist when Dax didn't seem to be taking the band seriously and Marcus took everything seriously... There was tension, yeah.

BARRETT: There was a lot of ego around that time. It gets to your head a little bit, when you blow up that fast. It made us a little blind to what was going on with Dax. We just thought he was being a dumb kid, out in the world for the first time, partying and experimenting. Maybe a bit too much, but he seemed pretty together compared to some of the other bands we toured with, so we didn't realize how bad it was until it was really bad.

JONAH: I don't know that it was just ego. There was legitimately a lot of shit going on, and no one really gives you a road map for it, so you're just kinda hanging on for dear life and hoping you don't get thrown off the ride.

Dax: I don't really remember a time I wasn't depressed. I was fronting this band that I'd basically fallen into, and I developed huge imposter syndrome, telling myself I didn't actually deserve any of the success Final was reaping. My depression and imposter syndrome fed into each other in a way that made me really self-destructive. I got on antidepressants at one point, but not the right ones—like, every bad side effect they warn you about? I had. And so I started taking more stuff—some prescribed, some not—trying to combat all that. I was medicated six ways from Sunday. When you're a part of something that big—something so much bigger than just *you*—there's no time for you to have a breakdown. People are counting on you to "be okay," so I was. I wasn't actually, but I figured out a system that allowed me to fake it.

Marcus: On the outside, we were having the best year of our life. On the inside...

Jonah: A lot of songs in the hardcore scene are about depression—ours are no exception. And yet, everyone seems surprised when they find out their favorite band members are fucking depressed. Like, "You should've said something." They fucking are. They're screaming it on stage every night. But when you're one of the biggest bands on the scene, no one wants to hear you complain about how beyond burned-out you are—

CAIN: Or how you miss your girlfriend back home and you're terrified you're gonna lose the best thing that's ever happened to you because you're gone all the fucking time—

BARRETT: Or that you're messed up over your dad dying and had to be back on tour two days after the funeral—

JONAH: We all just put on a brave face because no one wants to hear that the guys who seemingly have it all aren't happy. No one has time for your fucking feelings.

CHAPTER SEVENTEEN

The venue looks amazing—once I finally manage to get inside. The general-admission line is wrapped around the block, and concertgoers quickly recognized my friends as the band Post Humorous. I played photographer for a good twenty minutes before dragging them through the VIP door.

The space is fully decked out for Halloween, every column wrapped in gauzy fabric, with mummy hands and faces poking out between the gaps. Faux spiderwebs crisscross over the ceiling, the purple backlighting illuminating the giant spiders nestled in their webs.

Merch booths line the back wall, the venue floor split in half down the middle, the larger left side for general admission, the right side reserved for VIP. Along the right wall, under the overhang of the balcony, is a fully stocked, comped bar.

Some companies have holiday parties. *AP* has epic Halloween shows.

The VIP section is already filling up, my coworkers and tonight's acts milling about. I should be rubbing elbows with the bands and making connections, but I only care about my friends tonight. I've been waiting for this since they joked about coming out after their New York show, and the joke quickly became a plan. This wasn't possible when I was in California, them popping over from Boston. It's like coming home to myself, the chaos of all six of us in my one-bedroom apartment, talking over each other and pushing each other's buttons.

The general-admission doors open, and there's a mad rush for the barricade. Everyone came dressed in their Halloween best, zombie brides, goth dolls, and vampires spilling onto the venue's main floor.

I let Brooklyn pick my costume, and I should have known that was a mistake, but I was too caught up in work to pick one out for myself. She looks fantastic in her angel costume. Tiny wings protrude from her corset, and silver glitter dusts her cheekbones, matching her silver shorts. A dainty halo hangs over her head, reflecting on her shiny mane of black hair. Naturally, I'm her devil. Fortunately, the tight red dress is a comfortable cotton, but unfortunately, it rides up with every breath I take. I tried putting opaque tights on underneath instead of fishnet, but Brooklyn insisted freezing your ass off in a slutty Halloween costume was a rite of passage I wasn't allowed to disrespect. The gold stars she scattered across my cheeks like freckles even made me like my bumpy, twice-broken nose. The guys are all dressed as greasers, with thrifted leather jackets Brooklyn adorned with the T-Birds logo.

The six of us crowd into the photo booth along the back wall with effort, Brooklyn kneeling in front and toppling sideways in her stilettos every time we scramble to switch poses between shots. I'm grateful I opted for my Docs instead of the heels she brought for me, not needing to be any taller—or uncoordinated—than I already am naturally.

As we wait for the machine to spit out the photo strips, Charlie leans in to whisper in my ear. "Final is here."

My head whips to the side, watching as the five of them spill through the VIP door—and are immediately swarmed. Dax's gaze scans the room, and I avert my attention to the photos in Drew's hand, not seeing them. "Cool," I say, sounding the opposite.

Brooklyn huffs, shoving one of the photo strips into the top of her corset. "C'mon." Without waiting for my assent, she slides her hand into mine, steering me over to them.

"B," I plead. "This is unnecessary."

"You are profiling them," she says sternly over her shoulder. "It's weirder if you don't say hi."

I grumble under my breath. She's right, of course. I'm suddenly too aware of my body in the skintight dress. Not of Dax seeing me in it—he's seen me in far sexier and far less sexy—but of others seeing us next to each other. Dax can't kick everyone out of the room this time. I'd planned to avoid him all night. My coworkers can't get suspicious if they never see us together, but B has a point. I can only hope the ruse that worked on John works on everyone else.

"Hi, guys!" Brooklyn says brightly, bounding into the circle of them like they're old friends.

I suppose they are. She met them more than once that summer. Regardless of how well they know her, they all give her their undivided attention. Of course they do. She's a hot girl in booty shorts and she's also *Brooklyn*. She's magnetic.

I hazard a glance up at Dax, whose gaze is slowly raking over me.

"Well," he says as though from the bottom of a well. "I won't have to pretend to hate you tonight."

"What?" I huff, crossing my arms.

"Are you trying to torture me?" His face is a mask of haughty indifference, but his eyes tell a different story, his gaze intent upon mine. My blood turns to hot magma in my veins, obliterating everything in its wake.

To anyone else, we'd look like two people bickering. I shift my weight onto one foot, running my tongue over my teeth to hide the smile threatening to surface. "Is it working?" I ask with an irritated quirk of my head.

"Immensely," he purrs.

We glare at each other for a long moment, the mischievous glint in our eyes a secret only for each other. I like this new game.

He breaks our glaredown, his attention darting to the waist cincher B laced me into, and I swear the air around us heats an extra ten degrees.

"Don't even think about it," I hiss. I know where that look leads—my legs thrown over his shoulders, his face between them.

"Too late," he groans, tortured. "Way too late." He takes a half step closer, hovering over me so I have to tilt my face back to continue glaring at him disapprovingly.

"Dax." His name comes out like a laugh, my grip on our ruse slipping for half a breath. "Don't. Start."

He hums contradictorily. "I never stopped," he confesses under his breath. "Not for one fucking minute, baby."

He tugs gently on one of the corset's ties, and I feel that tug *zing* through my body like a pinball before pooling in my gut, hot and heady. I'm so heated my clothes may very well melt off of me.

"Okay!" Brooklyn calls, voice pitched high. "So good to see you again," she calls to the guys, simultaneously wrapping her hand around my biceps. "Let's separate these two before they start fighting."

I blink to clear the haze at the edge of my vision, having forgotten where we are, that we're not the only two people in the room—a problem that I have too often where Dax is concerned.

"Fighting to get their clothes off," she adds under her breath as she frog-marches me away.

"Sorry. And thank you," I breathe, all the heat in my bones exiting my body by way of a full-body blush.

Brooklyn's laugh twinkles out of her like wind chimes. "I honestly couldn't tell if you were about to fight or fuck."

I shake my head as we rejoin the guys by the bar. I accept a can of cheap beer from Charlie, pressing it to my neck. "We may have led everyone to believe we hate each other as a cover."

"Makes sense," Tyler says reasonably. I wait, because he never speaks unless he can be funny. "What's to like? He's just...hideous." He sighs wistfully.

Brooklyn titters under her breath, hiding her traitorous face behind her beer.

"So overrated, too," Reid chimes in.

"Biggest metal band in the scene? Never heard of them," Drew says, flinging an arm around my shoulders and tucking me into his side with an affectionate jostle.

"She hates us all," Charlie says before I can.

I give him a squinched smile.

It's an effort to keep my eyes off Dax for the rest of the night. I sigh in relief when he and the guys disappear into the rented trailers out back, the venue's greenroom not big enough for this many bands.

The VIP section grows uncomfortably full as the night progresses, the air thick from so many people. Before the Undead Kings set, Charlie, Drew, and I slip out from the bar wing and onto the VIP section of the main floor. Without a balcony overhead, the air is much cooler out here. We position ourselves in front of the sound booth.

Undead Kings are dressed—fittingly—as zombie royalty. After their set, I do my best impression of a professional journalist and not an unapologetic Undead Kings fan as I exchange contact info with their front-of-house manager.

It's been a long night, the *AP* Halloween show less a show and more like a minifestival. The crowd would have every excuse to be waning four bands in, but as the roadies flip the stage, Undead Kings' backdrop coming down to reveal the Final Revelations logo, the crowd roars louder than ever.

I rock backward into Drew as the force of it hits me like a physical blow. Drew's laughter is swallowed up by the crowd, but it rumbles against my back as he steadies me, his arms coming around me in a viselike hug.

I'm relieved I'm not backstage right now. I know Final Revelations' preshow routine like the back of my hand. My heart pangs uncomfortably, knowing I'm no longer a part of it. Dax's mouth won't find mine in the dark before he takes to the stage, his hand won't slide into my back pocket, squeezing my ass as he grins cheekily against my lips.

Brooklyn sneaks over to us, interrupting my morose trip down memory lane, and I hug her to my front, creating a three-person prom pose. It's more comfortable than it has any right to be, and I don't want to ever let go.

The lights flash, announcing the start of the next set, and a cheer goes up, the crowd pressing toward the stage in anticipation.

Red lighting descends upon the stage, Jonah, Marcus, and Cain strolling out, looping a guitar riff from one of their most popular songs.

I don't know who to look at first, trying to analyze their costumes. They don't match at all, but the red lightning across Marcus's face and Jonah's hat with concho hatband are immediately recognizable as Bowie and Slash. With his round black glasses, Cain is unmistakably Ozzy. Barrett appears on the drum riser. His costume is vaguely '70s, and I can't place him until he sits behind his kit. Of course he's paying homage to John Bonham.

"Where is Dax?"

As if in answer to Brooklyn's question, the crowd to our right parts, the telltale arc of flashlights heading toward us.

Dax posts up next to us like he's not supposed to be starting the show right now. His hand ghosts along the back of my arm, twirling a lock of my hair around his finger. He gives it a gentle tug that unlocks a cascade of memories, a montage of him grabbing my hair, holding me where he wants me while he slowly obliterates my self-control. His gaze snags on my lips before flicking up to meet mine, and my mouth goes dry. It's a watered-down version of our old preshow routine, but I'm as breathless as his kisses used to leave me. Knowing he hasn't forgotten our old routine any more than I have—

Not for the first time, I'm grateful Drew is at my back, keeping me upright. But for all the attention Dax pays to him, Drew may as well not be there.

Dax pushes away from us, his touch a brand against my skin.

"When the pit opens up, take care of that one," he says, finally acknowledging Drew, an unwitting third wheel to this entire interaction. "She's important to me."

If Drew weren't behind me, I'd topple over. Every cell in my body riots, needing to get closer to Dax, my brain waging war against that instinct, reminding me where we are, who is watching. Him coming to find me is risky enough.

"I think I just got secondhand pregnant from that," Drew whispers in my ear.

I notice Isaac for the first time, camera in hand, following behind Dax with two security guards. The stage lights flash out onto the crowd, Barrett's slap of his sticks like a war drum. When he does it again, Dax joins in. "Final," he growls, each syllable in sync with Barrett's drums.

Good god. This man is going to undo me. On a normal day, Dax is attractive, drawing people's eyes even when he's trying his damnedest to fly under the radar. Even if you don't listen to metal or have never heard the name Final Revelations, he has a presence about him that immediately lets you know *he's someone*. Dax dressed as Freddie Mercury wearing a literal crown and coronation mantle, no shirt, and the iconic white pants with the red stripes down the side? Lord help me.

"They're legends," Charlie says in near-reverent awe. He's referring to their costume theme paying homage to iconic rock bands, but also, Final Revelations themselves.

The crowd parts for Dax as he meanders through, he and Barrett perfectly in sync as their chant grows faster and faster, the crowd joining in. Dax climbs over the barricade into the gap in the middle of the venue floor, and I can sense security's dismay as he jumps the barrier to general admission. Isaac and the security guards struggle to keep up with him, but the crowd parts for him like a school of fish would for a shark, letting him make his way to the stage as the chant of *Final, Final, Final* reaches a near frenzied tempo, Dax somehow holding the note as security drags him over the barricade in front of the stage.

"He is fucking unreal," someone next to us breathes in awe.

My proud grin stretches more broadly across my face.

The room goes dark as Dax lets out one last, long, low guttural, the lights coming back up once he's on stage. He launches immediately into their first song, folding in half with a synchronized headbang with the three guitarists.

Dax is having far too much fun with his Freddie Mercury costume, prowling across the stage, fur-trimmed mantle trailing behind him. Fuck. Even the way this man *walks* turns me on.

When the song ends, Dax props the crown at the base of Barrett's kit, coming to greet the audience by bracing one foot on the riser, his crooked smile making his dimple pop.

The crowd cheers enthusiastically, only quieting when he brings the mic to his mouth.

"What's good, Cleveland?"

The room explodes again, and Dax shares a private smirk with the rest of the band, the crowd positively eating out of their talented hands. Final hasn't played a venue this small in years, and they're relishing it.

Dax slots the microphone back into the holder, and the way his hand slides down the stand is indecent.

As he works the crowd up, getting them to make some noise for the opening bands, Brooklyn glances back, brown eyes wide and sparkling more than the glitter on her cheeks.

I shake my head because I can't talk about it. He's so my id that it hurts.

They launch into their next song, and Dax straddles the mic stand between his legs, walking forward until it's parallel to the ground as he gets low, walking it back up...

Brooklyn leans back, resting her head on my shoulder so I can hear her. "I fear you're in a throuple with that microphone stand."

I shake with laughter, lust and longing rattling around inside me like a palpable thing. "Good thing I know how to fight," I joke.

"I don't think there's any competition," Drew chimes in fondly from behind me, his arms around both of us squeezing slightly. "That man has eyes for one person and one person only."

I flush, remembering Dax's comment from our faux fight earlier, how easily it slipped past his lips, leaving no doubt in my mind that it was true and not just part of our ruse.

I never stopped. Not for one fucking minute, baby.

I've had a lot of nicknames over the years. To most people, I'm Donavan. To some, I'm Boston. To my brothers, I'm Sammy—what they wanted me to be named, refusing to call me anything else for twenty-four years. But only one person has ever called me baby.

That person is currently putting on one hell of a show and having the time of his life doing it. The happiness on his face as he performs reverberates in my chest, an invisible string connecting him to me, his joy my joy.

And I know with absolute certainty that he's the only person I ever want to call me that.

CHAPTER EIGHTEEN

When Final Revelations exits the stage after their encore, I long to follow the magnetic pull backstage, to find Dax.

Reading my mind, Brooklyn nudges me in the ribs. *"Go."*

I shake my head. "I can't," I say meekly.

Indecision roots me to the spot. I can't go to him, but I can't bring myself to leave yet either. The crowd bottlenecks trying to exit the venue, and the four of us stay planted in our little corner by the barricade.

"Ooh," Drew says excitedly as my phone buzzes at my back—his front—where I tucked it into the waist cincher.

Easing it out, I nearly drop it when I see the name on my screen.

I swipe to open the text from Dax, and Drew rests his chin on my shoulder, not even bothering to pretend like he's not reading the message, too.

trailer 4. five minutes.

Drew drops his arms from around me, raising them in victory overhead. "I fucking knew it." He holds his hand out to me. "Five dollars."

I raise my brows at him.

"Oh, don't pretend like you're not going," he says with a click of his tongue.

"What?" Brooklyn asks. Cupping her hand behind mine, she angles my phone screen toward herself and then to Charlie.

Nosy motherfuckers, the lot of them.

"I'm not a part of your bet," I remind Drew, opting not to respond to his other statement because, yeah, I'm going. Taking my hand back from Brooklyn, I tuck the phone into the corset.

"See you at home?" Charlie asks. As our designated driver, he takes my keys from his pocket, twirling them around his finger before palming them.

"Someone could see," I say under my breath, uncertainty gnawing at my insides. I desperately want to go to Dax, but the logical part of my brain knows it's a bad idea. Unfortunately, other parts of my body are screaming quite loudly, drowning out logic.

I meet Brooklyn's gaze, her expression softening when she sees the panic no doubt in mine. Even in the harsh house lights, she looks damn near angelic. "Maybe we could avoid the crowd," she says slyly. "If we went out the back."

It takes the guys a minute to catch on, but soon they're nodding. "Yep, yep, great idea," Drew agrees enthusiastically.

We begin pushing our way across the venue, toward the back door that leads to the trailers, rather than the main entrance.

Once outside, I pause, turning back toward the door. "Wait, where are Reid and Tyler?"

Brooklyn ushers me on, her eyes scanning the numbers posted to the trailer doors. "We'll find them," she says, not at all worried. "That is not your problem right now."

With a gentle nudge, she guides me toward a set of trailer steps, a large *4* on the door.

"In fact," she says, taking my face between her hands, "you have the opposite of a problem right now." She winks. "Have fun, babe."

Before I can knock on the door, it opens, Marcus, Jonah, Cain, and Barrett spilling out of it. "We're going, we're going," Cain grumbles, as if I'd complained.

"Don't do anything I wouldn't do," Barrett says, laughing raucously. I don't think there's much he *hasn't* done.

The four of them link up with my friends, exchanging hugs, and I smile at the sight before slipping through the door. As it snicks shut behind me, Dax turns.

He's ditched his costume, back in his band tee and jeans, his fly undone as if he just pulled them on, a peek of his boxer briefs visible as he crosses the room to me. He presses his forehead to mine, walking us backward until my back hits the wall. The trailer must have showers, his scent wrapping around me like the evergreen inevitability of us.

He exhales as if he's been holding his breath all night, longer even.

Planting both hands on the wall beside my head, he leans back, taking in my costume unabashedly. His attention drags over me like an invisible hand, warmth spreading everywhere he looks. A flush tinges my chest pink as his attention goes to the modest swell of my breasts, the pleather corset belt, the dress that I've neglected to tug down, the black fishnets that disappear into my boots.

His left hand cradles the back of my neck, tilting my face up to meet his gaze, his amber eyes inky black with lust. "Do you know how hard it was not to stare at you all night?"

My mouth goes dry, and I swallow thickly. "Maybe I should dress sexy more often."

"You're always sexy," he says offhand, like it's ridiculous I could ever think otherwise.

I laugh through my nose. "Yeah? My oversized T-shirts really do it for you?"

Dax meets my gaze, and my pulse jumps beneath the grip of his palm. He ducks his head into the crook of my shoulder. "You have no idea"—he nips my neck affectionately—"how bad," he continues, his other hand coming off the wall to rest at my waist, "I want to slip my hands up under those shirts." His hand slides up to cup my breast, his thumb toying with the neckline of my dress as he squeezes gently.

A whimper slips out of me. I'm completely defenseless against him.

"So…" He pulls back slowly, his hand abandoning my breast to wind a lock of my hair around his finger. "Is not kissing me your only rule? Because I can do a lot with that."

My hands are on his chest, with no memory of how or when they got there. "Fuck it," I breathe. Hooking one finger through his belt loop, I tug him to me. My other hand goes to the hinge of his jaw, guiding his face down to mine. If kissing him ruins me, then let me be ruined.

Our mouths meet with a crushing eagerness, his hand at the base of my skull angling me to open up for him, his tongue guiding my lips apart at the same time as his knee nudges my legs to do the same. His other hand slides over my backside, squeezing roughly before drifting lower, hooking my leg around his hip. He hoists me up against the wall before bringing his body flush to mine. When our hips align, Dax moans into my mouth, the sound like something that's been trapped for years.

He pulls back for a fraction of a second, smiling softly as he brushes the tip of his nose against mine affectionately, before diving back in in a way that's both sweet and greedy.

"Fuck, I've missed you," he whispers against the shell of my ear, tugging on my earlobe with his teeth.

"It's only been a day."

He pulls back just far enough to fix me with a look. "And you know that's not what I meant."

Every particle in my body vibrates with happiness. Kissing Dax is like coming home after being away for far too long. "I missed you, too," I tell him, trailing a finger along his jawline, flicking his septum piercing playfully. He catches my finger between his teeth, equally playful, as if we have all the time in the world. But we're good at this, stealing moments, making the most of them.

Looping my arms around his neck, I pull him back to me. True to my word, I can't stop kissing him. I match the roll of his hips, smiling against his mouth as he sucks in a breath through his teeth. "Good thing you didn't pull me before going on stage or it would've been a different kind of show."

Dax smirks, resting his cheek on my forearm. "Bold of you to assume I didn't have to take care of that already." His hands at my hips squeeze, my dress bunching higher. His touch runs across my skin like lightning, gathering like a storm between my legs.

"Yeah?" I ask, laughing. The way he can make my blood fizzle with laughter and lust is unlike anything I've known with anyone else.

"No," he says with a cheeky grin, nipping at the tender flesh of my inner elbow. "But I did think about it." He places a kiss over the spot he bit before guiding my arm from around his neck, trailing open-mouthed kisses up to my wrist. He meets my lust-hazy gaze as he places a kiss into my palm. "I think about you all the time."

"Me, too," I confess automatically.

I already broke my no-kissing rule. It would be foolish to break any more. I'm about to vow to the insistent throb between my thighs that I'll take care of business when I get home, but then I remember my home has been invaded by five people I love very much but who have zero concept of privacy or personal space. A whine of frustration escapes me.

"What?"

I sigh heavily, tracing my finger along his cheek, drawing out his dimple. "I should go, but...I don't want to, and—"

"And?" The word is a rasped plea.

If I say this, I know exactly where this is going. If I say nothing, if I press gently on the center of his chest, he'll lower me down, help me fix my skirt, and we'll leave here having blurred no lines. Well, mostly unblurred. The ache between my legs hates that option, and I can already see myself tossing fitfully under the covers all night if this need goes unfulfilled. It's not a want at this point. It's a need.

"If I go home," I pant, "I can't exactly 'take care' of this with all the squatters currently there."

Dax's gaze sparks, a mischievous tilt to his lips. He hums against my skin, brushing his stubble across my forearm like a predator marking his territory. "I always knew the devil would come for me someday, but I like this version much better." He punctuates his sentence with a flick of the horns on my headband. I laugh, and he places another kiss to my arm. His hand comes up, enclosing mine where it traces anxious circles against the short hair at the nape of his neck. "Or we can go. You make the rules," he reminds me.

God, the way I trust him. If I trusted him less, my body would have made this decision for me ages ago. Instead, it's flushed and needy. The way he walks the line of respecting me and knowing how to utterly disrespect me—it's an art.

"What about you?" I don't know why I'm stalling. My body and my mind are already made up, but I need to hear it from him, even if his body is already telling me it's on the same page.

Dax laughs self-deprecatingly. "Whatever you want from me, take it. It's already yours."

I smile softly, tracing the lines of his mouth with my fingertip. Before him, I was embarrassed by my lack of experience, thought I should just "get it over with." I'm so glad I waited until I found someone who would take their time with me. After him, it was impossible to accept anything less.

"It's only ever been you for me," I confess without a hint of embarrassment. It will only ever be him. I don't care if it sounds hyperbolic—it feels true, and all I want in this moment is to *feel*, to hand over my control to him in the way I've only ever been able to do with him.

A growl sounds deep his chest, low and claiming. "When you left, I told myself I'd get over you, that eventually you'd leave my system and I wouldn't still crave you." He sighs in resignation. "I don't think I'm ever getting over you, Donavan."

"Don't." The word slips past my lips before he's even fully finished his sentence, and I'm pulling him to me, kissing him until I'm lightheaded. "Couch, please," I rasp as he kisses along my jaw while I catch my breath.

"Yes, ma'am," he rumbles. Encircling me in his arms, he hoists me off the wall, flicking the lock on the door before carrying me the few steps to the other side of the quaint trailer, of which I've paid zero attention to beyond clocking that there is a couch.

He lowers me down, pressing me into the cushions in a crushing kiss, and for half a breath, I think I'd be content doing only this. Then, his hips roll against mine and a strangled, needy mewl escapes me. At the slightest pressure of my hands on his shoulders, he stills, pulling back. Sliding one hand to the center of his chest, I guide him up and away, into a sitting position at the end of the couch.

He watches me curiously, waiting for me to clue him in on what I need from him.

"Rules," I pant, breathing heavily like I've done harder exercise than just wrangling my lust under control. "No touching."

He grunts, his head falling against the back of the couch. "How breakable is that rule?"

I press my lips together, opting not to answer, because truthfully, I don't know. I just made the rule and I'm ready to toss it aside, along with all my clothes and self-control. "We'll give it the old college try, yeah?"

The corners of his mouth quirk up crookedly. "I'm a high school dropout, baby."

I hum, nonplussed. "And yet, you're such a good student."

His gaze rakes over me the same way his teeth do over his bottom lip—roughly, hungrily.

I can't help myself. I'm kissing him again, as if trying to make up for the past three years in one night. I brush my knuckles along his jaw, trailing them down the side of his neck, his sternum. His abs tighten in anticipation, my finger teasing the waistband of his boxers.

"I love not touching," he breathes.

I grin against his mouth before placing one last long, lingering kiss there as my hand slips under his waistband. Guiding the elastic down, I free his erection, palming it with a long, slow pump of my hand.

He reaches out, trying to pull me onto his lap, but I encircle his wrist, bringing it down and wrapping his hand around himself.

With one last chaste peck of his lips, I lie back, propping one of the cushions under my head as I draw up the leg closest to the back of the couch, stretching the other one across his lap.

We've never done this before. Not quite like this, at least. I gave him so many of my firsts, and he took his time to learn me, to make sure each experience was enjoyable, patient and attentive to my body in a way no one else had been before. He had me show him how I liked to be touched before taking over, showing me new ways I hadn't known to ask for. And vice versa—he showed me the rhythms and pressures he enjoyed, readily gifting me the knowledge of precisely how to make him come undone.

I trail my hand up my thigh, my fingers catching on the diamond pattern of my fishnets, and he groans. "Fuck me."

"Maybe—if you're good," I promise with a cheeky grin.

He grunts, his grip on himself tightening, giving a slight tug as his attention leaves my face and locks onto my hand that's now dipping under the hem of my dress.

His eyes flick up to mine, pleading to be able to see.

I'm self-conscious for half a second, but the way he wants me makes it impossible to feel like any of this is worth being embarrassed about. I ratchet my dress up higher around my hips with my other hand, exposing the tops of my thighs and my incredibly practical black thong. Dax's bitten-off noise of need makes me feel like I'm wearing the world's most expensive lingerie and not a cheap costume from Spirit Halloween.

As I trace my finger over the damp fabric of my underwear, my head falls back, a gasp lodging in my throat. I can't see Dax, but I can hear the brush of fabric as he works himself, and the sound is just as effective. I tease myself, trailing my fingertip along the seam of my underwear, dipping underneath and pulling back, Dax's rapt attention like a brand on my skin.

Unable to hold out any longer, I slide my finger through the fishnet's diamond pattern and hook my underwear to the side.

Dax's free hand latches onto my ankle, and I inhale sharply at the grounding contact. Tearing my unfocused gaze off the trailer ceiling, my attention drifts from his long fingers encircling my ankle to the controlled way his tattooed fist works up and down his length, the pearlescent bead at its tip. My mouth waters at the sight, and Dax hums, knowing exactly all the ways I want him.

I meet his gaze, and we share lazy, lust-fogged grins. I drag a wet finger up my core, parting my folds, and my head falls back once more.

"So fucking perfect," Dax murmurs.

I circle my clit once, twice, before exploring myself, like I haven't done this countless times before, every time for the past three years done whilst picturing him. I'm trying to drag this out, the telltale twitch of my hips announcing that it won't take me long once I actually get going. I circle my entrance, and Dax moans like it's him I'm edging and not myself.

"Please." His grip on my ankle tightens, and I give in, plunging one finger inside. "Good girl."

I beam at his praise, at what I'm doing to him, the rhythm of his fist picking up speed.

Easing my finger back out, I turn my attention to my swollen and hypersensitive clit, swirling my finger around and around until my hips buck, needing more. Dax groans, shifting sideways. We lock eyes as his mouth comes down on my knee, biting gently. When I bring my other hand up, he sags against my leg, his pupils blown wide as he watches my fingers with unwavering attention.

He makes me feel like the sexiest woman alive.

"I'm close," I tell him.

Plunging two fingers inside, I use my other hand to continue the administrations to my clit and resist the urge to squeeze my thighs together against the rising tide of pleasure building inside me. If I were alone, I'd give in to the instinct, but I want him to see what he does to me.

My movements grow more erratic as I begin to tip over the edge. "Dax," I cry out as I lose control completely. My inner walls clamp down, spasming around my fingers as my other hand continues working my clit, drawing out my orgasm as it barrels through me.

I come back to myself in pieces, my inner thigh stinging where Dax's teeth sunk into it. With a shudder, I ease my fingers out of myself, shifting my underwear back into place. Wrapping his hand around my wrist, Dax brings my hand to his mouth, sucking the taste of me off my fingers.

Sitting up, I place a kiss at the hinge of his jaw before tracing the lines of the oni mask tattooed on his throat with my tongue, his Adam's apple bobbing as he swallows. "Are you close?" I ask.

He nods, his grip on his cock tightening. "Very. You may wanna—" His free hand squeezes my hip, where I'm leaning over him. He's going to spill all over my dress, all over himself. Without thinking, I slide off the couch, dropping to my knees between his spread ones. "Sloane—" My name comes out garbled.

I give him a sly smile before taking his tip into my mouth.

"I love not touching." His head falls back as he continues to work himself, my tongue swirling in tandem to the pump of his fist. His gaze meets mine, his mouth opening to warn me, I think, but it gets caught in a groan. I hum, letting him know it's okay to let go. His release comes a fraction of a second later, spilling into my mouth. I make a meal out of cleaning him up, dragging my thumb across the corners of my mouth primly as I swallow, Dax watching me in wonderment.

"You are—" His hand goes to the back of my neck, roughly guiding me up, onto his lap. I squeal as he presses me up against him. I'm grinning too hard to focus on kissing him right now, but he doesn't mind, busying himself elsewhere, everywhere.

When he finally pulls back, he studies me like I'm precious. He sighs contentedly, tucking himself back into his boxers before loosely encircling my waist. He drops his head to my chest, inhaling deeply.

"This," he breathes.

I hum in question, lazily tracing nonsensical patterns along the back of his bowed neck.

"Did I say that out loud?"

I laugh quietly. "Mm-hmm."

He presses his smile into my skin. "It's...it's a thing I've done for a while now, when I experience something I like, something I'm happy I'm still around for, that I would've missed." He brushes his lips against my collarbone before placing a kiss there, his gaze flicking up to meet mine. "This."

I hold him tighter, resting my forehead against his, my heart in my throat impossible to speak around. I don't know how long we stay like that, lazily tracing patterns with our hands while we catch our breath.

He speaks about it so plainly, his belief that he wouldn't live a long life, and I don't know what to say that doesn't sound trite. I'm still trying to figure it out when a knock at the door startles us both. We nearly jump out of our skin when the door handle rattles but thankfully doesn't open.

"Five minutes," a voice calls.

We both sag at the sound of retreating footsteps.

Dax meets my gaze with a mischievous quirk of his lips. "I can get a lot done in five minutes."

I laugh, smacking him lightly on the shoulder with the back of my hand. "I know you can." Easing off him and the couch, I stand on shaky postorgasm legs. Dax plants his hands on my hips, leaning forward and placing a kiss to the apex of my thighs.

"Dax!" I half moan, half scold.

He smirks, placing one last chaste kiss there. "Soon," he promises, before working down the hem of my dress so I'm covered.

I grab his chin, guiding his mouth to mine the way he used to do to me. He slips his tongue into my mouth, and I can taste myself, our flavors mingling in a kiss that quickly turns desperate.

Dax pulls back first.

"I told you I wouldn't be able to stop," I remind him.

"Do you hear me complaining?" Pushing off the couch, he crowds my space, his hand going to my throat as he brings my mouth back to his in a quick kiss.

I lean into him automatically, and he laughs, his hands going to my hips and angling them away as he begins gathering his things. I slip off to use the restroom because I simply don't have time to visit the circle of hell that is a UTI. When I return, Dax is throwing the last of his things haphazardly into his bag before looping it over his shoulder. He holds out his hand, and I cross the small space, sliding mine into his. We can't hold hands outside of this room, so I squeeze his a little too tight. He pulls me closer by our conjoined hands, dragging his mouth over mine once, twice, before bringing me in for one last bruising kiss. Dropping my hand, he smacks me on the ass before opening the door.

I suck on my teeth, shaking my head at him disapprovingly, and he grins shamelessly.

We only make it a few steps out of the trailer before we run into the last stragglers of the event.

"Donavan!" someone calls, and I whip around. It's one of the Nicks—there are three at *AP*. I don't know him well, or why he's flagging me down until he glances toward the trailer Dax and I just came out of. "Alright?" he slurs, a knowing look in his eye.

Fuck.

I cross my arms. "Yeah," I grumble. "Just nailing down some details for the article." To Dax a few paces away, I call, "Don't leave. We're not done." I give him a meaningful look that I hope he can translate.

Nick titters under his breath, and I'm relieved to see the sly look is gone. "I heard that wasn't going well."

I huff, rolling my eyes. "What're ya gonna do?" I say with a frown. "Musicians and their egos."

Nick gestures over my shoulder, and I glance back, repressing a proud smile that Dax got my memo.

"Hey!" I call after Dax's slowly retreating form. To Nick, I say, "See you Monday!" before chasing after Dax. Louder than necessary, I chastise him. "You are not off the hook yet."

"I hope not," he says in a low rumble when I reach him.

"Sorry." I keep my arms crossed so that for all intents and purposes, we still look like two people bickering and not two people who just came for each other. "I know this ruse is a lot."

"It's fun," he says with a shrug. "But it would be nice to not have to pretend."

It's an effort not to soften my combative posture. "Yeah."

"Do you think that's possible?"

I chew on the inside of my cheek, giving the idea actual thought. Dax and I together, openly. I nod, slowly at first, and then more eagerly. We're far enough into the parking lot now that it's safe to smile at each other. "I don't think it would be too detrimental if everyone believed we connected through this process. It'll be...a lot at first, probably, while everyone wraps their heads around it. Well— It'll only be bad for me. You'll probably get congratulated." Dax grunts in agreement and annoyance. "I don't think we could tell the full story, but if we can control the narrative, I think we could drop the act after." Our hands brush against each other as we walk, and I interlock our pinkies. "I don't want us to be a secret forever. Just a little bit longer."

His car lights flash as he unlocks it, and I can't get inside fast enough. Once we're behind the safety of his tinted windows, we reach for each other before doing anything else.

"Just a little bit longer," he echoes, nudging the tip of his nose against mine.

I pull him to me, and his hand goes to the back of my neck, holding me there as his tongue tangles with mine until we're both panting. He pulls back, grinning, running his thumb down the column of my throat. He hums contentedly, gaze roaming over me, and I want to crawl over the console and straddle him. I want to tell him I love him. It's too soon and three years late, all at once.

"I know, baby." He leans in, brushing his lips across mine. "Me, too," he mumbles against my mouth.

"I didn't say anything." Not for the first time, I wonder if he can read my mind.

"You didn't have to."

It's like he's trying to tell me something, but I'm too slaphappy from kissing him and punch-drunk from how late it is, losing myself in yet another kiss that I don't want to end. He leans farther over the console, pushing me back into my seat, and I smile against his mouth, ready for more. He reaches past me, locking me into place with the seat belt. "Devil woman," he mutters, flicking the horns of my headband affectionately.

As he leans back, I stare goofily at the clock on the dashboard. Half past midnight. Meaning struggles to make itself known amidst my kiss-addled brain.

I gasp, turning to him. "Happy birthday."

His mouth curves upward shyly. "Thank you."

Twenty-nine. Two years longer than he thought he'd get. I slide my hand into his, bringing our conjoined fingers to my mouth, kissing each of his knuckles in turn. "It'll be a feat," I say mischievously, "to top this for your thirtieth, but I'm up to the challenge."

"Oh yeah?" he says around a laugh.

"Mm-hmm." I peer up at him, resting our conjoined hands on the center console. "I'm really glad you're here."

He meets my gaze for a moment that could be a second or years before looking away, squeezing his eyes shut. He nods, knowing exactly what I mean by it. His grip on my hand tightens for the span of a few deep breaths that rattle his chest. "Me, too," he says at last, with finality.

He looks over at me, saying nothing, but it holds everything, the things he can never say, never convey, even if I spent a lifetime interviewing him.

I lean in, our kiss slow and sweet this time, like a promise.

It's not my birthday, but I make a wish anyway: for twenty-nine more years, then twenty-nine more.

[Excerpt from Sloane Donavan's Final Revelations interview transcript]

2002: Nobody's Fucking Business

MARCUS: Ah, yes. The infamous Reverie Fest.

BARRETT: I don't know, man. That shit was embarrassing, for sure, but I've always maintained that's Dax's story to tell, if he wants to. If not, it's nobody's fucking business.

JONAH: I've run back the events of that day multiple times, but the thing is... I don't remember *seeing* Dax until right before we were supposed to go on stage.

CAIN: He was clearly fucked up, but that wasn't exactly new at that point.

MARCUS: He'd always pull it together somehow, right before going on stage, so we just rolled our eyes and figured it'd be like every other show Dax was half-present for.

CAIN: Even halfway gone, Dax is still better than most guys.

MARCUS: Except he wasn't even half-present. He had no idea where he was. I don't even know how he found his way to the stage, much less on time, to be honest. I feel like shit saying this. Do we have to talk about it? I guess everyone knows already...

CAIN: I wish I could say this part of our story isn't true, isn't as bad as it looked, but... Yeah, it was that bad.

JONAH: Right before we went on, I remember thinking, *I don't know that he's gonna pull it together this time.* I wish I'd said something, but then again, butterfly effect, y'know? We all knew Dax wasn't okay, but you can't force someone to get help if they don't want it. That show was mortifying, but it was also a wake-up call.

Dax: Do I want to talk about Reverie Fest? No. But I guess I have to, huh? [**per SD, to be redacted:** My family had never come to any of our shows. So when my sisters asked to come to Reverie Fest, I was stoked. I met up with them for breakfast and I remember making a deal with myself not to take too much that day so I could be present for them. But when we got back to the festival, I got them through security, and...my parents were waiting. My mom and I had kinda talked, mostly through my sisters. My dad and I—we hadn't spoken since I got expelled from school. He could tell I was strung out, and it ended up in a fight.

Now, I'm not blaming my dad or anything. I got myself into that mess all by myself. That day was a roller coaster, and I had been numbing myself to the roller coaster for nearly a year at that point. I was scared shitless to start feeling stuff again, because I knew how much I hadn't been dealing with, that there would be no dipping a toe. I'd drown. So, instead of sobering up and proving everyone wrong, I went back to our van and...got incredibly fucked up. Took more than I usually did, took things ahead of schedule. Yeah, I had a schedule. It allowed me to believe that I was the one in control, that I didn't have a problem.]

Marcus had to sing almost all of that set by himself. I don't remember any of it. I don't remember falling backstage afterward, but I got this. [*points to dimple*] I do remember waking up in the hospital, sober for the first time in I don't know how long. And I was drowning. They were getting ready to discharge me, and I remember being mad, like, don't they know what I'll do the instant I'm out of here? As if they were the irresponsible ones. And I realized that it wasn't anyone else's responsibility to fix me. I'd thought I was in control, but that day, I broke all my rules. And now that I had...I was scared of what I'd do if left to my own devices.

I'd spent the past few years trying to pretend I wasn't a kid, but in that hospital bed, I was every bit the kid I was. I called my parents, crying, asking if I could come home. They said yes—on the condition that I got help, and I agreed. They picked me up, set me up in my childhood bedroom, and— They'd never even met my bandmates before that day, but I remember walking downstairs the next morning to find my band, my parents, and my sisters at the dining room table, making calls. They got me into rehab a few days later.

CHAPTER NINETEEN

My paranoia was warranted.

I drag the red button back to watch it again, to torture myself. Mike Song sits in front of his snobby wall of perfectly curated vinyls, giving his weekly vlog update. "To everyone who caught *AP*'s Halloween fest two nights ago, I hope you stayed until the end for Final Revelations. Two weeks ago, I hinted there may be a new album from the band, but I've since learned this isn't the first time they've been in the studio since their fifth album, *Purgatorium*. I don't know what happened with the sixth album they recorded, but we all know about the long-standing feud between frontmen Nakamura and Bailey, so it's not really a stretch to assume what the issue was. A source close to the band confirms this seventh album will be their last—if it doesn't go the same way as their sixth, that is. So, if you caught Final Revelations' *AP* set, count your blessings. It may have been one of their last performances. We are in the end times of Final Revelations."

Slamming my laptop shut, I roll over in bed and scream into my pillow, a few frustrated tears leaking out. I count backward from five and then from ten before forcing myself to get out of bed.

My apartment is still half-destroyed from my friends' visit, and I wish they'd stayed one more day so I had someone to hold me together right now.

How does this keep happening?

I'd opened my laptop to check on my video with Marcus and Dax that went live today, only to find Mike Song's vlog trending much higher.

How does he know? How is he still one step ahead of me, privy to information I've barely managed to wrangle out of them?

I pause in the middle of brushing my teeth. Unless—

I push the thought aside. No. This is my exclusive. There's no way a member of Final is leaking info to Mike Song of all people. Which only makes it worse. If it were *anyone* other than Mike, it wouldn't feel so damn personal.

Outside of the band, there's John, Robb, and me, but we're all NDA'd up to our eyeballs. Expanding my mental scope of suspects, I feel slimy adding Final's family and friends and, begrudgingly, my own—I told Brooklyn everything. I don't actually suspect her, but the point is people *do* know. There's Isaac, who has sold images to *The Offbeat* before, but I don't think getting paid makes him a villain. Then there's Hudson, but why would he turn on his mentors? There are lots of sources "close to the band." I can't fathom who would sell us out, who would have something to gain from it.

None of this is my fault or my responsibility to resolve, but it still feels like it is. I have to go into a meeting with Robb and John in an hour, a meeting about the article I can't seem to get right, even when rewriting it based on their feedback. The foundation for the life I've spent years building is crumbling under my feet—again. Will the article go the same way as Final's sixth album—nixed? Has my big opportunity slipped from my grasp? If I'd been more focused, less caught up in Dax, would I have cracked the article already? Would I know who the leak is if I'd been paying attention to my career and not my feelings?

I rub the scar on my ring finger the entire drive into the office. *I know*, I tell it. I want Dax with a surety I've only ever felt for him, but if I fumble my career now, I'll regret it for the rest of my life. I have multiple missed calls from him, but I can't talk to him yet, not until I know what's going on with the article.

I'm fairly certain I leave my stomach in my Jeep, the crunch of the gravel beneath my Docs sounding in my ears as I approach the office like I'm walking to the gallows.

I barely make it one step in the door before Robb corners me.

"Get out of here," she says under her breath. She glances over her shoulder to Dolores, who pretends not to see us.

"What?" I ask.

"Go home. Write. Write like your life depends on it—because it kinda does."

I glance around wildly, tears springing to my eyes. "But our meeting—"

"I got it," she says urgently, gripping my shoulders. "John is livid Song scooped us, but him making you feel like shit for something that's not even your fault isn't going to help. So go before he sees you."

"Who is doing this?" My voice cracks, my bravado cracking with it.

"Would knowing help you write the article?" she asks with a tilt of her head.

She's right. I decide here and now to drop it, to bury my journalistic instincts and not dig into it. I don't have time to go down that rabbit hole. All I can control is the article.

I stare at her for a long moment before nodding resolutely. I've never hugged her before, but I don't hesitate, wrapping my arms around her like a kid. I've waited years for someone to have my back like this, to take me under their wing and push me out of the nest at the same time. "Thank you," I breathe.

"Make this worth it," she says with a pointed raise of her brows. She gives me one last squeeze before spinning me around toward the door.

I drive back to my apartment in a daze, silencing my phone as I toe off my boots in the foyer. I have no idea where to start, how to write this article right. I've tried dozens of times, dozens of angles, every single draft coming back from Robb like it had gone through a wood chipper. I drop my phone onto the mail pile, pausing when it clunks loudly. Shifting the top envelopes to the side, I spy the clear case Dax dropped off a few days ago.

I only have the energy to lightly flagellate myself for not listening to it yet. I can't even muster the energy to be nervous about what's on here about me.

I settle onto the floor in front of my record player. The long wooden table it sits on is one of my most prized possessions, my dad building it for me when it became clear my obsession with music was not a phase. The middle is the perfect height for slotting in vinyls, the two cabinets on the side concealing my piles of CDs and the wires connecting my equipment. The speakers on top of the table were a graduation gift from my friends, and much nicer than the ones I had when this table was built. Today, however, I plug my headphones into the stereo. Some albums are car albums. Some are shower-concert albums. I have a feeling this is a lie-on-the-floor album, a need-the-music-as-deep-inside-my-ears-as-possible album.

Taking a bracing breath, I slide the CD into the stereo and nock my headphones into place.

As the first notes fill my ears, I go still. I don't know what I expected: heavy riffs, haunting melodies, guttural growls. Instead, the slow strumming of an acoustic guitar introduces the first track. When Dax comes in, he sets the record for how quickly an album has ever made me cry.

"Hi, my name is Dax and I'm an addict. I've been sober for six years."

The first verse is aggressively upbeat, a sleight of hand. Heavy lyrics with bubblegum pop vocals. It's simultaneously *not* Final Revelations and *very* Final Revelations. Dax sings about his struggles with sobriety, and I'm not ready for the chorus. He switches from clean vocals to gutturals, and I recognize the lines for what they are: every article ever written about him questioning his sobriety. I blink, and tears track down my face because I know without a doubt that the choice to sing these lines this way... This is Dax's inner monologue, repeating the worst things ever said about him as he's holding on to his sobriety with a white-knuckled grip.

The song ends with a primal yell, and I hit Pause. The need to relisten is immediate, but I take a shaky breath before hitting Play on the second track.

The rest of the album is in the same vein. Dax versus his demons, wanting to throw in the towel because what's the point when everyone already thinks the worst of him, while simultaneously wanting to prove everyone wrong, the crushing weight of being told his music saves lives when he's barely treading water himself. Just when I thought the album was taking a happier turn in the middle, it jumps abruptly back to dark, the flow of the record disrupted, robbing me of catharsis. It fits the theme of the album. Dax has been fighting invisible battles no one else can see, every victory overshadowed by a legacy he doesn't see himself in. His view of himself is so low it breaks my heart.

As it loops back to the first track, I realize how short the album is. While there are no songs about me, I understand why he was nervous for me to hear it.

Dax and Marcus's arguments over the album make so much more sense now. I get why Dax wouldn't want to put it out there. It's incredibly personal. I could write articles about each song, about the glimpses into not only his psyche but the issues each track tackles: sobriety, mental health, parasocial relationships, industry expectations, imposter syndrome. I know *Nixed* is a reflection of Dax's experiences, but I can see myself in each song, the catharsis it could bring others, and I understand Marcus's point of view, too. These songs are much more literal than their previous albums, and there's a vulnerability in Dax finally letting the literary veil drop. Wiping my cheeks, I realize my tears haven't stopped flowing since that first note.

Their decision to do this article has been years in the making. Even still, it's no wonder Dax struggled during our interview. He doesn't feel in half measures, bite-sized for public consumption. He feels in ways that are uncomfortable to bear witness to.

But fuck, isn't that what punk is for? The misfits who feel too much, who refuse to go numb to the machine of a society that relies upon our collective complacency to undermine the promises made to us. Real art *should* make you a little uncomfortable; a mirror for truths you have to make peace with in order to stare back at it.

I restart the first song and make good on my initial instinct: I lie back on the floor, staring up at the ceiling as Dax's musical diary rewires my brain chemistry.

This should be his interview. He doesn't need me to tell his story. Everything he wants to say is already in this album.

This is some of the best music I've heard in a long time.

It is, without a doubt, their best work.

And no one will ever hear it.

So how, *how*, do I write an article that can encapsulate this, honor this?

[Excerpt from Sloane Donavan's Final Revelations interview transcript]

2002: Blubbering Babies

Dax: I turned twenty-one in a rehab facility. Not exactly what you picture when you're growing up, y'know? Most of my life wasn't how I pictured it. Most of it was better than I'd dreamed. I just had to stop fucking it up on purpose so I could actually be present for it. I was really nervous, leaving rehab, reentering the real world, going back to work. I didn't totally believe in myself. To be brutally honest…I still don't, some days.

Jonah: We all showed up to pick him up. We all crashed at Barrett's that night and then moved Dax in with me since Barrett's house was party central and the last place Dax needed to be.

Marcus: It felt really good to get back to work.

Cain: Listen, none of us were fucking saints, okay? We were all up to shit, just not to Dax's level. But it *could have been* any of us, y'know? We all cleaned up our act after that.

Barrett: It's gross the way people were almost rooting for the kid to fail.

Marcus: Fuck Mike Song.

Cain: Fuck *The Offbeat*.

Jonah: Fuck that article.

Barrett: If I were stuck in the woods with the world's worst case of diarrhea and no toilet paper, but I had that article? I still wouldn't use it to wipe my ass.

MARCUS: We wanted a fresh start after Reverie Fest. We'd fucked up. We'd betrayed our fans' trust, and we wanted to let them know we took that seriously.

BARRETT: I hope Mike Song's pillow is hot on both sides.

JONAH: The article we wanted was not the article we got. Far from it.

BARRETT: I hope his belt loops catch on every doorknob he walks past.

CAIN: I wondered for a long time what we did to get on that guy's bad side, and I don't think we did anything. He knew what kind of article would put *The Offbeat* on the map, so he wrote that, regardless of what he actually saw from us that day.

BARRETT: I hope he never has enough creamer for his coffee, and that the creamer he does have? Is spoiled and chunky.

MARCUS: That was a kick in the nuts. We were so full of hope, eager to get back to work. Dax was doing fucking fantastic. And then that article.

BARRETT: *Fuck* that guy.

JONAH: That article rattled Dax. Not so much that he wasn't ever going to be allowed to move past his worst moment, but that none of us would be able to either. I think he felt guilty.

DAX: Let's be real here: There's a lot of guys in this scene who have done much worse than me, haven't changed, and went on to have great careers, every opportunity laid at their feet in the name of "separating the art from the artist." But they're white, and I'm not, so of course I was held to a different standard. And to have the article condemning me come from Song, one of the only other persons of color on the scene? [*two middle fingers up*]

CAIN: Deciding not to do press anymore was the easiest decision we ever made. Our label hated us for that, but the feeling was mutual—but that's another story.

MARCUS: Our first show back, I was so nervous no one would come. We'd postponed the tour because Dax was in rehab, and after that article, we feared no one would claim their tickets for the rescheduled shows. I remember waiting in the wings before our set, all of us dead silent. I kept trying to come up with something meaningful to say. It felt like one of those moments where you should make a speech or something. But we were all mutely quaking in our boots. The venue was packed, sure, but were they just waiting for the chance to boo us off stage? Which sounds absurd to say out loud, but then they *did* start chanting, except— [*grins*] They were chanting for us.

BARRETT: [*air drums*]

CAIN: Fi-nal.

JONAH: Fi-nal.

MARCUS: Fi-nal.

DAX: We've started every show since with that chant. I don't know how the crowd knew what we needed—what *I* needed—in that moment, but they did. We left them chanting for a long while because we were all fucking blubbering babies. As an artist, you don't always know if what you do matters to people. You don't always get to know it while it's happening. But in that moment...we knew. One article didn't get to define us unless we let it. The fans were trusting us with a second chance. And we've spent every day since working to never break their trust again.

MARCUS: I'm sure there were people who were hoping we'd fail. That in the vacuum of our downfall they'd get to be the ones at the top. Sorry. [*laughs*] I'm not sorry at all, actually.

CAIN: That Euro tour was some of the best shows we've ever played.

JONAH: We wanted it so bad. I was sober that entire tour. Partially out of solidarity with Dax while he was learning how to be sober in an industry that decidedly *isn't*, but really, it was just...I didn't want to miss one fucking second.

⚡ CHAPTER TWENTY ⚡

TV detectives have nothing on my murder board.

After playing *Nixed* multiple times through, I text Dax to let him know I've listened to it. While I wait for him to respond, I decide to go back to the beginning.

Hearing Dax tell his own story—through our interview and through the *Nixed* album—I decide to do the same for all the guys. I throw out all my notes, every outline Robb and I ever made, save for my interview transcripts.

I feel lighter just being rid of it all, too many voices in my head to hear my own. More than that, it was the guys' voices who were being drowned out, and wasn't that the whole point of this anyway?

Settling down on the couch with a mug of tea and a granola bar, I pull Barrett's transcript into my lap. By the time I finish, his pages are flecked with tea from all my spit takes. As I pick up Marcus's pages, an idea begins to take root. I don't even finish the first page before I'm reaching for Cain's and Jonah's pages, cross-referencing.

I catch my hip on the kitchen counter in my haste to grab my scissors from the junk drawer. I check my phone, opening the missed text from Dax.

with the fam for my birthday.

Under the text is a selfie, Dax's face squeezed between his parents, his three sisters making silly expressions behind them.

Then another text: **my dad said to stop distracting you. call you tomorrow?**

I stare softly at the photo, how casually he sent it, the affection in their identical smiles. For most people, it would mean nothing, but I know for Dax, it's everything. He may have reconciled with his parents years ago, but this ease is something new, something precious.

I text back in the affirmative, before tossing my phone on the TV stand. Picking back up my interview pages, I sloppily highlight each guy in a different color and begin cutting, weaving an oral timeline of their history. I don't totally know what I'm going to do with it, other than it feels *right*—more right than anything I've tried so far.

By the time I get to the end, it's the next morning. I got a few hours of sleep before waking up energized, ecstatic about this new direction and eager to get back to it. After rereading the whole thing, I rearrange the final quotes for maximum impact. I'm breathing heavily like I ran a marathon—which, by journalistic standards, I have, this article coming together in one all-nighter.

Pushing off the floor, I step back to take in my handiwork. I quickly ran out of room on the coffee table, and now both it and the couch have been pushed out of the way, my floor now covered in the timeline of Final Revelations, as told by Final Revelations. I'm lightheaded, either high on my own brilliance or low on blood sugar, yesterday's granola bar opened but uneaten. My stomach growls threateningly.

A knock at the door startles me, and I jump. I have to walk along my couch to get to the front door without stepping on the chaotic genius papering my floor.

I can't take my eyes off of it, fearing if I look away, the spark will disappear, the angle I've been chasing under my nose the whole time.

Opening the door, I do a double take.

"Dax!" I exclaim. Did I manifest him by thinking about him too hard?

His gaze drags over me from head to toe and back up, from my threadbare T-shirt that's more holey than Swiss cheese, my high school gym shorts that I should've stopped wearing years ago, to the haphazard bun I'd thrown my hair into so I could concentrate better.

Dax makes a noise of intrigue, like I'm wearing a tantalizing outfit and not my ratty pajamas.

"Oh, shut up," I grumble. "I'm working."

His attention sweeps over my destroyed living room, his eyes going wide before flitting back to mine. "Are you...okay?"

"I think I figured it out," I whisper, afraid to curse it.

He smiles back. "That's my girl."

My whole body flushes, and I step back to let him in. Maybe he should stay. Celebrate.

No, Sloane.

"Not that I don't love your recent habit of showing up at my door unannounced—" It's only then I notice the paper bag in his hands. My stomach growls loudly. "You can't stay," I say regretfully, needing to establish that right out of the gate, knowing how quickly I'll crumble in his presence.

"I did try to call first," he says, shifting nervously from one foot to the other, holding the paper bag in front of him like a shield.

"I didn't hear—" *Fuck.* I hopscotch over my scattered papers, slipping into my bedroom to grab my phone from my nightstand, where

I'd left it to charge when I woke up to a dead battery. On the lock screen, there's a handful of missed texts and a call from Dax. "I forgot I put it on silent," I call out, disappointed in myself.

As quickly and carefully as I can, I pick my way back across the living room, arms extended toward him.

He laughs at the spectacle, and I'm sure I deserve it. "You fucking weirdo," he says affectionately.

I make my movements more exaggerated as I near him, and he laughs harder, turning his back to me. Undeterred, I wrap my arms around him from behind. "I'm sorry," I say, my voice muffled as I press my face between his shoulder blades.

"It's okay," he rumbles. He guides me around to his front, staring at me for a long moment. "So... you liked it?"

The way he says it, it's like he expected me to run for the hills. There was nothing on *Nixed* that he hadn't told me already. Expressed in a much rawer way than he usually allows, sure, but it was all him.

I place my hands on either side of his face, and he leans into the touch. "Yes," I breathe. "Thank you so much for sharing it with me. It's... It's fantastic. It's unflinching and honest and it's really brave. It's *you*." I shrug. "Of course I love it. You should be really proud." He drops his gaze, and I duck my head to keep it. "I'm so proud of you. If you want to talk about it in detail, we can, now or later or never—I'm not going anywhere."

I watch as the worry melts from his features, the line between his brows disappearing, his eyes softening as the corners of his mouth turn upward. For a moment, he looks like he's going to say something, but then he leans in, peppering rapid-fire kisses to my cheek and neck until I'm laughing and squirming out of reach.

He nudges the couch an inch to the right to get into the kitchen, and I cry out in alarm, but the pages on the floor remain undisturbed.

He holds his free hand up defensively. "Is that our article?" he asks, eyeing the taped-together scraps with a bemused smile as he unpacks the paper bag.

"Yes," I say defensively, crossing my arms. "I'll show you later." Fetching a clean fork from the dish rack I haven't emptied, I open one of the containers and stare down at the contents, mouth watering at the yakisoba noodles and thinly sliced beef. He didn't just bring me enough food to feed me for days. "You cooked for me?"

He opens the door to the fridge, surveying the nearly empty shelves with a dissatisfied purse of his lips before loading them up. "Technically, my dad did."

My eyes widen. "What?"

"He's very excited about the article and wanted to help."

My chest aches. It's not lost on me how much this gesture encapsulates, the work they've put in to fix their relationship, for this man I've never met to be looking after me from afar, all to ensure his son's legacy is penned correctly. "Tell him thank you for me," I say softly.

"Thank him yourself when you come over for dinner after the article's done. Mom insisted she gets to take care of you, too," he hedges.

I blink, not fighting the smile that stretches across my face, not overthinking what this means for us, only about what it means to Dax. "Okay."

His eyes light up. "Okay?"

"Okay," I repeat, nodding.

He ducks his head to hide his own smile, his gaze straying to the chaos on my floor. "My dad also reiterated that I not distract you, so I'm not staying. I just came to bring you fuel."

"Fuel?"

"Mm-hmm." He gestures to my now-stocked fridge. "And motivation."

"Motivation?" My exhaustion must be catching up to me—I'm incapable of making sentences, only echoes.

Dax eases the Tupperware from my hands, setting it on the counter beside me. I whimper in protest, the sound getting caught in my throat when I meet his gaze. I'm not the only hungry one in this kitchen.

Dax's hands go to my waist, hoisting me onto the counter. My arms and legs wrap around him automatically. He grips my chin between his thumb and forefinger, halting me from leaning in. He nudges his nose against mine, a relieved exhale sighing out of him before he slots his mouth against my own in a languid kiss.

I try to behave. I do. But our kiss quickly turns heated, hands roaming, his dropping from my face to palm my breast. I know the exact moment when he clocks it, his thumb brushing over my nipple once, twice, confirming what he felt. He pulls back, bracing both hands on the edge of the counter.

"Sloane," he breathes. "Did you . . . ?"

He doesn't need to finish the question, his gaze bouncing back and forth, my threadbare T-shirt unable to conceal the hard press of my nipples—or the piercings there.

A groan tears out of Dax, and he has to walk away for a second, hands dragging down his face. "When?" he asks from across the kitchen, before biting down on his knuckle.

"Two years ago." We'd been broken up for a year and I hoped having some part of me that he hadn't touched would make moving on easier. (It didn't, but it *did* make me love my tiny tits more.) I brace my hands on the counter behind me, arching my back in invitation.

A wicked laugh tumbles out of Dax, and he's in front of me again in two strides. He hoists me up off the counter, and I lock my legs tight around his waist as my arms loop behind his neck. His hands grip my rear, holding me up higher as he dips his head. His mouth closes over me, his tongue flicking the piercing through my shirt. We both moan appreciatively. He repeats the gesture on my other breast, teasing me with his tongue until the cotton of my shirt is soaked through.

"Is this you *not* distracting me?"

He hums, nuzzling his face into my neck before bringing his mouth back to mine in a bruising kiss. His hands knead my ass, his fingers ghosting back and forth at the apex of my thighs, just shy of where I want them. When one long finger grazes exactly where I want it, I gasp like I'm coming up for air.

Dax grins lazily, setting me back on the counter. Leaning down, he takes my earlobe between his teeth and tugs gently. "Not distracting—*motivating*," he murmurs.

I *humph* in disagreement, pulling at his shirt to get him closer.

He doesn't budge. "Motivating," he repeats, moving his hands to my shoulders and holding me in place as he takes half a step back. "If you want more—" He gestures to himself, then to my hacked-up paper and raps his knuckles against my laptop on the counter.

My jaw drops, and I have to wiggle it back and forth to get it to slot back into place.

Dax smirks and his dimple winks as he begins slowly backing out of my kitchen, every inch between us taut like a bowstring.

"I cannot fucking stand you," I call after him as he laughs the entire way out of my apartment, leaving me flushed and panting in my kitchen.

But y'know what? I'm fucking motivated.

[Excerpt from Sloane Donavan's Final Revelations interview transcript]

2003–2006: A Bit Feral

MARCUS: We released our third album, *Shadow Psalms*, in 2003, and it ended up being an apt metaphor for the next few years.

JONAH: *Shadow Psalms* was the second album we recorded with Dropkick Records, who we had a three-album deal with.

DAX: We decided rerecording our first album, *Sacrament* [previously recorded with Garage Door Records], fulfilled our contract of three albums.

JONAH: They did not agree.

CAIN: They owed us a fuckload in unpaid royalties. We made them so much money and we barely saw any of it. But we saved every penny we did get, and as soon as we had enough—

BARRETT: We sued their asses.

MARCUS: They did not like that. Our name was already in the mud from that *Offbeat* article—and every other reporter parroting Song's shit—so everyone believed Dropkick when they started bad-mouthing us to anyone who'd listen. [*mocking*] *Dax and Marcus are divas. They're impossible to work with.* The only difficult thing we did was ask to get fucking paid.

DAX: We already weren't speaking to the press, but even if we wanted to, we couldn't while the case was ongoing. So we just had to take it on the chin.

JONAH: Every band on their roster was being screwed. We were just the first band that could afford to take them to court.

BARRETT: It took two years, but we won. We fucking won.

MARCUS: That was a nice paycheck.

BARRETT: I paid off my dad's medical debt with that.

DAX: I finally got my own place with that check.

CAIN: I proposed to my girl, moved us out of our tiny apartment.

JONAH: I invested it. That's a boring answer, isn't it?

MARCUS: I started my own label. A lot of Dropkick alumni signed with me. Funny, that.

JONAH: We were a bit trigger shy to sign with anyone too soon, and we had a whole album we'd written but couldn't release while still locked in the lawsuit.

MARCUS: We ended up releasing it under my label, just to get it out there to the fans.

DAX: That album, *Prodigal Son*, is special to all of us for a lot of reasons. Mostly because we produced and released it ourselves, but for me...People think—*I thought*—good art is made in the mess, that whole tortured-artist schtick. I definitely bought into that when I first started. But by *Prodigal*, I'd been sober for a few years, had some perspective, and I'm really proud of the lyrics Marcus and I wrote for that. And we were all, like, simmering with rage and energy, waiting to see how the lawsuit would pan out, and it translated.

BARRETT: There's something a bit feral about that album. We were like animals caught in a bear trap, waiting on the judge's ruling, ready to gnaw our own legs off to get free. And once we were—

MARCUS: I know a lot of fans have nostalgia for our early records, but I think we hit our stride around *Shadow Psalms*, and *Prodigal Son* and *Purgatorium* kept that momentum going.

DAX: There were multiple points in our career where I'd thought, *It can't possibly get better than this*—and every time, I was wrong. Getting free of that label felt like a new start. Seven years and four albums in, and we felt like we were just getting started.

CHAPTER TWENTY-ONE

"You're probably wondering why I gathered you all here," I say dramatically, suddenly very nervous. I've never had the dream of showing up to class in your underwear, but I imagine it feels like this. Except watching a bunch of guys read the article I wrote about them is infinitely more mortifying. But necessary.

"We were already gathered," Marcus points out with a bored quirk of his brows.

"Thanks, Barrett." I wink at him, my coconspirator, tipping me off that everyone would be at his place to write the final song for the album. "Anyway," I say, plowing on, "I've finished the article—almost. It's unconventional and not necessarily what you asked for—what anyone asked for," I admit under my breath. "But I think this is better. But—"

"Two *but*s? That's never good." Cain laughs.

I make a face at him, still avoiding Dax's gaze from the moment I crashed the end of their session. I called him last night to float this idea past him before proposing it to everyone, and the call ended with a "long-distance practice session"—aka phone sex—and I don't trust myself not to blush if I look at him. That, and I never let the subject of my article review the piece beforehand, and I'm incredibly nervous about them reading it—him more than the others.

"But," I continue, "if you're on board with this, I need a little bit more from you, since you conveniently left out some parts the first time." I flash them a saccharine smile, and they have the grace to look abashed. Well, all of them but Marcus, who isn't even slightly abashed. "First—" Clearing my throat, I slide the binder-clipped bundles from my backpack, handing them to each guy in turn.

I save Dax for last, and when I hand him his, he doesn't need to graze the back of my hand to take it from me, but he does it anyway. I meet his gaze, and there's no trace of nerves or hesitation in his eyes—just pride. I smile weakly before retreating to the bottom of the basement stairs to wait, mentally reciting the article in my head.

♪ ♫ ♬

[DRAFT] Finally, Revelations: The Reintroduction of Final Revelations

By Sloane Donavan for Alternative Press

When one of metal's biggest bands asks you to do their first interview in nearly a decade, you don't say no—even when the frontman is your ex.

But I'm not here to tell you if Dax Nakamura is a good kisser (he is) or the best places to sneak around on a bus ([redacted]). I'm here because if anyone is going to tell you exactly how it is, it's the girl who spent a summer on their bus a few years ago and doesn't have anything left to prove—to them or to you, dear reader.

Final Revelations isn't new. Everyone knows them—or thinks they do, despite them not giving an interview in eight years. Yeah, you know the one. After that article, it would make sense they'd never speak to another reporter again.

I'm here to tell you that you don't actually know Final Revelations.

Are they curmudgeonly? Yes.

Do they only want to talk about the music? Yes. And no.

Do Dax and Marcus hate each other? No; they bicker like an old married couple—with love.

Did Dax make a deal with the devil to sound Like That? The demon I made a deal with to get this article says I'm not allowed to disclose that.

Is this actually their final album? Yes.

If you ask them what to expect off this record, you'll get five different answers, only half of which make sense. For example, when I asked Cain, he made a jerk-off motion, so do with that what you will. But weirdly enough, I know what he means.

The album isn't done yet, but if I tried to describe what I've heard so far, I'd say it goes a little something like this: It's like when you were a kid and you'd sit at the bottom of the swimming pool and see how long you could hold your breath. You're fighting to stay under, to not give in to the screaming of your lungs, believing that maybe if you just hold on a little longer, some magic will happen and you'll sprout gills. But then, eventually, you accept the limits of your mortality and allow yourself to surface. And when you do—the air is crisp and fresh the way it is after a storm, and it tastes all the sweeter because you'd forgotten what a gift it is to breathe easy.

So yeah, (insert jerk-off motion here).

You either know what I mean or you don't.

You can decide for yourselves what the album feels like in March. For now, here's their story, as told by Marcus, Cain, Jonah, Barrett, and Dax—no "source close to the band" needed.

See below for part 1 of their interview, and stay tuned for part 2 in the January issue.

♪ ♫ ♬

I allow a trickle of pride to slip in as Jonah laughs within seconds of starting to read. I can't claim ownership of most of this piece—it's just them being them—but by the time I had their transcripts satisfactorily interwoven, the intro I wrote poured out of me easily, as well as a smattering of joyful tears because finally—*finally*—the voice in my head, the one on the page, was mine. So I take Jonah's surprised laugh and Barrett's mischievous chuckle and even Marcus's intrigued brows to heart.

I try not to watch Dax too closely, but I can't help the way my gaze slides back to him, his only reaction a slight crease between his brows as he reads.

"You little shit," Cain mutters, tossing a guitar pick at Marcus, who dodges it.

"What?"

"Page three."

"How are you on page three already?" Barrett crows.

Dax doesn't even look up at their bantering, his eyes sweeping across the text, a full page ahead of them all. He finishes first, staring at the last line like he's waiting for more to appear, before starting over.

I hold my breath. I'm vaguely aware of the others as they finish, can feel them watching me watch him, until all of us are watching him, because really, this article is about all of them, their collective name dragged through the mud, but none so much as Dax. I couldn't allow myself to think about it too hard while writing, but I'm rewriting their history. Or I'm the vehicle for them to rewrite it. I don't know if I'll ever write anything that means as much as this ever again.

Dax reaches the end for the second time and is halfway out of his chair when his eyes meet mine. I loose a shaky breath, and he's already to me, taking my face in his hands. He's bending over, bringing his mouth to mine and he's pushing me back into the stairs. He's sighing into my mouth like he's putting down a weight he's been carrying for eight years. He's painting my cheeks with his tears, and I'm wiping them away with my thumbs, tasting his invisible burdens on my tongue. He's pressing his forehead to mine, his staccato breaths like the slap of drumsticks counting down the start of a new song.

"Thank you for seeing me," he whispers just for me.

"I liked it, too, but I'm not gonna kiss ya, Boston," Barrett calls irreverently from the other side of the room, effectively cutting the tension.

I laugh, and so does Dax, our amusement intermingling. I wipe his cheeks and then my own before meeting everyone's gaze.

Marcus nods, and the others nod their approval as well. I sag in relief.

"So what do you need from us?" Jonah calls, scanning the article.

"*Nixed*. And the final Final."

"We don't want this—"

"—to read like an obituary," I say in tandem with Marcus. "I know," I assure him. "I mostly want to talk about *Nixed* before a brief segue into setting up the future. It won't be an obituary because you're not fucking done yet. You have this album and then tour. Let me finish your story up to this point. That's all I'm asking."

All the guys' attention drifts to Dax. *Nixed* is their album, but it's Dax's stories.

"That's who you gotta ask for *Nixed*," Marcus says with a nod to Dax.

"I've already heard it."

Marcus's brows shoot up, and he and Dax exchange one of their silent conversations.

"Something I should know?" I ask blandly.

The corners of Marcus's mouth turn down. "Guess not."

"Great. You should release it."

They splutter and choke on their words.

"Yes," Marcus agrees the instant he gathers himself, the two of us on the same page for maybe the first time ever.

"Come full circle—leak it like the EP," I say. "Or go out on a double album. Dax sent me the final Final last night, and— The juxtaposition of those songs versus *Nixed*, the perspective of when you're *in it* versus when you're *through it*—that's a story worth telling. Obviously, I'm not a member of the band," I hedge. "But as a fan, I've had points in my life where I needed both albums."

They exchange loaded looks, and I hold up my hands. "You can discuss later, when I'm not here. But if I could steal one of you to—"

I don't get to finish, to qualify why I want to speak to them individually, same as before, rather than as a group, Dax taking me by the hand and dragging me upstairs.

"*Not* in my room," Barrett calls after us.

"We're not going to scandalize your furniture," I promise around a laugh. "Dax knows the rules."

"Do I?" he questions, glancing back with an arched brow as we reach the top. He pulls me closer by our joined hands, backing me up against the kitchen wall. Leaning in, his breath ghosts across the shell of my ear as my hands fist in his shirt, pulling him closer on instinct. "Do you?"

I scoff, shoving him away.

He smiles, holding out his hand. I slide mine into his, allowing him to guide me up the next flight of stairs and down the short hallway. "I meant what I said to Barrett."

He grins at me over his shoulder, pausing at the end of the hall. He swings the door open, revealing a small guest room with a sloped ceiling. I glance at him in question.

"This is the room I lived in after my dad kicked me out—and for probably more years than Barrett would've preferred," he says on a laugh.

I slip past him into the room. It's neutral and plain now, but I can imagine eighteen-year-old Dax hitting his head on the sloped ceiling, mattress on the floor, his guitar tucked into the dormer, his Vans neatly stowed under the dresser.

He sidles up behind me, encircling me in his arms, his steady breathing ruffling my hair. "Are you sure about including us in your article?"

Us. We're slow-walking our way back together, at least until the article is done, but there's nothing slow about the affection warming my insides at the word.

I chew on the inside of my cheek, nodding slowly. "Yeah. Enough things have been written about you from dubious sources. It's better I come out the gate with it than have it come out some other way."

He hums against my neck, and I twist around to peer at him. "Are you okay with it?"

His expression softens. "More than okay with it."

"But what if we—" I can't say *break up*. "The article will be out there forever."

"I'm not worried about that."

I nod, not entirely sure which part he's referring to. It feels too soon to be making references to forever. "You're the only one I don't need to reinterview," I remind him. He gave me his *Nixed* sound bite last night before our call took a turn that was definitely off the record. "Unless you've figured out your plans for what's next?"

"You," he says without hesitation.

I frown up at him. "That's not a real answer."

He laughs. "Why not?"

I rub the scar on my ring finger automatically. "Because—" Because I've lived in the aftermath of what happens when you make someone your whole world. I don't know why I'm about to qualify his unserious answer with a too-serious one. I swallow the words, counter with the other question swirling in the back of my brain. "Why was Marcus so surprised you shared *Nixed*? The album is dark, sure, but I'm not that fragile," I joke.

His arms drop from around me as he moves to the edge of the bed, sinking onto it and guiding me to stand in between his legs. "Because he doesn't know I didn't send you every song." My hands still, halting my absentminded tracing of the fraying seam at his shoulder. "There's a song I couldn't finish, a song for you, that I wasn't quite ready to share yet."

"I see," I say on an exhale. "Do you—" I pause, taking a deep breath as Dax interlaces our fingers. "It's okay if not, but do you think you'd ever share it?"

He smiles softly up at me. "Yes."

"Yeah?"

His grin stretches, his dimple winking into existence. "Yeah."

"When?" I whisper.

A laugh gusts out of him. "You want me to get a calendar?"

I shake my head, sinking down onto the edge of the bed, straddling his lap. "No, not a date. More like a moment?" Pushing him back onto the bed, I guide our conjoined hands over his head. "Would you share it before or after we finally"—I tug on his earlobe with my teeth—"have sex?" The groan that escapes him is tortured. "Before or after we tell people about us?" At that, he beams, and I can't help but mirror it, the thought like sunshine in my chest. "Before or after you leave me to go on tour?"

The reminder is like an ice bucket over us, the inevitability that he will be leaving for long swaths of time over the next two years.

"I can't answer that yet."

Disappointed, I let go of his hands, sinking back onto my heels. He props himself up on his elbows.

"Is it...bad?" I ask, forcing the words out.

He shakes his head. "No."

I lick my lips, and I'm acutely aware of the way he tracks the movement with his eyes. "I do see you, Dax. I hope you know there's nothing you could say that's going to scare me."

He stares at me for a long moment, a disbelieving huff escaping him.

"What?!"

He pushes up, pressing his forehead to mine as he encircles me in his arms. "I see you, too, Sloane Donavan. Well enough to know there *are* things that scare you."

My face screws up, and he smiles softly, smoothing the crease between my brows.

"I want us to get it right this time," he whispers against my cheek.

"Me, too," I whisper back.

"Do you trust me?"

"Yes," I say automatically.

"And I trust you"—he sinks his teeth into the side of my neck and I squeal in surprise—"to finish this damn article with the quickness, because I fucking miss you." His arms tighten around me, pressing me to him, a certain part of him pressing into the backs of my thighs, letting me know how many different ways he misses me.

I grin into his dimple before placing a kiss there. "Well, then, you better leave me to get back to work."

And like the asshole he is, for the second time in as many days, he does.

Only this time, before slipping out the door, he turns back, extending his hand to me. He drags me back downstairs, pulling a chair out for me at the breakfast table before hollering down the basement stairs. "Oi, one of you fucks get up here."

⚡ CHAPTER TWENTY-TWO ⚡

"This isn't the article I asked for." John studies me over the rims of his readers, and I'm too exhausted to feel scolded. I stayed up until midnight piecing together yesterday's interviews in order to hit my deadline. What little sleep I did get was fraught with nightmares of this meeting, of it going exactly like this.

It's *not* what he asked for. It's not what Robb asked for, either, and I only hope me going rogue doesn't reflect poorly on her. To her credit, she tried. She tried so fucking hard to wring the article out of me, but it refused to come together until this iteration. I just hope John never looks at my original transcripts, all the stories that I redacted because the guys got a little too comfortable with me and forgot they were "on the record."

John leans forward, folding his forearms on the edge of the desk. I wait for him to scream or be quietly disappointed. Instead, he beams. "It's better."

I'm already sitting down but I feel like I need to sit down harder. "Sir?"

He gestures at the screen. "This is incredible, Sloane. It takes a lot of maturity to put your own ego aside and remove yourself from the equation entirely to let the subject shine. An impartial article is exactly the right call, given their history."

I bite down on my tongue to keep from crying I'm so relieved. "Thank you."

"I'll get you my notes in the next few days, but I don't think I'll have many."

I'm sinking and floating at the same time, unsure what to do without the weight of the article looming over me.

"In the meantime," he says, leaning back and gesturing with his readers, "do me a favor?"

I raise my brows in question.

"When this publishes and all the big names start trying to poach you, don't make any decisions without talking to me first."

I blink in surprise. Even in my most indulgent of daydreams, I'd never considered the idea of a bunch of publications fighting over me, but now that he's planted the idea... I don't hate it. Like a zombie rising from a grave, my buried dream of *Rolling Stone* twitches back to life. "Okay," I say around a disbelieving laugh.

He smiles, gesturing toward the door. "Go celebrate. You did good, kid."

I loop my bag over my shoulder, pausing when he calls my name as I'm halfway out the door.

"But Sloane—don't ever lie to me again about your relationship to a source."

I meet his gaze, nodding once. "Yes, sir."

I keep my head down the rest of the way out of the building, waiting until I'm safely tucked into my Jeep to flail happily. Hugging the steering wheel, I take a few steadying breaths, placing a kiss to the scar on my ring finger. I'm fucking doing it. Finally.

♪ ♫ ♬

I send off a few half-incoherent texts in all caps with too many exclamation marks to my group chats for Final Revelations and Buncha Punks, letting them know John accepted the piece. I leave Robb a voicemail that perhaps only a dog could hear.

I don't know what to do with myself, my workload empty for the first time in weeks. I drive home with a dopey smile on my face, soaking in that it's *done*. By the time I hit the highway, my phone is buzzing around my cupholder with incoming texts from my friends—both from afar and the community I'm starting to build here, too. For the first time, I feel like I'm really, truly, *finally* settling in here.

I park, and I'm a hundred feet away from my apartment when I see him. Everything in me sighs contentedly, my grin stretching more broadly, my strides lengthening.

He hasn't spotted me yet. He's staring down at his phone, one foot propped against the wall outside the gated entrance to my apartment stairs.

Through the rip in his jeans, I can see the demon inked on his knee. The dragon on the back of his hand comes alive as he types, only its face visible, the rest of it hidden beneath his hoodie. As if sensing my gaze, he glances up, septum piercing glinting in the light. His default stony expression softens when he spots me, and I pick up my pace. The way he puts his phone away, I know he's gonna do *the thing*. Two paces away, he opens up his arms, and I'm bounding into them. With one arm, he picks me up, my legs wrapping around his waist as his other hand cups my face.

"Hi," I breathe, resting my forehead against his.

"Hi, baby."

It's a chilly November day, but I feel the sunshine for the first time.

"I did it," I murmur, squeezing my eyelids against the tears prickling the backs of my eyes.

"Yeah, you fucking did."

Looping my arms around his neck, I pull him closer. I'm not sure how long we stay like that—probably longer than we should, making a bit of a scene—but I can't bring myself to let go for a long while, needing to revel in it a moment longer. When I finally tap his shoulder, letting him know he can put me down, I keep one arm around him as I buzz us into the dark corridor, taking him by the hand up the stairs.

Unlike my friends, he doesn't complain once about the hike.

When we reach my door, he leans a shoulder against the doorframe, blocking me from unlocking it. "So," he says meaningfully.

I raise my brows. "So?"

He ducks his head, a blush tinging his cheeks. "If John's read the article and accepted it...?"

I know what he's asking, but it's still cute to watch this man who commands crowds of hundreds squirm for me. I mimic his posture, propping myself against the door, facing him. "Yeah?"

He laughs on an exhale, knowing I'm fucking with him. I follow the path his tongue traces on the inside of his cheek as he feigns being exasperated by me. "Are we still pretending we're not doing this?"

Heat pools in my stomach as he snags my gaze and refuses to let go. My heart is in my throat and it's difficult to breathe around. If I open my mouth, it may float out and leave me for him, as if it hasn't been his ever since the first time he said my name.

He raises his eyebrows at me, not letting me off the hook for an answer, as if it's even a question. He crowds me, not touching me, caging me by bracing his forearm against the top of the doorframe, his other hand cupping my cheek.

I toss my hair back as if his proximity doesn't send my pulse racing. "Why? You wanna call me your girlfriend or something?"

He glances away, fighting a smile and losing, only turning back to me once he's wrestled it under control. "I want to call you a lot of things, Sloane Donavan, but sure, we can start there."

Looping my fingers through his belt loops, I pull him closer, arching onto my tiptoes so I can brush my mouth against his. He inhales sharply before angling away, placing a kiss at the corner of my mouth instead. "I'm asking," he whispers against my cheek, "because I need to know"—he places a kiss at the hinge of my jaw—"if I should check some of my filthier thoughts at the door."

"They're more than welcome," I rush out, overeager, already fumbling with my keys. I only have two and I somehow manage to grab the wrong one twice, my vision lust darkened and unable to focus on anything but the way Dax brushes my hair off to the side, placing lazy kisses along my neck as I complete the arduous task of focusing long enough to unlock my door.

Thankfully, I don't have to focus on much once I do manage to get us through the door. I barely get my shoes toed off before Dax's hands are at my hips, pulling me back into him. He pushes my hair to the other side, busying himself with the side of my neck he hasn't yet claimed. All the while, his hand trails down my arm, easing my keys from my hands and tossing them blindly toward my foyer table, where they skitter across the top before dropping to the floor. If he notices, he doesn't show it, attention focused on my neck as he clumsily kicks his shoes off and into a haphazard pile in the corner, so unlike his usual neat self.

I don't know why, but Dax losing his careful grip on his self-control is what does it for me more than anything else. I suck in a shaky breath, swallowing thickly, which he clocks instantly. Circling around in front of me, he holds my face in my hands. "Are you okay? We can slow down."

A watery laugh escapes me, and I shake my head adamantly. "No. Fuck, no. I just—" I place my hand on his shoulder, my thumb dipping beneath the collar of his shirt to trace the divot of his collarbone. "I've had to be impartial about you—or try to be, at least." I laugh because the notion is ridiculous. "But it's all hitting me. I finished the article, yeah, but so did you." My brows draw together as I meet his gaze. "I'm really proud of you."

He averts his gaze because despite his ego, he cannot take a compliment.

"You're really fucking special. And I don't know *what* you saw in me three years ago or last month when you asked me to do this, but I'm really grateful you did. I'm glad we got to do this together. Thank you for trusting me with it."

His gaze is fierce when it meets mine again. "It never could've been anyone else. Only you."

When he kisses me again, it's not the fevered, sloppy kisses from when we stumbled through the door. It's slow, intentional. Our hands grasp at each other, as if now that there's nothing keeping us apart, even a whisper of space between us is unbearable.

"This," he whispers against my mouth. "I've gotten a lot of things wrong in my life, but this? *Us*. This I got right. I'm going to get it right this time."

A rush of affection for him swells inside me, the improbability of this moment, this second chance neither of us knew we'd get, hitting me like a freight train, making me cling harder to him, arching into his touch. He pours everything into his kiss like he's realizing it, too. I deepen the kiss, guiding his hands up under my shirt. He slides his hands underneath my bra, not bothering to unhook it. The brush of his calluses over my breasts steals my breath and all conscious thought, a needy whimper eking out of me as he flicks my peaked nipples with the pads of his thumbs.

Reaching behind me, I unhook my bra, slipping it and my shirt off in one go as he sinks to his knees. His breath coasts across my skin, eliciting goose bumps. He nips at the underside of my breast before soothing it with a swipe of his tongue that comes close, so close, to where I want his mouth, but he doesn't give it to me. His hand comes up to tease my other breast, circling, circling, closer each pass, before pulling back and starting over. My head falls back against the door in frustration.

His cocky laugh dances across my ribs, and he gives me the barest of flicks but not enough to take the edge off. "I've waited three years to do this again. Did you think I was going to be quick?"

"No," I huff. "But it's not like you to leave me wanting either."

Heat flares behind his eyes, like I knew it would. The air between us goes taut as I wait for his next move, the moment hanging suspended. My breath hitches at the wicked tilt of his mouth because I know that look. It's the same one I've been picturing for the past three years while wishing it were his hand between my legs and not my own.

He has my pants unbuttoned and unzipped in a flash, guiding them down my hips, taking my underwear with them. He frees my right leg from my jeans, guiding it up onto his shoulder. Dax's priority is never to get my clothes *off* so much as *off enough*. He kisses his way up my thigh, indulging in one just-shy-of-painful bite that has me hissing in a breath, before he soothes it with a swipe of his tongue and a kiss.

He goes down on me like this is the breakup sex we never had and makeup sex, all in one. He tastes me like he's savoring it, like it's the last time and not the second first time.

His thumb joins his mouth, making tortuously slow, tight circles around my clit as his tongue explores me like he's going to make a topographical map of my pussy later. When my hips buck forward of their own accord, his left arm curls around my thigh over his shoulder, taking more of my weight, my leg planted on the floor growing increasingly unstable. This time, when I rock my hips, he hums in approval, his lips vibrating against my clit. I gasp, nearly shooting up the wall at the rush of sensation, but his grip holds me in place.

Fingers digging into his shoulders, I give up what little sense of decorum I have left and ride his face. He groans in approval, his free hand drifting up to toy with my nipples until the gentle rock of my hips grows desperate. I sink a few inches lower on the door, and he has me, his right hand going to my hip, pinning it against the door.

It's been three years, but you'd never know it from the way he still remembers exactly what I like, teasing, flicking, sucking. He feasts on me until I have to squeeze my eyes shut, becoming nothing but a giant ball of sensation. I arch against his mouth, my orgasm taking what little control I have left. My toes curl with the intensity of it, and my heel digs into his back as my other leg straightens, before giving up any pretense of holding me up and going limp. He works me down with gentle laves of his tongue, holding on to me until I come back into myself enough to stand.

He frees my ankle still trapped in my jeans before pushing off the floor, dragging his hand over his wet mouth. I barely let him finish before planting a kiss on him, walking him backward toward the couch. Maybe one day we'll make it all the way to the bedroom, but right now, my need is too much. A light push to the center of his chest and he sinks back obediently onto the cushions, and I settle atop his lap.

I don't waste any time divesting him of his shirt, hands roaming across his chest, pulling him closer by the chain around his neck and kissing him before pressing him against the back of the couch. He buries his hand in the hair at the nape of my neck, not letting me break our kiss. My hands drift south, deftly undoing the button there and then his fly. "Condom?"

"Yes." His raises his hips for me, and I slide my hand into his back pocket, fishing out his wallet. Once I have the foil packet I seek, I toss his wallet onto the coffee table. He shoves his jeans and boxers down to his knees, which brings his face to my breasts, his tongue darting out to flick the piercings there as he kicks his clothes off the rest of the way.

Our chests rise in tandem on a deep breath, the smile on my face mirroring his.

"Hi," I breathe.

"Hi." His hands coast up and down my thighs, and I lean in, hand going to his throat as I place a soft kiss on his lips.

I quickly get lost in our kiss, pressing my chest up against his, rocking against him gently. His touch drifts lower, a long finger teasing me. I gasp, and he seizes the opportunity, sliding his tongue into my mouth and a finger inside me at the same time.

I grind against him until I can't take it anymore, a guttural noise escaping me. Leaning back, I place a hand to his chest to keep him from chasing my mouth with his own. I roll the condom on, tossing the wrapper over my shoulder, not caring where it lands.

I guide his arms onto the back of the couch.

"It's my turn to take care of you, okay?"

He looks tortured, but he gives me an infinitesimal nod.

I slide my fingers between my legs, getting them good and messy. Dax watches hungrily, his cock jumping impatiently. I wrap my fingers around him, giving him the pressure I know he likes, working him for a few strokes before easing up onto my knees. I slide over him once, twice, taking pleasure in the way he can't take his eyes off us, his pupils blown wide, his hands gripping the back of the couch.

Then, slowly, I notch him at my entrance. His attention flicks from where we're joined to my face, my mouth dropping open on a silent gasp as I slowly work down his length, sliding down and back up, taking more of him each time. He groans when I finally take all of him and grind against him with a circle of my hips. Planting one hand against his chest, I brace my other arm behind me as I begin to roll my hips.

When he calls me "baby," it's a curse—and a prayer.

My entire body flushes with heat and pride at his praise, and goddamnit, I'm already close. I try to draw it out, undulating against him deliciously slow, but soon my rhythm begins to stutter, and I'm aching to pick up the pace, to increase the pressure.

"Dax," I breathe, and he knows exactly what I want, what I need.

His arms come around me, pulling me into a kiss. One hand drifts down to my hip, holding me there as he takes control, picking up the rhythm I lost, increasing the tempo. Our kisses grow sloppy, tapering off until it's less kissing and more a sharing of breath as we drink in the other's gasps. I pant out his name, teetering on the edge of release, and he grins wolfishly.

"Come with me," I plead.

"I will," he promises. He picks up the pace, and I cling to the back of his neck, our breaths intermingling as he watches me, waiting for the cues that tell him I'm tipping over the edge. He places one hand at my lower back, the other on my abdomen, applying just the right amount of pressure and—

Every muscle in my body locks up as my pleasure reaches its peak, before unlocking in a shudder that ripples through me.

Dax moans, and his eyes drift to where he thrusts into me again and again. The continued press of him against my clit is too much, and his attention snaps to mine when he feels the telltale flutter of my inner walls.

"Yeah?" he asks with a cocky smirk. He's so damn pleased with himself for how he wrecks me.

I nod, coherency a lost art.

"One more time for me," he whispers against the shell of my ear, not breaking his perfect rhythm. This time, he doesn't need to read my clues, a cry ripping out of me as a second orgasm piggybacks my first.

He buries his face in my neck as he follows me over the edge, kissing me everywhere he can get to. He takes me with him as he sinks back against the couch, and I collapse onto his chest, sated, the only sound our labored breathing.

After our hearts have slowed from a gallop and our breaths are mostly normal, I ease off of him, my sweat-slicked skin letting go of his reluctantly. I want to collapse sideways on the couch and rest, but I get up, holding my hand out for him. He accepts, trailing after me into the bathroom, turning on the shower to let it heat up while I pee and he disposes of the condom. It's an easy rhythm, one we've done before, albeit not many times, our first go at this disproportionately short compared to how much room it's taken up in my heart the past three years, like a squatter refusing to move out.

As we slip into the shower, I wrap my arms around him, pressing my cheek to the reaper at his back. I hope that we get longer than a few weeks this time. That we never got our epic ending the first time because we were meant to be epic, not end.

CHAPTER TWENTY-THREE

"Congrats, babe," Robb says with a warm smile, tapping her champagne glass against mine with a crystalline *clink*.

"Thank you." I flush. The restaurant we're in is incredibly swanky, and I'm underdressed in spliced plaid pants, a frayed sweater, and Docs. Thankfully, Robb is equally as casual in her simple cotton dress and plaid jacket. They definitely tucked us away in the corner of the bar on purpose. "This is... We could've just gone to a brewery."

Robb waves this away. "Work expense," she says with a smirk.

Should I have been saving my receipts? Then I realize that's probably a staff perk, not a freelance perk.

"How are you feeling?" Robb asks before taking a sip of her drink.

I ferret around the cheese board between us, stalling. The waiter explained what pairs best together, but I forgot the instant they walked away, so I grab two random items and hope for the best. "Great," I say, popping the cheese and dried fruit into my mouth.

Robb raises her brows from behind her cat-eye glasses. Then she shakes her head. "Sorry—yes. You should feel great. You wrote a great fucking article."

"But?" I ask suspiciously.

Robb hems and haws for half a second. "Are you happy?" she blurts. "At *AP*?"

I nod eagerly. "Yeah," I reassure her. "All I've wanted since graduating was someone I could learn from. After *The Offbeat*—" I shake my head. "Thank you so much for believing in me. I couldn't have done it without you, and I hope we get to work on more things together."

Robb smiles softly. "I hope so, too. But that's not really what I asked."

Something heavy settles in my gut, like I ate all the cheese on the table in one gulp. "Am I happy at *AP*," I repeat, trying to riddle out what she's really getting at. "I mean, obviously I would like to not be freelance anymore," I hedge. I got the interview of the year. It feels classless to complain, but I would *really* like to have a steady paycheck, benefits, health insurance, a 401(k).

"Has John offered you anything?"

I open my mouth to say yes, then close it.

When this publishes and all the big names start trying to poach you, don't make any decisions without talking to me first.

"Not an offer, exactly," I realize. The hopeful balloon that I've carried in my chest since that meeting with John deflates like a whoopee cushion. "Just not to accept any offers without coming to him first."

Robb snorts, sinking against the back of her chair. "Of course he said that."

I lean forward. "What do you mean?"

"I mean it lets him off the hook, doesn't it? For actually having to pay you. Are you looking elsewhere?"

My skin goes clammy. "Should I be?"

Robb's eyes bug. "Yes, Sloane. You just wrote what will become part of scene history. You shouldn't be getting paid scraps."

The neck of my sweater is suddenly too tight, and I tug at it. "I mean, yeah, but I finally found someone I like working with," I say meaningfully.

Robb smiles sadly at me from across the table. "I've really enjoyed working with you, too, watching you grow."

"But?" I say again, the word left hanging unspoken at the end of her sentence.

"But..." she begins again. "I'm putting in my notice tomorrow."

My spine hits the chair as I rear back. *"What?"*

"All the guys on the writing staff make way more than me, which I could stomach if I were still growing as a writer, but—" She exhales heavily. "Everything I pitch beyond the same beat I've been doing the past ten years John shoots down." I nod in understanding. "I applied to *Rolling Stone* as a way to get a competing offer, to force John's hand to pay up, but the counteroffer he made—" She shakes her head. "The *Stone* offer stopped looking like a bargaining chip after a while."

I nod again, unsure what to do, what to say, feeling selfish that my predominant thought is grief over losing my mentor so soon. "I get it—I hate it, but I get it. I'm really going to miss working with you."

"What if...what if you don't have to?" Taking a deep breath, she bends over, retrieving something from her bag. Flicking open a manila envelope, she hands me a heavy piece of card stock. I can't make anything out other than the *Rolling Stone* header.

"Come with me." She taps the paper in front of me, and I really see it for the first time. My name at the top, my title—*staff writer*. My eyes bulge at the number next to the word *salary*.

"They need writers based on the West Coast and they're letting me build my own team in San Fran. When they asked me who I wanted, I told them all about you," she begins. "They want you—bad. They know you'll be able to go anywhere you want after the Final piece goes live, so this is a very competitive offer to lock you in before it goes out."

I don't know what to say. *Rolling Stone* has always been my dream job. I thought Mike was my in, and when that internship went sour, I put my dream on hold. Working with Robb is all I want, the mentorship I've waited years for, and I'm losing her—unless I follow her.

"Think about it," she pleads. "And just—" She grimaces. "I love Dax, I do, but don't stay here for a guy."

I scoff on autopilot, because the idea of giving up my dreams for another person is antithetical to my very being. I spilled my own blood on a rooftop promising that I wouldn't. While I may have been too young to fully understand it in the moment, over time, it became a cornerstone I built my life around.

But... what if he's the *guy?* I can't say it out loud, can barely think it inside my own head. It feels like tugging at a thread that's kept me stitched together for years. I've spent my entire adult life working toward an offer like this. But... I want the community I've begun cultivating here. I want Dax. I want *AP*. And yet, I know that wanting alone isn't enough to make something reality. Plans make things happen, and I have a very real new plan sitting in front of me. Not just any plan—my dream, served up on weighty card stock. I'd be a fool to pass this up without considering it. If I take it, would I regret it? If I don't, would I always wonder, *What if?*

"You have until the December issue to decide. I hope you'll come with me," she says. "And if not, there will be an opening at *AP*. It should be yours. But I can tell you right now, it's not *that*." She taps the paper in front of me.

I nod, easing the paper off the table, the *Rolling Stone* header like a half-remembered dream. I slide it into my bag carefully, as if I'm handling a bomb. I may as well be, the way this would detonate everything I've started to build here.

♪ ♫ ♬

The rest of our happy hour goes smoothly, a reminder of what I'll be giving up if I don't go with Robb. But I can't ignore the pit in my stomach at the thought of going back to San Francisco. It feels like getting back together with a toxic ex and expecting it to go differently. Except I wouldn't be working for Mike, but Robb, who was unfailingly patient with me while I struggled my way through this article, even when the article should have been hers all along. She couldn't be less like Mike. And while I like John, I don't know that he'd mentor me in the same way, nor has he made any moves to secure me a permanent place at *AP*.

My head spins the entire drive home, and I slog my way up the stairs to my apartment, the job offer like a ten-pound weight in my bag. I want Robb. I want Dax. I want a steady paycheck and benefits. Neither option allows me to have all three.

I toe off my boots once I'm inside my apartment, and I can't ignore the lift in my spirits when I spy Dax on my couch, guitar in hand. He stops playing when he sees me.

"How's Ro— Whoa, what's wrong?" he asks, pivoting when he catches my expression.

Fuck, I forgot to school my face. I need to tell him about Robb's offer, but I want to riddle out how *I* feel before I discuss it with him. Including him in making a massive decision about my future—I prefer to dip a toe into the water to test it before cannonballing into the deep end. It's a conversation we need to have, but I'm too scared of the answer to force it. Everything about this situation is a little too familiar, a distorted funhouse mirror of what ended us three years ago. Him leaving for tour, me fixing my eyes on the *Rolling Stone* horizon, us at a crossroads.

Dropping my bag by the door, I half expect the offer to leap out and announce its presence. It doesn't, and I trudge over to Dax, climbing on top of him and wrapping all my limbs around him. We only *just* uncomplicated things. I want to stay in this bubble as long as possible.

"Robb's leaving *AP*," I whisper into the crook of his neck, his oni tattoo glaring at me like it knows the other half of that statement and is judging me for omitting it.

Dax's arms wrap around me, rubbing soothingly up and down my back. "I'm sorry," he breathes. "Do you want to talk about it?"

I shake my head, rolling off him and sideways onto the couch.

"Can I say one thing?" he hedges.

I gesture for him to go ahead.

"Means you should be getting an offer soon, though," he says around barely restrained excitement.

I smile weakly. "We'll see." I turn my attention to my coffee table, strewn with scraps of paper not unlike the chaotic plotting of my article. Only Dax's chaos isn't printed interviews; it's napkins and receipts and ripped papers, all scrawled with his messy handwriting. "What're you working on?"

"Final song." He pinches the bridge of his nose. Their band name makes for multiple meanings, but I know what he means before he clarifies, "Last song on the album. We still need one, but nothing we've tried feels right. It... We're a bit too in our heads about it, trying to write something, the *last* something, that will be satisfying for the fans."

I hum in understanding, studying the organized chaos on the table. "Can I say one thing?"

He smirks at my echo, mimicking my gesture from before.

"Since when have you written catering to anyone? Do whatever the fuck you want."

His dimple winks at me, his attention on the papers before him, like they're a puzzle he doesn't know how to begin assembling. "Yeah," he says noncommittally. "The problem is I want a lot of things. Half of them don't even sound like Final, but I keep coming back to them anyway. But they make no sense all together."

I nod. "Can I say one more thing?"

He huffs, grinning. "Yes."

"No matter what you do, it'll sound like Final, because you *are* Final." Leaning forward, I plant a kiss on his shoulder. Sliding my legs off his lap, I plant them on the ground, padding over to my record player and dropping to the floor. Rifling through the cabinets, I begin piling CDs and vinyls at my feet.

"What are you doing?" he asks.

I pause to hold up one of the albums. "Studying. Records with killer last songs."

He grunts thoughtfully before pushing up off the couch and coming to join me on the floor. I ease a CD into my player, skipping to the last song.

We go like that for hours, Dax breaking out his iPod at one point, the two of us lying side by side on the floor as we take turns queueing up songs, talking over others, dissecting what makes them work.

As Dax selects another song, I roll onto my side, curling into his, one of his arms coming around me automatically. I'm not paying attention to the song, my mind on the offer in my bag, how accepting it would mean losing this.

I want to stay in this bubble forever, but as our current research session reminds me, good things end, even when you don't want them to. But that doesn't make them any less beautiful or perfect.

If this is our swan song, then perhaps I can make peace with it, because this moment is both beautiful and perfect.

CHAPTER TWENTY-FOUR

Three weeks pass. Robb puts in her notice, and I try not to cry while helping her pack up her closet of an office. With every passing day and every meeting where John doesn't accept any of my pitches, I begin to lose faith *AP* will ever make me an offer.

Each morning, I wake up and try to convince myself that *today's the day*. Every day, I promise myself I'll talk to John, and every day, I chicken out. I'm frozen in the balance, needing to make a decision but terrified of the fallout.

Rolling over, I meet Dax's gaze across the pillows. With hardly any work to do, I've disappeared into him, the two of us almost always together, staying at each other's places. But the bubble is about to burst. The first time, when the bubble of tour burst, we ended. And now, reality is knocking at the door of this secret, precious thing we've been building. I have to give *Rolling Stone* an answer next week, and I'm no clearer on what to do than I was when Robb presented it to me.

After today's pitch meeting, I'm flying home to spend Thanksgiving with my family. I still haven't told Dax about the offer, but by the way we've been inseparable, it's like he knows, can feel the proverbial needle pressed to our bubble and is as determined as I am to squeeze as much "us" into the coming weeks as possible.

We spent last night apart—him at the studio and me at a show, scouting for Artists to Watch—and I was fast asleep when he let himself into my apartment late last night. Now, I wrap as many of my limbs around him as I can, desperate for the contact.

We lie like that for a while—me flopped half on top of him while he lazily strokes up and down my spine—before Dax presses a kiss to my temple and says, "I want to show you something."

I arch a brow, glancing down pointedly, the hard length of him apparent even through the duvet.

He laughs throatily. "I mean, I can multitask." He rolls us over, pressing me into the mattress with a kiss before extricating himself from the tangle of limbs and blankets. Grabbing his phone, he unwinds the headphones wrapped around it before slipping them into my ears.

He doesn't say anything, but he doesn't have to. It can only be one of two things: the *Nixed* song he never sent me or the final song on the album, which they've spent the past few weeks writing and recording.

He hits Play before laying his face on my stomach. My breath hitches immediately. It's the melody I've heard many times from the next room over. They haven't done a soft song since their first album. Dax is using a harsh vocal style I've never heard from him before—there's no other way to describe it other than it sounds like heartbreak. I'll need to listen again to fully absorb the lyrics, but true to his word, it's not *bad* about me, but it's definitely about me. The way he went back to the memories of us over and over—the same way I did—rereading our chapter and wishing for an alternate ending. I realize this is both the *Nixed* song he never shared with me *and* the final song on the album. The beautiful guitar medley ends and what comes next can only be described as a screamed confessional. Dax half telling me to go, half begging me to stay, promising to wait until we can try again, when he's better and I'm ready. Then the rest of the band comes in, and it's so different but so *them*. It's an anthem and a victory cry, the life he dreamed of becoming real. It's no longer just a song about me, but a song for all of the guys. It's an epilogue and a blank page all in one. It's hope for a future.

It ends, silence ringing in my ears in the aftermath. I glance down to find Dax watching me nervously. Angling his phone toward me, I restart the song, tapping the button to auto-repeat. I feel more than hear his laugh, and he places a kiss against my stomach, on the exposed strip of skin where my T-shirt has ridden up. His lips graze an unhurried, scorching path to my hip, my thigh, the apex of my legs, before he drags my underwear down, making good on his promise to multitask.

Go, I'll get better

He's making promises in my ears and between my legs.

Come back, I'll be worthy

He doesn't know he's always been worthy.

Go, don't let me drag you down

The drag of his tongue over me has my back arching, my hand fisting in the sheets.

Come back, let me hold you up

His arm bands around my legs, holding me in place.

Go, live your dreams

He did this in my dreams last night.

Come back, you are mine

I can't believe I'm his—or that I'm already about to come. I tug the headphones out of my ears, unable to focus on anything but what he's doing to me, undoing me. The melody is barely audible from where it continues to play from the earbuds, intertwining with the rustling of bedsheets and, *fuck*, the sound of Dax's other hand working himself.

As he sends me over the edge with a flick of his tongue and brings me back down the same way, I let the rush of endorphins make me optimistic, that everything is going to work out. I drag him up to me, kissing him until he groans into my mouth, spilling onto my stomach as he comes.

Reality creeps back in, the song still playing on his phone restarting, and I hit Pause as we catch our breath. Dax flops onto his back and I press a kiss into his shoulder. "I love it," I tell him.

"The sex or the song?"

I swat him with the back of my hand. He knows what I mean. He grins over at me. "Do you?" I ask.

He nods, smiling softly at me. "Yeah," he breathes. "I love it."

Somehow, we ended up sideways on the bed, and we stare at each other over the crumpled duvet. My heart rate should be slowing down by now, but the way the word *love* hovers in the air between us has my pulse racing all over again. We never said it before, but didn't we? We said *I love you* a million times, just never with words.

The way he's watching me now, I think he might. I think I might. He wrote me a song, proclaiming it, but somehow those three words still feel bigger. They're on the tip of my tongue, stuck in the back of my throat, a future I want but am afraid to grasp. I want to implode all my plans and make new ones with him at the center, but it scares the absolute shit out of me. If I can get an *AP* offer, I can have it all without imploding anything. I don't know if that makes me a coward or an optimist.

I get why he never showed me the original song. It would have been too much then, when we were just starting again. Even now, it's a lot to take in. It's the same reason I can't bring myself to show him the offer from *Rolling Stone*. It feels too big, too much, too soon. This thing between us is both new and old, solid but also precious, fragile. It's too early for a test of this magnitude. I've never done this before, always having been on my own. I've never made plans with someone else in mind. I thought we'd have time to navigate smaller firsts before we got to one like this, time for this fledgling thing to get its legs beneath itself, to walk before it had to run.

"Come home with me," I say impulsively.

He blinks. "What?"

"For Thanksgiving," I say. We've been in a bubble, and I want to see if we can withstand a few small tests before I throw a really big one into the mix. And if we can't, if our days are numbered, then I don't want to waste a single one of them away from him.

"Are you serious?"

I shake my head, confused. "Why wouldn't I be?"

Dax readjusts his pillow under his head, stalling. "Because I... I'm not really the guy you take home to meet your family. I'm not the guy dads dream about their kid ending up with. I'm the guy your dad gets gray hairs over."

I wave this away. "He's a single dad of five. The man's *been* gray."

Dax laughs, the sound throaty and deep.

I place a kiss to the hollow of his throat, the metal of his chain cool against my lips. "Please." He studies me warily, and I place a kiss to the sinister oni at his throat. "You are so kind, Dax Nakamura. And you are so good to me. And you make me come, like, all the time." He smirks at that, and I flick his septum piercing playfully. "You feed me, you let me talk your ear off about everything and nothing, you believe in me even when I don't believe in myself, but mostly, you make me really, really happy." I press my lips against his stubbled jaw. "And for that reason alone, I know my dad would want to meet you."

He pulls me in for a kiss. When he slides one leg between mine, I squirm out from his grasp, knowing exactly where that will lead if I don't eject myself from the bed immediately.

I slip into the bathroom to clean myself up, and Dax follows shortly after. "I know you have plans with your family, so if you don't want to miss that, I get it," I hedge, preparing for rejection.

"I'll come home with you," he says with a smile.

"Yeah?" I ask, trying to keep my excitement at bay and failing. I can practically see my Dax-days counter filling back up, regaining the time I would have lost going home.

"On one condition," he says slyly.

I narrow my eyes at him. "What's that?"

"You have to ask John to make you an offer today."

I grumble, resting my hip against the bathroom counter and burying my face in his chest. I wrestle with myself internally. I've waited weeks hoping John would bring it up so I wouldn't have to. I rationalized it, thinking he was waiting until Robb was gone to offer me her spot, but in the week since, nothing.

"What if he says no?" I mumble against his skin.

"Then at least you'll have your answer," he says sagely.

I can't meet his gaze, so I stare off to the side blankly. The real reason I haven't pushed John for an offer is because if he says no, then I only have one choice left. A choice that, on paper, is the better choice but feels like putting my heart through a shredder. But damn if every day spent waiting isn't death by a thousand cuts.

"Okay," I concede with a sigh. "I'll ask him after the meeting."

Dax tips my chin up before grabbing me by the shoulders. "You got this."

I try and fail to smile. "I hope so."

"I know so." His gaze softens, drifting over my face.

"Tell me it's all going to work out," I whisper.

Dax's dimple winks at me. "It's gonna work out," he reassures me, and I wish I could believe him. He leans over, planting a kiss on me and blowing a raspberry on my neck that has me squealing away from him. He turns on the shower for me, cranking the knob as hot as it will go. As soon as it heats up, he smacks me on the ass. "Now, hurry up before you're late for work."

I rub my smarting cheek dramatically as I step into the shower.

He slips out of the bathroom, returning with his laptop and sitting on the counter with one leg up, searching for flights to Boston. I finish my shower and get ready around him. There are no seats left on my flight, nor on any flights today, so he books the only available flight tomorrow morning while I scramble to gather my things before I actually *am* late for work.

"Have you seen my—" I call from the kitchen, dumping my backpack upside down, searching for my keys. They're not in the bowl on the foyer table, and I rifle through the contents of my bag, which I didn't realize had accumulated quite so much junk at the bottom.

Dax emerges from the bedroom, my keys in hand, and I sigh in relief.

"In the bathroom," he tells me, and I remember my mad dash to go pee last night after getting stuck behind a train on my way home.

"Thank you." I plant a kiss to his cheek, and his hand goes to the small of my back, holding me there until I give him a proper kiss. "I cannot fucking stand you," I murmur.

He smiles softly. "I know. Me, too."

I've given up trying to decipher what he thinks that means. He might not remember our old bit, but maybe it's okay to make a new one as this new version of us.

"I'll clean that up later," I call as I shove my shoes on, gesturing to the mess on the kitchen counter formerly known as the bottom of my bag. I pause by the door, grinning.

"I'm really excited you're coming home with me."

He matches my grin. "Me, too. Now, go get that job offer," he says with a jerk of his head toward the door.

My thumb goes to the scar on my ring finger, but I don't allow myself to trace it. For once, I let myself hope, my cheeks aching with how hard I'm smiling.

It's going to work out. *Please* let it all work out.

⇝ CHAPTER TWENTY-FIVE ⇝

The vibe at the office is...*weird*.

When I first landed the Final Revelations article, there was some tension with a few of the senior staff writers that I'd been the one to get it. Once the shock wore off, they warmed up. But today feels like before. I pour myself a cup of coffee in the break room, adding more sugar than I should, and I can feel eyes on me. Only, when I look up, everyone is engrossed in whatever they're doing. Unnaturally so.

I try to shake it off, to focus on the excitement of Dax coming home with me for Thanksgiving. I called my dad on the way in to let him know I was bringing a friend, and after an overlong silence while he processed, he pretended to not be completely surprised that I was blindsiding him by bringing someone home for the first time. He loves a plan as much as I do, and I know he's already recalculating his grocery list and menu for Thursday.

I'm thinking about that—and not the way people's eyes seem to stick to me as I make my way to the conference room for the Monday pitch meeting—when I knock on John's open office door.

"Morning," I call.

"Sloane," he says distractedly, typing away. "Can I steal fifteen minutes on your calendar after the meeting?"

Hope buoys in my chest. *It's finally happening. He's going to make the offer, bring me on full-time.* "I was going to ask you the same."

"Great," he says sans his usual enthusiasm, clicking on his computer. My buoy of hope bobs as a storm of paranoia rolls in. Before I can ask, he plows on. "Say hi to the new guy when you head into the meeting—Trent. Today's his first day. He's... Well, his dad was way before your time, but he was a fantastic writer, so here's hoping he's the second coming of Christopher."

My hope sinks to the bottom of the ocean as I nod numbly, turning on my heel and walking to the conference room on autopilot.

What fucking new guy?

I do not greet the new guy. I barely hear a single thing the entire meeting. Every time I blink, I see red. I've done everything right and they hire a fucking *Trent* whose unoriginal pitch gets approved and mine doesn't, for the third week in a row. I'm gutted.

When I trudge into John's office afterward, I plop gracelessly into the farty leather chair while I wait for him to finish chatting with Trent in the conference room. Taking my meeting time after taking the job I've been busting my ass for is just adding insult to injury.

It's an effort to stifle my youngest-child petulance, but honestly, my upset is justified. What was the point of me working so fucking hard, for so fucking long, for the job to go to some nepotism hire?

"Sorry, sorry," John says by way of greeting as he strolls in. "Okay." He stares at me for a long moment, as if trying to remember why we're meeting. Which, to be fair, I have no idea why I'm bothering anymore. There's no way Robb's departure created enough of a budget to afford two new staff writers. "Right. I know we already ran your piece through the fact-checkers, but given recent events, I gave it another pass—"

"Wait..." I interrupt, blinking in what feels like slow motion. "What?"

John purses his lips, studying me from across his desk. "The internet?" When I continue to look confused, he sighs heavily. "Oh boy. She doesn't know," he tells his ever-present invisible audience. "Okay, let's backtrack, yeah?"

I nod like, *You think?* I'd like to backtrack all the way to when and why he decided to hire Trent and not me, but one thing at a time.

"The video you did with Final Revelations...We didn't catch it before we posted or we would have chosen another take, but, ah, the fans caught that Dax's arm is around you—" My eyes flutter shut as I'm instantly portaled back to that day, his hand on my back until that final take, where it dipped lower—and into the frame, apparently.

I already know where this is going, and I yank my laptop from my bag. I nearly snap it in half trying to open it, navigating to the video as fast as my fingers can type. John doesn't say anything more, letting me discover the damage for myself.

> **pdubz86**: i'd give my first interview in eight years, too, if the reporter looked like that
> ↳ **svpernova**: call me crazy but i swear his arm is around her
> ↳ **jessicuhhh**: no it totally is, you can see his hand by her hip
> ↳ **mrs.revelations**: tell her to get away from my man
> ↳ **sceneXqueen**: who tf is she, she has like one (1) other article online, how did some n00b get this

↪ **baddiec0re**: ok i did some digging, i think she used to date someone from post humorous? she's all over their page; check the Punkapalooza 2007 MySpace blog posts
↪ **final_rachelations**: check the final revelations YouTube tour vlog from that summer, too, im 100% she's in the background at the 4:08 mark, next to Dax
↪ **xX__taylorrr**: omfg it's definitely her!!
↪ **metalmami**: she could just be a friend y'all, chill
↪ **0phelia**: ha no, i worked merch at punka that year, her and dax were def a thing
↪ **mrs.revelations**: SAY IT AINT SO
↪ **sadchad**: so we finally get new FR content and...it's written by a fucking groupie?
↪ **plaguez**: what a joke

The happy bubble I've been living in pops.

I shut my laptop, not needing to see more. And there's a lot more. The internet terrifies me. I don't have a single photo of Dax and me from that summer. And somehow, the internet was still able to link it together, thanks to 0phelia.

"I mention that Dax and I dated in my article," I say hollowly, knowing it's useless.

I meet John's gaze, where he's studying me from behind his interlaced hands. "Right, which was helpful to get out in front of, but we are now behind," he finishes with a grimace.

I hold back a swear with effort. "The article's basically a transcript, so surely it's still okay?" If this gets pulled, if I have to tell the guys it's getting pulled—I can't even think about it. My chest aches.

John nods noncommittally. "Right," he agrees. "Factually, we're sound."

I wait for the *but* I know is coming. He tugs a manila folder from his bifold, flipping it open and sliding it over to me. It's the unedited transcripts I submitted to the fact-checkers weeks ago. The ones I hoped he'd never read. My stomach sinks as I reach up, flipping through them, John's red pen in the margins circling and underlining all the things I left out.

"The issue with this coming out now is your integrity is being questioned. People are going to say you went easy on them because of your connection to them, and after looking into it...you did."

I blink, the red ink of John's pen still overlaid in my vision.

"We go to print in three days, and to make sure we're not accused of pulling punches—"

I already know which page he's thumbing to. Reverie Fest, Dax's backstory about his family, how his parents surprised him by showing up and it sent him into a spiral. The backstory I chose to omit at the last minute. "No," I say automatically.

John freezes as if I'd slapped him, his brows rising slowly. "No?"

"I'm not adding anything back. They wouldn't want it in there."

"It's on the record, Sloane. If they didn't want it used, they shouldn't have said it."

I shake my head. "The internet can say what they want about me. They're not *owed* every detail of Dax's life—or any of the guys' lives. Reverie Fest has been discussed enough. It's tired. There's no integrity in forcing Dax to self-flagellate for the masses. Including that, catering to the lowest common denominator—" I take a steadying breath, forcing my voice to stay level. "*That* would be compromising my integrity. It's a good article. You agreed until this morning. So no,

I'm not changing it. And I know you have final say, but if you include that...take my name off it."

I didn't mean for it to come out so heated, but fuck it, I am heated. All this work to find my voice again, to get this article right, and I'm being Mike Song-ed. I wish Robb were here.

"I have an offer," I say abruptly, nothing left to lose at this point. "You said to tell you—if I got one."

John blinks, drawing the manila folder back to himself and closing it. "Who from?"

"*Rolling Stone*." I fish blindly around in my bag for the offer, to lay out the specs of what I'd like *AP* to match. I promised Dax I'd talk to John about this, and while the timing couldn't be worse, I don't think timing is my biggest problem right now. My chances were slim before this meeting, but after telling John no...I don't allow myself to hope. I just need an answer, a plan, some semblance of security.

John huffs. "I knew Robb would try to poach you."

Wrenching the top of my bag all the way open, I realize my bag is empty save for my laptop charger and my keys.

I dumped my bag on the counter this morning.

I dumped my offer from *Rolling Stone* on the counter this morning.

I dumped my offer from *Rolling Stone* that my boyfriend doesn't know about, my boyfriend who is incredibly clean and will likely clean up my mess for me and see the offer that would put us on opposite sides of the country once again.

Fuck.

"I need to go," I blurt.

I barely register John's comically bewildered face as I bolt out of his office, shoving my laptop into my bag as I speed walk to the parking lot as fast as I can without running.

♪ 🎵 🎶

I circle my block twice looking for parking, cursing when the only available spot is too small because the other cars are parked like assholes. I find a spot a few blocks away, hands shaking as I half walk, half run to my apartment.

By the time I scale the steps to my door, I'm a panicked, sweaty mess under my winter layers. I fling the door open, my hope hanging by a thread that he didn't clean up my mess, that the chaos on the kitchen counter is still there.

The thread severs half a step into my foyer. Dax is waiting for me on the couch. I don't need to check the kitchen counter—the letter is lying in front of him on my coffee table. I want to be mad, but I can't—I left it sitting out. Of course he looked, the *Rolling Stone* header like a beacon.

I toe off my shoes, drop my bag, lock the door, and drop my keys into the bowl—all the autopilot habits my body can't not do even when my heart is across the room. I perch sideways on the couch, close to Dax but not touching him. I want to wrap him in my arms and explain, but the distance between us right now is more than the centimeters between my knee and his hip.

It feels a lot like three years ago. Me, him, a bench in Boston, the last night of tour—for me but not for him. I was going back to school to finish my degree and then to San Francisco for the *Offbeat* internship I hoped would catapult me to *Rolling Stone*. He had another tour lined up right after. And then another after that. He had to go live his dream and I had to chase mine, so we let each other go, let the dream of us remain perfectly preserved in the amber of that summer.

Three years later, on a couch in Cleveland instead of a bench in

Boston, we've found our way back to each other, back to the same dilemma: him leaving for tour, me leaving for *Rolling Stone*.

Somewhere on the drive from the office to here, the reality of my situation sank in. I get it now, how Robb's *Rolling Stone* offer went from a bargaining chip to a lifeline. Similarly, her offer to me went from something to consider to a Hail Mary.

"When do you leave?" he asks, staring a hole into the wall, rhythmically running his finger along the chain at his neck.

I can feel the *push* like a physical force. "I have to give them an answer before the article comes out."

"So, next week." He turns his attention to me, but he's a million miles away, he's three years ago, he's now, he's here, he's already gone. "Stay."

Pull.

"Did you talk to John?" he asks, fishing for hope.

This morning's optimism feels like another lifetime. I nod.

He raises his brows. "And?"

"And he hired a legacy instead of me."

Dax sits up straighter, regarding me beneath pinched brows, searching for some sign that I'm joking. *"What?"*

I blink, and tears fall, and I'm shaking like a leaf as I allow myself to feel it all fully for the first time, to mourn how close I was to having it all. I feel both numb and like my insides are vibrating. "Don't worry—it gets worse," I say around a humorless laugh. I tell him how the internet discovered our history, how it prompted John to review my transcripts. "He wanted me to add in so much stuff about you, and your family, and Reverie Fest—"

"Do it."

"What?" I pull back to look him in the face, my eyes stinging with every blink.

"Do it. I don't give a fuck anymore."

I shake my head. "*No*. I'm not compromising my integrity as reparations for...for what? Being twenty-one and into someone?" *Being twenty-one and in love* I almost say but don't. I take a steadying breath. "I told John no and to take my name off the article if he adds it in."

Dax sinks back against the couch, running his hands over his face forcefully, knocking his septum piercing askew. "You are so good, you know that?" The way he says it doesn't exactly sound like a compliment. *Push*. Then, more softly, "You are good in a way I cannot fathom, in a way I don't deserve, but fuck, I wish you could just—" He exhales heavily.

My spine stiffens. "You think I should have folded? This is my name at stake, Dax. I thought...I thought we were in this together, taking it back—our names, our integrity. I've compromised mine before, trying to impress a boss that was never going to hire me. I'm not doing that again."

"And you think *Rolling Stone* won't ask that of you? They're all the same, Sloane."

I push off the couch, needing to move. I've never done this before—fight with a partner. I don't know how to do this. This is too big a thing to tackle without training wheels. We were supposed to fight over something inconsequential first, like types of peanut butter or which way to face the toilet paper. "No," I insist. "I'd be working with Robb."

He frowns, opening his mouth to say something before shaking his head, seeming to think better of it. "Don't leave."

Pull.

"And do what?" I ask helplessly. "What's here for me? And don't say you, because you're going to be gone on tour a lot the next two years."

Don't leave. I'm gonna fight, he promised me. I hold my breath waiting for him to make good on his promise. He stares at me for a long moment, his expression unreadable, and my heart is turning blue waiting for him to give me the key to the cipher.

"Fine. I'll go with you."

It's what I wanted him to say, but never in my hopeful imaginings did he say it so reluctantly, so baldly confirming my biggest fear. "I can't ask that of you."

He leans forward, bracing his forearms on his knees. "You can."

"This is your home, Dax. You think you won't miss it, but you will. Ask me how I know."

"Sloane," he says gently. "I've been on the road the past ten years. I'm used to it."

"And you're quitting Final because it's not what you want anymore! So don't pretend like it's not a big deal when it is." I force my tone to remain soft even as fear threatens to throttle my vocal cords. "Don't say what you think I want to hear and then quietly resent me." I pace back and forth, a numbness prickling my fingertips and spreading slowly, leaving a hollow tingling in its wake.

Dax cocks his head. "Okay. You're right. I don't want to leave Cleveland. But I don't think you do either. Do you even want to go to *Rolling Stone*, or are you just running scared?" The unsaid *again* hangs heavy in the air between us.

Push.

We're not yelling, but he's fighting me, at least, and hope sparks feebly in my chest. *Pull.*

I rub the scar on my finger, the taut smoothness comforting. My heart is jumping ahead of my body, already back in Boston. On the rooftop outside my bedroom window, where I made a pact to never give up on my dreams for a boy. A promise I've only ever questioned twice, a promise that's guided my choices for the past few years, only to put me right back in front of the only person I've ever considered breaking it for. "I can't stay here for you when you'll barely even be here. I have to do something. I can't... I can't just sit and wait."

"That's not what I asked," he says quietly.

I shake my head, because I honestly don't know how to answer him. I'm scared to go and I'm scared to stay, paralyzed with indecision.

"How long have you been talking to *Rolling Stone*?"

I take a deep breath, trying to keep my cool as all my plans, my hopes for the future spiral out of my grasp. We're two mature adults. He's trying. I'm trying. Surely we can figure this out. "I haven't. Robb made the offer before she left."

He drags his hand over his face roughly. "I'm sorry, but I have to ask: Did you know she was the leak?"

I stagger back a step. "What?"

"The leak," he repeats, as if I didn't hear him the first time. "Did you know it was her?"

"She couldn't be," I breathe. "She signed the same NDA I did."

He shrugs like that's an inconsequential detail.

I stare at him in disbelief, unsure what to focus on first. Betrayal wins out, but not Robb's—his. "Do you actually think I'd know and not tell you, that I'd sabotage my own article?"

He rubs the stubble on his chin, staring at the offer on my coffee table like it offends him. "The two of you getting big offers from the parent magazine of where it was all leaked to—doesn't look like sabotage to me."

I inhale sharply. *Push*.

I'm ambitious, yes, but I'm not *that* ambitious. The fact that he could suspect me feels like a slap in the face. I stop myself before I start pointing out all the motives for his bandmates to have been the leak. I don't know much about fighting with a partner, but I know there are some things you can't unsay. If Dax is wrong and I'm right... I could never live with myself if Final ended sooner than scheduled because of it. I wouldn't do that to him. If he needs to believe it's me, fine. I cross my arms to hide the way my hands are shaking. I feel hollowed out, gutted.

His expression shutters. "I'm sorry. I...I don't actually think it's you. I don't know why I said that."

I nod like it's okay, but I don't feel okay, because *we* are not okay.

He lets out a frustrated growl. "I just want to be with you."

Pull.

"I know," I say emphatically. We're still fighting, but I allow a trickle of hope that we're fighting *for* us now. "I want this, too. I just...I thought we had a plan, and it was all going to be okay, and now...I don't know how we do this without hurting each other."

Dax shakes his head. "No—I want this. Full stop. Fuck the plans. Fuck it if we hurt each other. I want this—you, us. Unconditionally. Long-distance, here, there, when it's hard and when it's easy. I don't need some perfect plan where everything works out to know this is what I want. I want you even when it's inconvenient."

He takes a steadying breath. "You're ambitious, and I love that about you, but...I don't know that I can be with someone who's never going to put us first. I know you're trying to prevent us from hurting each other, from asking too much of each other, but you have to stop. Ask too much of me, Sloane. Get fucking messy with me. I'd rather be with you, and hurt, than just give up. Stop taking me out of the race to spare me some potential future heartbreak we don't even know is coming. Because I'll keep showing back up to the starting line, but I need to know that you'll eventually let us see this through."

I can't tell if that was a push or a pull or both. The lump in my throat feels like I'm going to throw up my heart all over the hardwood.

I don't know what to say to make this okay. I'd give anything to go back to this morning, when getting what I wanted felt possible and not like trying to solve a riddle with no answer.

Dax exhales heavily. "I let you go before so you could chase your dream, and I still want that for you, but I... I guess I don't know what it is you want here. Do you want to break up?"

"No," I say automatically.

"Do you want to do long-distance?"

"No."

"Do you want me to come with you?"

Everything in me sags. My grip on my cool demeanor slips as the truth spills out. "Yes, of course I do, but I feel like an asshole for wanting it, for wanting you with me when your life is here. I'm scared you'll do it because you're *you* and you're selfless, but then you'll be there and you'll miss home and you'll resent me for everything you're missing out on, and what if you're right and *Rolling Stone* is the same as everywhere else and I'm making the wrong choice and I dragged you there for nothing? But if I tell you to stay here while I'm there, I'll miss you and I'm scared that will break us in a way we can't fix, and what if you're right and Robb is the leak, then I can't take the job and if I choose to stay here because *you* are what I want but then you're gone on tour, I'll miss you and have no offers and no work to distract me from missing you, and what if I'm my mom and end up holding that against you even if it's not your fault and—" I suck in a breath, feeling dizzy as I forcefully brush my hair out of my face.

Dax's eyes widen before softening. "You are not your mom, Sloane."

I can't look at him. I'm staring at the wall as I roll my lips inward to keep my chin from quivering, blinking rapidly to keep the tears at bay.

Silence falls, hanging heavy in the air between us as we both process everything we've said in the past few minutes.

"Thank you," Dax says quietly.

"For what?"

"For finally telling me what you were thinking."

I throw my hands up helplessly. "But where do we go from here?"

He rakes his teeth over his bottom lip roughly. "I don't know."

My phone buzzes incessantly in my back pocket. Tugging it free, I silence the reminder that reads "Airport!"

"Fuck," I mutter. I grab my backpack, slipping into my bedroom and blindly throwing clothes into it. I'm in the middle of shoving three times the amount of underwear necessary for my short trip into my bag when Dax says something from the next room that I can't parse. I poke my head out just as the front door slams shut behind him.

All the air leaves my lungs.

Don't leave. I'm gonna fight.

He left. He's not going to fight.

Push.

A sob rattles my chest but I repress it. How did this get so messed up? Why couldn't the bubble have lasted a few more days, given me time to figure things out? How to have everything—the job and the guy. Instead, I'm trying to figure out how in the world I'm going to afford airport parking. Dax was supposed to be my ride.

All I want is to go home. It's the only thing that feels right about all of this. I want to be with my friends, my brothers, my dad. Dax was supposed to be there, too, but him getting on the plane tomorrow feels like a pipe dream. Everything has imploded so quickly, and I don't have a plan for any of this or how to make a new one from the pieces.

I trudge on heavy feet out of my apartment. When I reach the bottom of the stairs, my heart leaps into my throat to find Dax in the loading zone, leaning against the side of his car.

He opens the back door for me to dump my bag, then wordlessly opens the passenger door. I sink into it, unsure what to do with my hands after buckling my seat belt. I sit on them as Dax slides into the driver's seat, cranks the car, and pulls out into the street.

We hit the highway, and neither of us has said a word. Dax shifts gears, smoothly accelerating, merging until he's in the left lane. His thumb traces the top of the gear shift in a rhythmic pattern. I place my hand atop his, squeezing, and he hooks his thumb over my pinkie.

I'd say anything to fix this right now. If what he said is true, if Robb was the leak, there's no way I can take the *Rolling Stone* offer. Which leaves me with no offers, stuck in a freelance gig that hired someone else, that hasn't given me work in weeks. I know what he wants me to say. That I'm staying, that I'm picking him, and I want to, but putting everything I've worked so hard for on the back burner...

Robb's voice echoes in my head. *Don't stay here for a guy.*

I don't want to lose him again, but I don't know how to keep him. I walked away before, and it sucked, but we both survived, didn't we? Maybe I have to not be greedy. Maybe I have to let him go again. Maybe we'll cross paths in a few years. Maybe the third time's the charm. Maybe if we don't hurt each other too much this time, we'll be able to try again. Or...maybe we've already hurt each other too much to try again, and we'll just be friends. And we'll pretend we haven't spent the intervening years searching for each other's gaze across rooms to share in a private laugh, and I'll pretend I don't want to sink into his gravity when he stands next to me. We'll make small talk as if we didn't once make pillow talk, and I won't stare at his mouth like I know it so well I could make a topographical map of his dimple when he gives himself over to a rare, true smile, and I won't let on that I'm mourning the way his smiles are no longer for me.

Fuck that.

Too soon, Dax is pulling over at the departures curb, and I'm turning to him, wild-eyed.

The instant our eyes meet, the distance between us narrows, the hurricane of my panic slowing. He's in the eye of the storm with me. I'm not flying home today, because over the past few weeks, it stopped being home. I've built a new one. He is my home. I don't remember drawing up the plans, but it's here, its bones rattling in the storm raging around us. It's here and it's solid and I love him—*god* do I love him—and I've never told him and now's not the time and I have to go but—

"I don't want to leave," I blurt, hoping he hears every single way I mean it.

He smiles softly at me, but it doesn't reach his eyes, which are churning with the same helplessness I feel.

"You have to," he says.

I'm not leaving. He'll be back with me tomorrow. This won't be like last time. This isn't our ending. This is an interlude, not an encore. "Let's just..." I chew on the inside of my cheek. "Let's take the day apart to think, and we'll talk tomorrow?" *Pull.*

He nods. "Okay."

It's the same thing he said last time, and suddenly I'm twenty-one all over again, and my heart is breaking and I can't do a damn thing to fix it.

A security guard comes over to glare at us for idling too long, waving us on. I fling my door open to let him know I'm moving, then turn back to Dax. Leaning over the console, I cradle his jaw, guiding his mouth to mine for a goodbye kiss that feels a little too heavy on the goodbye.

Push.

CHAPTER TWENTY-SIX

"Thanks for picking me up," I mumble into my dad's chest.

Boston is fucking freezing. Or maybe I'm just worn out, wrung out, from all the tears I cried on the way here.

The woman who sat next to me on the plane had walked into the airport bathroom as I dried my tear-soaked shirt under the hand dryer. She looked like she wanted to ask if I was okay, but thank god she didn't. I don't know that I have any tears left to cry, but receiving motherly concern for possibly the first time in my life might undo me altogether.

Splashing water on my face did little to erase the splotchiness of my skin or the puffiness in my eyes, but I blame both on the biting cold and lack of sleep when my dad's attention lingers on my red-rimmed eyes. I realize he sees right through me when he says, "Unfortunate your friend couldn't book the same flight." The way he says "friend"—somehow, fatherly instinct perhaps, he knows the person I was bringing home last minute was not *just* a friend.

"Yeah," I mumble before slipping into the front seat, cutting off that line of conversation. I was bummed Dax wasn't on my flight when he booked his this morning—this morning feels like a week ago so much has happened since. Now I'm grateful for and terrified of the time apart. I'm grateful for the space to sort through what's eating at me so we can talk about it with our heads on straight. I'm haunted by the way he said, *Okay*, like he did three years ago when life sent us in different directions and he let me go without a fight. I'm terrified he might do the same again, that when I go to the airport tomorrow to pick him up, he won't have gotten on the plane.

He doesn't push further, because he's my dad, and he's never pushed us kids to talk more than we're ready to. Occasionally, growing up, he'd sit us down and force us to tell him what was going on, but only when he was concerned we'd gotten in over our heads. Somehow, he always knew when that was. Otherwise, he trusted us to figure it out ourselves. With five kids to raise on his own, he didn't really have the time to coddle us all. We knew the reason the gray at his temples rapidly took over after Mom left was the stress of doing it all on his own, so we did our best not to get into any real trouble. We didn't want to lose him, too. As far as dads go, he's a pretty great one.

We don't speak as he navigates the congested airport traffic, and I study him from the passenger seat. His close-cropped hair is fully gray now, and the cut of it screams ex-military. His angular face has more wrinkles now than it used to, and it's weird watching him age more and more each time I come home.

As we finally hit the highway, I try to view him through Dax's eyes, what it would be like to meet him for the first time, if Dax does show up tomorrow. Would he ask Dax to call him Mr. Donavan, or would he let him call him William or Bill?

"Your brothers are excited to see you," he offers, cutting through the silence.

"Yeah?" I say, smirking. "Did they say that?"

My dad scoffs in the back of his throat. "Of course not. But they did set up the old Nintendo."

I grin. Five kids and four controllers were responsible for easily a dozen Donavan-sibling wrestling matches. "Apologies in advance for all the screaming."

"I bought earplugs on the way to pick you up," he says as he pulls onto our street, gesturing to the drugstore bag at my feet.

He still lives in the house we grew up in, and sometimes it makes me sad to think about him in this big house all alone, but I'm always happy to see it when I come home. The brick and mortar are an extension of our family.

Next door, a light shines from the narrow basement window. I won't see Charlie and the rest of the Post Humorous crew until tomorrow night, but there's comfort in knowing Charlie is only a wall away.

As soon as the car is in park, my door is open. Snatching my backpack from between my feet, I throw it over one shoulder as I head for the basement door around back. I can't remember the last time anyone entered our house through the front.

I drop my bag as I kick my shoes off on the cold cement floor, my brothers' voices drifting to me from the basement living room that was ours to destroy. The couch down here is broken in more places than not, so unlike the untouched, pristine sitting area upstairs my dad frequents with a J. R. Alastor thriller and a whiskey.

My dad shuts the door behind him, and my brothers' voices cut off immediately.

"Sammy?"

"SAAAAM!"

"Sam! Sam! Sam!"

"AY, SAMMAY!"

It's been twenty-five years since they found out they weren't getting another brother—who they'd decided would be named Sam—but instead, a little sister: me. They have *never* let it go, refusing to call me by my name. I hope they never do.

The smile that breaks across my face is nearly painful, my socks sliding on the cement floor as I rush into the living room, throwing my arms in the air like a gymnast landing a particularly difficult floor routine.

All four of them are sprawled out on the tan sectional with the telltale sag in the middle. Nate, the oldest and tallest of us, is on the left-hand side, his hair sticking up at all angles probably from a wrestling match I just missed. No matter how old we get, if you put us all together, we're right back to being delinquent little shits. With the same brown hair and brown eyes, Nate, Bryce, and Austin look like triplets, despite there being two years between them all. They're all clones of our dad.

Gray and I are the only ones who got our mom's blond hair and blue eyes. I head for the right side of the couch and wrangle Gray into a hug. We've always been close, but even more so since he dropped out of college and moved back home my senior year. It was another one of those times where my dad somehow innately knew what we needed, letting Gray come home to lick his wounds before pushing him back out the door again a year later.

I smell the popcorn before I see it, pivoting around as a petite brunette woman comes downstairs. She seems vaguely familiar, but I can't place her until Bryce hops up off the couch to grab the third bowl of popcorn she's barely managing to balance. I recognize her as his on-again, off-again high school girlfriend. Are they...back together? I cut a silent look to Gray, who rolls his eyes in the way I know means both *long story* and *tell you later.*

"Sammy, you remember Anna," Bryce says, providing her name helpfully.

I nod and wave.

"Hi, Sloane," she calls to me before sitting down in the middle of the couch—in the saggy, broken middle of the couch.

Popcorn flies everywhere as she sinks down, slowly consumed by the quicksand section. As buttery popcorn rains down, our golden retriever, Biscuit, appears, summoned by the smell of food.

I manage to hold back my laugh as Anna tries and fails to extricate herself, but the chaos of Biscuit jumping on her to help clean up combined with Bryce's unsuccessful attempts to haul her out of the sunken middle because he's laughing too hard—it undoes me.

My dad disappears, muttering something about a vacuum, but not before an unspoken game begins as all of us try to shove as much popcorn into our mouths as possible before Biscuit can get to it. It's a miracle I don't choke on a kernel I'm laughing so hard, shoving more into my mouth in some crunchier version of chubby bunny.

"Wait, Sammy," Nate calls around a mouthful of popcorn. "Dad said you were bringing someone."

I take my time chewing and swallowing my now-soggy popcorn, trying not to get teary over how cute Bryce and Anna are picking popcorn out of each other's hair while Biscuit dutifully hoovers up the fallout. "Yeah, but his flight is tomorrow," I say. *And I hope he gets on it*, I don't say. I want to break down, to admit how scared I am by our first fight, but I can't bring myself to let that be the first impression I give my family of him. Plus, I know what my brothers would say—to take the job and not look back. But then I watch Bryce and Anna, and I'm not so sure.

"*His* flight?" Bryce clarifies.

Pushing Gray's feet off the chaise section of the couch, I drop gracelessly onto it before shooting Bryce a look, silently telling him to be cool. I've never brought someone home before, never had anyone I cared about this much.

Bryce, of course, is not cool about it, exchanging looks with my other brothers like, *Did you know about this?*

"What's his name? Age? Profession?" Bryce barrels on, not one for delicacy. Anna squeezes his knee, and he looks at her like he has no idea he's obnoxious.

It's not lost on me that my dad is using a broom on the carpet so he doesn't have to turn on the vacuum and, thus, can eavesdrop.

I shake my head, smiling at the ground as I wind a loose thread from one of the couch pillows around my finger. "Dax. Twenty-nine. Musician."

Bryce grunts, dissatisfied with my minimalistic answers. "And who is he to you?"

I chuckle as Anna swats Bryce for being so pushy, but I expect nothing less from my second-eldest brother. He's always been the one who will say what everyone else is thinking—even when you wish he wouldn't.

I hesitate. Dax was my boyfriend. I hope that's still true. I want to believe one fight—the *same* fight—won't end us *again*, but this is uncharted territory for me.

Gray nudges my foot with his. "Didn't you already date a guy with that name?"

I nod. "Yep. Same guy."

Austin laughs. "Wait—are you pulling a Nate right now?"

I grin, understanding his meaning instantly. Our eldest brother is so private that we've always joked he'd just show up one day and announce he's married, none of us the wiser that he'd even been seeing someone. "No," I say around a laugh. "We just reconnected when I moved to Cleveland. I wrote an article about his band."

Anna coos, and Austin narrows his eyes, picking lint off his Vassar sweatshirt. "Isn't that, like, not allowed in your profession?"

I press my lips together, puffing out my cheeks before releasing the breath. "Yep," I say, popping the *p*. "I mean, it's not *not* allowed, but it's frowned upon. I told my boss, and I thought it was fine but then the internet figured it out and now the article that was supposed to launch my career is under scrutiny and the risk I took freelancing for *AP* in the hopes of it turning into a job offer is... Well, there's pretty much a zero chance of that happening now," I rush out, as if it'll be less painful to say it quickly. "Anyway, should I make more popcorn?"

Without waiting for an answer, I launch myself off the couch and bound up the stairs to the kitchen, ignoring my brothers' cries calling me back.

My dad wanders in, dumping the floor popcorn into the trash as Biscuit watches mournfully. He busies himself in the kitchen as I wait for the kernels in the pan to pop, making himself available to talk if I want to. The sigh I let loose when I dump the popcorn into a bowl must speak volumes, because he eases the bowl from my grasp. "I can take this down if you want."

I'm about to say I can do it, when I realize he knew what I needed before I did. I nod, not ready to face the inquisition that will resume as soon as I set foot downstairs.

I trudge upstairs, down the hallway to my room, not stopping until I reach the window that opens over the roof and climb outside. I suck down the cold November air and watch the blinking of airplanes in the night sky as they pass overhead.

Before long, the window scuffs as it opens, Gray's head poking out. "Can I join you?"

I nod, patting the shingles next to me. He launches a blanket over to me before climbing out, and I drape the Roof Blanket over myself. It's a tattered, knitted afghan, the one we won't let our dad throw away even though it's half-unraveled from years of roof hangs.

Gray settles next to me, and I laugh as he eases an entire bottle of our dad's fancy Scotch out of his sweatpants pocket before lying back to stare up at the sky with me. He uncorks it with a faint *pop*, taking a swig before passing it to me. I swallow a small sip, wincing as it burns all the way down, my insides warming.

"Billiam's beside himself that you're bringing a guy home," he tells me. Our dad went by Bill when we were little, but when he took his professor job, there was already a Bill in his department, so he started going by William. We found that hilarious and started calling him Billiam instead. "I'm pretty sure he ironed the curtains."

I smack him lightly with the back of my hand. "He did not."

He takes the bottle of Scotch back from me saucily. "Okay, he didn't, but he's rearranged the den so many times everything's back in its original position."

I grin, and we fall silent for a minute, passing the bottle back and forth. I love all my brothers, but as the youngest, Gray and I had to team up against our older, bigger brothers, so we've always been the closest. Likewise, Nate and Bryce are close, and Austin...is an enigma, the quintessential middle child who is all of us and none of us.

"So, what's up?" Gray asks, nudging me gently with his elbow.

I exhale heavily, watching my breath cloud in the air above me. "Dax and I had a fight before I left."

Gray nods slowly, threading a finger through the holes in the blanket. "Do you want to talk about it?"

I think for a long moment, not sure where to start, if I want to start. "Do you remember that blood pact we made on the roof?"

He holds up his left hand, the scar on his ring finger shining in the moonlight. "We thought we were so clever."

"How do you mean?"

Gray scoffs. "I mean, we were kids. We didn't know what the fuck we were talking about. And yeah, it sucks Nate gave up his dream college to follow a girl that dumped him two weeks into the first semester, but I dunno... I've made dumb choices for a guy before, but I'm still glad I made them, that I tried, y'know?"

I blink up at the sky, mulling that over. "So... you never took that oath seriously?"

"No," he says around a laugh, then sobers up. "Wait—did you?"

I cover my face with my arm.

"Oh, Sammy," he says pityingly. "It's not a bad pact," he admits. "You're literally cooler than all of us for it, with your big plans, big dreams."

I snort. "I don't feel very cool." Then quietly, I confess, "I think I fucked everything up."

"The job or the guy?" he asks knowingly.

"Both."

"Which one are you most upset about?"

I blink, thinking, but I know the answer immediately. "Dax. And that scares me."

Gray falls silent for a beat, then murmurs, "Do you love him?"

My heart squeezes. "Yes," I breathe, watching the admission swirl in the air above me.

"Well, the way I see it," he begins slowly, studying the scar on his ring finger in the moonlight, "the only way we turn out like her is if we walk away without trying. And you, my badass sister, who is, in fact, the coolest of us all"—I laugh disbelievingly—"always end up getting everything you want. You'll figure it out."

"I don't get everything I want," I counter.

"You're the most driven person I know. Always have been." He fixes me with a look, counting off on his fingers. "You were a sophomore in college by the time you graduated from high school. You applied to *one* college—your dream school—and got early acceptance. You locked down your dream internship before you'd even finished your double fucking major. You got back the guy you spent years mooning over—"

"I did *not* moon," I protest. "And that internship was a flop."

"So?" Gray scoffs. "Everything working out isn't the point. My point is, when you want something, you make it happen. Figure out what you want and go for it. And if it doesn't work out, make a new plan, but at least you tried. You're not her so long as you're trying."

I inhale sharply. *Figure out what you want.* I know what I want. But more importantly, I know what I don't want. And I think I've known since Robb first slid me the piece of paper, but I wasn't ready to let go of my old dream, to trust my heart over my head.

"Do me a favor?" Gray asks.

"Hmm?"

"Get it right so I can believe in it, too."

I place my hand over his, squeezing, surprised when he grips me back twice as tight. I wait a minute for him to talk if he wants. When he doesn't, I loose the joke on the tip of my tongue.

"What, Bryce and Anna aren't selling the dream for you?"

Gray honks a laugh. "Fifth time's the charm, huh?"

"Please," I say gravely. "They're at least on try number seven."

Gray chuckles. "Hey, at least they're trying."

"Ugh," I groan. "I can't let *Bryce* show me up."

"Oh god, no," Gray agrees. "I'd never let you live it down." He holds up his hand, extending his ring finger to me like a pinkie promise. "New pact—"

I link my finger around his.

"Try."

I wait, but he doesn't say anything else. "That's it?" I laugh.

He nods slowly. "Yeah. I think it's that simple."

I shake our linked fingers, sealing the deal. "Okay," I agree. "To trying."

I hope my brother's belief in me isn't misplaced, and as a plane arcs overhead, I begin making a new plan, hoping against hope that Dax's silence isn't the before kind, the three-year kind, but him making his own plans, too.

CHAPTER TWENTY-SEVEN

I trudge down to the kitchen the next morning, nursing a small hangover despite only having a few sips of Scotch. I follow the smell of coffee over to the pot in the corner, where my dad is already pouring me a cup.

"Heard you on the stairs," he says by way of greeting.

"How'd you know it was me?"

He smiles at me as he pours sugar into my mug. "You're the only one that doesn't walk like they're angry at the ground."

I laugh, knowing exactly what he means. My brothers have all the grace of a bull in a china shop.

"How'd you sleep?" he asks, handing me my cup.

"Like the dead," I confirm before blowing on my coffee and following him over to the breakfast table, where the newspaper crossword and his coffee await him.

"When are you heading to the airport?" he asks, folding up the paper.

I sink into my chair—two to his left, all of us having unofficially assigned ourselves spots at the table for as long as I can remember. "In an hour, but, about that—" I take a deep breath.

"Oh, thank god," he mutters. "I thought I was going to have to ask."

I pause, forgetting the other half of my sentence. Instead of dropping the bomb I was about to, I start at the beginning. I tell him about Dax—the first time, the now time. I tell him the truth about my *Offbeat* internship and how I gave up my voice in the hopes of getting a foot in the door at *Rolling Stone*, and how I finally have that offer now, how I turned it down via email this morning, and about the email I sent to John with a few last-minute edits to the Final piece, addressing the gossipy YouTube comment section directly. I tell him about the fight Dax and I had, the dumb pact my brothers and I made on the roof, the conversation I had with Gray last night.

I can't remember the last time I talked so much with my dad. It feels good. It doesn't feel like the dozens of times he'd sit me down at this table and attempt to extract truths out of us, my brothers and I coordinating lies to keep ourselves out of trouble. Now it feels like the only way out of what's troubling me is to talk about it with the only people who could possibly understand why I am the way I am, the only other people who lived through it. All of us have scars on our hearts from when Mom left.

"So anyway," I say, attempting to wrap up my deluge of feelings, "I bought a standby ticket to Cleveland, in case he doesn't show."

My dad smiles softly at me, nodding. "Good for you."

"You're not mad if I miss Thanksgiving? I know you've been planning for weeks—"

My dad waves this away. "I'm proud of you."

A strangled, wet laugh escapes me. My life is in shambles. I can't see anything worth being proud of. "Why?"

"Because you already had a flight back to Cleveland—in five days. You could wait, but instead, you're going for it. You're not waiting until it's too late to fight." Regret flashes across his face, and my chest pangs painfully.

"You don't think I'm being foolish?"

"Sloane, of all my children, you are the least foolish. In fact, I think you should be a bit more foolish."

For all our shenanigans as kids, I was along for the chaos but was rarely the source. I was the one who came up with the plan on how to get us *out* of trouble, not *into* it. "It's a risk, though, turning down that job for…" I gesture vaguely. I don't have high hopes *AP* is going to make an offer. There's only one thing keeping me in Cleveland.

My dad hums thoughtfully from behind his mug, taking a sip before speaking. "Does it feel like a risk?"

"No," I say, the answer sighing out of me. It doesn't make sense how sure I am about Dax when we have literally nothing figured out, but I'm sure about him, his presence in my future an indisputable fact. He's woven into my life the same way my friends are. No matter how often I get to see them, whether we go days or weeks without talking, I know they're going to be in my life forever. Dax feels like that.

I blink back to the present, and my dad is filling in the squares on his crossword, letting me disappear into my own head.

"How did you do it?" I blurt. I've spent so many years focused on not becoming my mom when I should have been focused on becoming my dad. "Five kids and a career?"

He puts his pen down. "Well, I had to feed you gremlins somehow," he says dryly. "But…thanks to your mom. We didn't get it all right, obviously, but we leaned on each other. She put her dreams on the back burner to raise you kids while I chased mine so we could be financially stable. But you can't— It can't be one thing all the time. It's got to be give-and-take. That's where we got it wrong. I was pushing so hard to get into a position to provide for us all that I burned her out, shut her out. If I'd taken my foot off the gas, let her dreams have room to breathe rather than her suffocating them to support me, you kids, things may have turned out differently.

"I was up for a promotion," he says suddenly. "When she left. I'd been promising for years to slow down, once we were comfortable financially, once you kids were all in school, so she could do more than just be a caretaker. And we were comfortable, and you were all in school, but I was still pushing. If I'd taken that promotion—and I wanted to—I would be at home even less. And that was the breaking point. She didn't believe things were ever going to change, and I hadn't given her any reason to believe they would. She left, and I didn't take that promotion, because I couldn't. I had to be home with you guys. And I wish I'd just...done that anyway, not made her force my hand." He traces the wood grain on the table. "Even if it means I didn't get to provide for you all as much as I would have liked, I'm glad I didn't miss everything. In the end," he muses. "I won't miss not working more, but I would have never forgiven myself for not getting to know you kids."

"Even though we made you go gray?" I tease.

He runs a hand over his close-cropped hair. "I think it suits me," he says with a wry grin. His gaze drops to my left hand wrapped around the warm coffee mug, and I realize he's staring at the scar on my ring finger. "Your mom and I... Neither of us had good relationships with our parents, so we rushed into getting married and making the family we never had. And I don't think we ever really got to be *just* kids because we were trying to be for our children what we never had, and I never wanted that for you all—especially you."

"Because I'm the favorite?" I ask slyly.

He purses his lips. "Favorite daughter, for sure."

I roll my eyes. He's made that joke a million times, and somehow it still gets a laugh out of me.

"'Especially you' because...you were such an introverted kid, very private, very practical. I think you somehow stole your brothers' shares from their DNA because they're so—" He pinches the bridge of his nose as if decades of shenanigans are flashing before his eyes. "As much as I didn't want them to be a bad influence on you, with them, you let yourself just be *a kid*. And Charlie, and the band, they got that silliness out of you, too, but in public, you always seemed to keep it hidden, a secret side of you that you reserved only for those you felt safe to be yourself with. Which," he concedes with a nod, "you come by that honestly." He gestures to himself. "And it wasn't until you started writing for your friends' band that I saw you share it publicly. It came alive in your writing. You came alive."

I roll my mug between my hands, my brows furrowing. "So, you think I shouldn't have turned down the job?"

He takes a slow sip of his coffee, choosing his words. "I think you're twenty-four and could be a bit easier on yourself for not having everything figured out. I think you should do whichever allows you to be the most *you*."

It's such *dad* advice. And yet, it makes perfect sense, taking the tangled mess of my situation and boiling it down to one simple factor. I've spent so long trying to find my voice again, and at the end of the day, it wasn't Robb or *Rolling Stone* or *Alternative Press* that helped me find my way back to myself: It was Dax. He's always been my safe space to land.

"The question is," my dad continues casually, attention back on his crossword, "when you get everything you want, are you standing alone or is there a certain someone you want next to you?"

I understand Dax's point for the first time. Maybe it's okay if I don't have a plan right now, or if my only plan is him, us, figuring it out together, because at the end of the day, I don't want any of it more than I want him. I love him. I love who *I* am with him. It's not just the person you want by your side when you get everything you want. It's the person who's still there when all your plans fall apart, showing back up to the starting line, ready to begin again.

My phone vibrates in my pocket, and for the second time in as many days, I silence the "Airport!" alarm. Only this time, I'm not leaving Dax but leaving with him.

I hope.

⚡CHAPTER TWENTY-EIGHT⚡

The first two hours of airport parking are free, and I don't allow myself to read the rates for anything beyond that. If Dax doesn't show, if I do have to leave my dad's car in the lot, I don't want to know how much that's going to cost me. But Dax is worth it.

I leave my bag in the trunk because I need to have hope that Dax will show. I squash the image of me having to come back to get it before waiting on standby.

I may have scared the person working the information booth with my numerous questions about where Dax's flight would let out. They reassured me many times which carousel the luggage would be unloaded onto, but I doubt Dax checked a bag. I'm worried I'm coming across less star-crossed lover and more fanatic, so I thank them and go to study the arrivals board. There's only a handful of other flights landing at the same time as Dax's.

It occurs to me that I could just *text him*, but I want the dramatic reunion. I want him to know (1) I'm an idiot, (2) I love him, and (3) I'm not giving up on us.

I honestly don't know what to expect, with the way we left things. I'll use my standby ticket if I have to, but god do I hope he just shows up. I'm not leaving him, and I'm willing to fight for us, but I want him to fight for us, too.

My phone buzzes in my back pocket, and I ease it out to silence it, pausing when I see the name on the caller ID. Swiping to accept, I bring it to my ear in a daze.

"Robb," I say by way of greeting. "Thanks for calling me back."

"Sorry, I was in a meeting. Honestly, there's a special circle of hell for anyone who schedules a meeting right before a holiday weekend. Anyway, what's up? This better be a celebratory call because if you called me with bad news right before Thanksgiving—"

"You might want to sit down, then," I say hollowly, sinking onto the uncomfortable plastic airport seating.

Silence greets my words, followed by shuffling on the other end of the line and the groaning of a chair as she presumably sinks into it.

"Was it you?" I press.

"What—"

"Don't," I cut across her, pinching the bridge of my nose. "Were you the leak? I need to know. Please don't lie to me."

Robb sighs heavily. "Do you want the long answer or the short answer?"

My stomach sinks, what little hope I had that she hadn't stabbed me in the back wheezing out of me. "I want the truth."

A pregnant pause, then, "I wasn't the leak—at first. Mike already knew they were recording. The same source told him about *Nixed* and their retirement, but that was a lot harder for him to verify since so few people knew. He asked me since I was working on the article with you. I told him to fuck off, but then...Sloane, he knew about you and Dax. Mike was at Punkapalooza that summer. There's photos of the two of you backstage. It was either confirm what he already knew so he could run it, or he was going to implode your credibility before the article came out. I knew we could bounce back from the leaks, so I chose the lesser of two evils."

Even though she can't see me, I nod, feeling wrung out. "Well, it all came to light anyway."

"I saw," she says sadly. "I'm sorry. Is John having a meltdown?"

Despite myself, it all comes spilling out of me. The changes John wanted me to make to pander to the internet mob, me telling him no and squandering the tiniest chance I had of getting an offer after he'd already nepo-hired someone. I don't know if I'm mad at Robb or if I understand her—or some combination of both—but she was my rock at *AP*, and I desperately need an ally in the industry right now. "Oh, and I turned down *Rolling Stone* this morning."

A sad noise comes over the line. "I understand." There's a beat of silence before she speaks again. "For what it's worth, I'm really sorry, Sloane, for how . . . for how it all went down. Please don't let this stop you. If there's anything I can do— Actually," she says, her soft tone shifting, sharpening, "I cannot believe he— I'm sorry to cut this short, but I need to make a call. Chat soo—"

"Wait," I interrupt. "Who was the leak?"

Robb hums. "I can't say, but Final may want to rethink their tour lineup next year. Pay attention to who *The Offbeat* has in their next volume. Tell Dax I say hi and that I'm sorry."

The call disconnects, and I feel a strange mix of relief and betrayal. The tour lineup isn't public, not even close, but I know Dax's mentees—Hudson and Hollow Graves—were in consideration as openers. If I'm right, it's certainly better than the leak being a member of Final, but to be betrayed by the very person they've been Mr. Miyagi-ing . . . I take a deep breath, shaking the mix of emotions out of my limbs. I have a bigger issue to tackle right now.

A gaggle of passengers push through the security door and begin making their way toward the baggage carousel for the Cleveland flight, and I leap out of my chair, heart in hand. The edges of my vision go fuzzy, and I realize I've forgotten to breathe. I remind myself not for the first time to look into calming breathing exercises, but I settle for breathing in through my nose and out through my mouth.

A strangled noise escapes me when I spot him, half a head taller than everyone else. He looks the same as he always does, and it's so goddamned comforting.

I'm practically crawling out of my skin as I wait for the crowd to mosey along. He's looking down at his phone so he doesn't see me until he's nearly right in front of me. He looks up as he's about to pass me, as if on instinct. His whole body seems to relax, a smile spreading slowly across his face, and it might be the most beautiful thing I've ever seen.

His duffle thuds against the ground as he reaches me, one arm coming around me to pick me up, the other looping behind my back, holding me close. I wrap my legs around his waist, my hands cradling the back of his head as he rests his forehead against my collarbone.

"I'm sorry."

I don't know which one of us says it first, but it's all we say for a moment as we cling to each other. I've been home for nearly twenty-four hours, but I finally feel it here, now, in the circle of his arms.

"I'm so glad it's you," he murmurs into the crook of my neck.

I pull back a fraction to study his face. "What?"

A blush blooms across his cheeks. "I may have texted B to pick me up, but Gray told her you'd already left to get me."

I suck on the inside of my cheek, shaking my head at the ceiling. Of course they were all scheming behind my back. "I'll always come for you."

I hear how it sounds the moment the words are past my lips, and Dax grins up at me. "Yeah you do," he growls in my ear.

I roll my eyes as he lowers me to the ground.

"I hate fighting," I breathe.

"I know, baby. Me, too." He sighs, pressing his forehead to mine as if we'd entered some sort of touch deficit and he needed to rectify it immediately. "We're gonna have to sometimes, and we might not be able to figure it out in one conversation, but as long as we keep talking to each other, I think we can make this work—I *want* to make this work."

I open my mouth to speak, but he holds up his hand.

"Sorry, I...I've been rehearsing this in my head the whole flight, and I really need to get it out."

I smile softly, nodding for him to continue.

"I think I fell in love with you the first time I saw you."

My breath hitches. I should've gone first. *Of course* his apology will be a fucking masterpiece worthy of a museum. Mine will be the word-vomit equivalent of a kid's macaroni art, barely worthy of the refrigerator door.

"You were backstage at...I can't remember what band because I was only paying attention to you—"

"Lay it on thicker, please," I goad him, fanning myself.

He shushes me with a dopey smile. "Everyone else was socializing but you were completely oblivious, locked in on the stage. You weren't dancing, weren't moving, maybe not even breathing, because when the set was over, you took this massive inhale like you'd been holding your breath. The band came off stage and you immediately began networking with their crew. I had no idea who you were or what you were doing, but I could feel how badly you wanted to be there. And I...I'd been in survival mode for so long I couldn't remember the last time I'd wanted something like that." He swallows thickly. "Afterwards, I was on a mission to find you, to be around you, to know you, to be wanted by you. And then when you said we should end it—"

I slide my hand into his, squeezing gently to let him know I'm listening.

"I'd spent a long time thinking I wouldn't be around, so what was the point in wanting, in fighting, in making someone stay, in them making room for me in their life, when I wouldn't be—" He shakes his head, rolling his lips inward and pressing them together. "I didn't know how to ask for that three years ago. I didn't think I was worth all that. But I've got a whole life I didn't think I'd get, and I...I've got to figure out what I want to do with it.

"I don't have big dreams like yours, because I've had mine. And yeah, I really want to enjoy this last era of Final, but more than that, I want you. I want to enjoy it with you. I want to call you after a long day on tour and feel grounded just hearing your old-lady smoker voice—"

I huff, rolling my eyes. I came out of the womb sounding like I smoked five packs a day despite never having touched a cigarette in my life.

Dax ducks his head, placing a kiss to the hinge of my jaw before whispering, "And to have filthy phone sex with you."

I shove playfully against his chest and he rocks back, taking me with him. "I want to fight with you because we're determined to get it right this time. And between tour stretches and after it's all done, I want to wake up with you and bring you coffee in bed. I want to cook you dinner and bend you over the kitchen counter—" He lowers his voice for that last part, thank god. "I want your shit fucking everywhere because you're kind of a slob—"

"Hey now, I'm clean in the ways that matter—"

"I want to follow you wherever you get a job, whenever that happens, because it's going to happen. You're so fucking talented and I cannot wait to watch your career take off, and if you think that means *Rolling Stone*, then let's fucking do it. And if we hate it, then okay. We'll do something else. And we'll keep doing things together and building a life because the details of it don't really matter to me as long as it's us."

My heart lodges in my throat. *As long as it's us.*

"I know you worry I'd regret following you, but I think this era of my life is coming to an end now so I can be there for your big dreams, because *you* are my big dream, Sloane Donavan. And I know it'll be hard with me on tour and you in California, but—"

"I turned down *Rolling Stone*," I blurt.

"What? Why?" Dax leans back, eyes scanning my face.

"Because I realized I didn't actually want it. I think I would've been miserable there, even if Robb hadn't—" I don't want to get into the Robb and the Hudson of it all right now. This moment is ours, and they've taken enough from us already. "I've spent half my life trying not to become my mom. I thought working hard and staying independent would keep me from living with regret like she did. I've left families, friends, cities behind, all to chase what I want, and now...what I really want is to not be so fucking lonely. In trying so hard *not* to be her, I ended up becoming her anyway. I can see that now." I shake my head. "And I know it's ridiculous that I'm so fucked up by a woman I barely knew, but...I'm working on it," I say with a self-deprecating laugh.

Dax hums contrarily. "I think I corner the market on 'fucked up' in this relationship."

A laugh wheezes out of me. "Dax!"

He smirks, squeezing my hand to let me know he's listening, too.

"What I need to figure out is what my mom never did—how to do both. *Rolling Stone* has been the goal for so long and I thought I'd regret turning down my dream job, but it's not my *only* dream, and I'd regret missing out on everything else so much more." I thread our fingers together. "Your dreams are my dreams, too. I want Cleveland. I want you. I am so fucking excited for you, the band, this album and the tour. I want to be there for you as you see this through. And then when it's my turn—"

"I'm there," Dax promises without hesitation.

I've had blinders on, and in my focus, the world outside my tunnel vision grew very, very small. I want a life that's big and loud and a little chaotic. By choosing Dax, I can see a new plan loosely falling into place, his dreams merging with mine. I may have to wait a bit longer for mine to take off, but I'll be cheering him on while he sees his through. Then, he'll be in my corner while I chase mine, and whatever shape they end up taking, it'll be more than enough. *As long as it's us.*

Stretching up onto my tiptoes, I press a kiss to his lips. "Lastly, I'm sorry I've never said this before, but god, I love you so fucking much, Dax Nakamura."

A contented noise rumbles in his chest, and he's pulling me farther into him. "I know, baby. Me, too."

I lean back a fraction, gaze bouncing around his face as realization dawns, what he's been telling me all along. We've never said those three words to each other before, but haven't we been saying them all along anyway? The words tumble out of me automatically, and I mean them in every iteration. "I cannot fucking stand you."

He grins. "I love you, too." His hand goes to my hair, threading through the locks at the base of my skull, holding me there as he brushes his mouth over mine. "Stop flirting with me."

My breath hitches. *He does remember.* "I would never." It couldn't be less like the way I said it three years ago, before our first kiss, still in denial of my attraction to him.

"That would be disgusting," he agrees, smiling against my mouth.

"Completely abhorrent." This time, when he presses his lips to mine, it's the same rush as three years ago. But it's also different. There's still a little bit of disbelief that he wants me but none of the insecurity of what to do with him wanting me because it wasn't a part of my plan. This time, I don't freak out and run away. This time, I stay. I hold him tighter, pour everything into the kiss like I'm pouring the foundation for the future we'll build together.

I pull back, eyes narrowed. "I thought you'd forgotten. Why didn't you say it back before?"

Dax's thumb strokes along the side of my neck, making my pulse jump. "When you said it outside the studio two months ago..." He shakes his head. "I didn't forget. I felt it, too, but if we were going there again, I didn't want to dance around it or hide behind it. That summer..." He pauses. "We found a lot of ways to say how we felt without actually saying it, and I wasn't going to say it first, because if we did—if we called it what it was—then it would've been a hell of a lot harder for me to let you go. But this time, I knew I was playing for keeps. I love you so fucking much, Sloane Donavan. I'll say it every possible way you want, but I wanted the first time I said it to be plain, not hiding behind anything."

Every part of me hums happily, and I tell him I love him at least a dozen times on the walk to the car, trying to make up for every time I didn't say it. It'll take a lot longer than that, but it's a start.

I pop the trunk for him to throw in his bag, and he frowns when he sees my backpack.

"I may have bought a standby ticket in case you didn't show," I explain.

Dax smiles softly at me. He tosses his bag into the trunk before easing it shut. His hands go to my hips, and he hoists me on top of the car, stepping between my legs. "I'm always gonna show," he promises. He nudges his nose against mine, and I grin against his mouth before claiming his bottom lip.

I wrap my arms around his neck, rubbing the scar on my ring finger, remembering the new pact I made last night. *Try.*

"I know, baby," I tell him. "Me, too."

CHAPTER TWENTY-NINE

I give Dax a brief tour of all my old childhood haunts—my high school, the skate park, and the make-out spot I never used before but that we made good use of now. When I pull into the driveway, the silence in the car is content. I've never done this before—meeting the family—and neither has Dax, but we're doing it together, figuring it out together.

He fetches both our bags from the trunk and starts down the path to the front door, but I incline my head for him to follow me to the basement door. Once inside, we toe off our shoes, Dax subconsciously straightening my Chucks with his Vans as he slides them into place next to mine. When his duffle hits the ground, the adjoining room goes silent.

"SAMM-AY!" my brothers crow as one.

Dax's brows pinch together at the nickname, and I shake my head and laugh. "Not Sammy, just a burglar," I call.

"Oh, thank god," Austin says, sighing in faux relief.

I hover inside the doorway, glancing back to silently check in with Dax. He ducks his head, pressing his forehead against mine.

"I love you," I whisper.

A low grumble comes from Dax, almost like a purr. "I love you."

Sliding my hand into his, I tug him behind me into the basement living room. "Hi, everyone. This is my—" I freeze, not sure how to qualify Dax. *Boyfriend* is both too big and too small. Biscuit comes thundering down the stairs at the promise of someone new to beg for attention from, golden tail wagging happily as he wiggles in Dax's general direction, too excited to walk straight.

"This is Dax," I finish in an attempt to cover my blunder. The evil grins my brothers are shooting my way make me uncomfortable, so I turn back to Dax, who is dutifully scratching Biscuit behind his ears. "Dax, this is...everyone." I jerk my head toward him, and my brothers jump off the couch to introduce themselves, remembering their manners.

My dad, Bryce, and Anna wander downstairs at the sound of voices, trays of snacks in hand. Introductions are made, hands are shaken, and miraculously, my dad doesn't comment on the tattoos or the septum piercing, though I can tell he's making a concerted effort *not* to fixate on Dax's gauged ears. His eye contact is a little too intense.

I lost my grip on Dax's hand during all the introductions (Gray insisted upon a hug because of course he did), and I slide my hand back into his and guide him onto the nonbroken chaise section of the couch. As we settle into the corner, Gray mouths to me, *Mooning*.

I shoot him a glare and he snickers, preemptively ducking out of reach of the punch I'm already preparing to land on his biceps.

"Nintendo!" Nate says suddenly, squishing himself between Gray and me on the couch and effectively ending the impending squabble. As if a game of *Super Smash Bros.* has ever defused anything in the Donavan household. The sag in the middle of the couch is a direct result of Bryce Falcon punching Nate off the spaceship one too many times in a row and the wrestling match that ensued.

In a rare moment of awareness, Bryce slides off the couch and switches out the *Smash Bros.* cartridge for *Mario Kart.*

Austin is already on the floor, drawing up a new bracket to accommodate the five of us plus Anna and Dax. With more kids than controllers, tournament brackets were a peace-keeping necessity.

"Whoa," my dad calls. "I want in."

All of our brows shoot up, but Austin says nothing as he erases the board and starts over. We haven't been able to convince my dad to play any game other than Scrabble in years.

My brothers and I exchange wicked smiles.

"Same team?" I ask.

They nod. "Same team."

"What does that mean?" Anna asks in alarm.

My dad sighs. "It means they're teaming up against us to make sure we"—he gestures between himself, Anna, and Dax—"lose. My children are ruthless. I'm so sorry, but also—" He gestures to Anna and Dax. "You *chose* them. And I'm stuck accepting I raised them this way. So let's kick their ass."

The jaws of all five Donavan children drop in unison. Our dad never swears.

"Hell yeah," Anna agrees, bumping fists with Dax.

I exchange a wary look with Bryce. "I don't know how I feel about this."

My brother shrugs. "Doesn't matter. They'll lose soon enough," he says confidently. Anna attempts to tackle him, but she's so much smaller it has little effect.

"My dad never plays," I mumble to Dax, settling between his legs with my back to his chest. "He's showing off for you. Well…he's going to be terrible, so it's not so much showing off as he's trying."

Dax's laugh ruffles my hair, his arms coming around me and

grabbing the second controller in my lap. He twirls and flicks the joystick beneath his thumb in a move that my body automatically responds to, and he smirks when he catches me crossing my legs. "I can't believe you wouldn't call me your boyfriend."

I flush. "Are you?" I ask under my breath.

His chest shakes with laughter behind me. "Probably not after I kick your ass at *Mario Kart*."

I feign offense, my head tilting back to look him in the eye. "You wouldn't do that to your sweet girlfriend, now, would you?" I bat my eyelashes at him and he snorts.

"You forget you're not the only one with too many ruthless siblings. You can't flirt your way out of a *Mario Kart* ass kicking, baby."

I raise my brows. "Me, flirt? I would never."

"That would be disgusting," he agrees.

"Completely abhorrent," I intone automatically, the memory, the words, imprinted on my heart like a tattoo.

When he pulls back after placing a chaste kiss to my lips, the smile that spreads across his face has me melting farther into him, and goddamnit, I *am* mooning.

Final Revelations' *Self-Titled*: Reviews

"With this final installment, Final Revelations is selling tickets to their autopsy. The self-titled album starts off with a sound akin to their early days, the style progressing more toward what we know them as now and ending on an unexpected note, almost a tease of what they could have become had they not thrown in the towel. For longtime fans of the band, this album will scratch the itch and then leave you jonesing for a fix that will never come."

—*Rolling Stone*

"[…] but the real shining star of the album is the final track. It's the song we didn't know we wanted from Final Revelations until they gave it to us. It's not a ballad, but with soft cleans we so rarely get from Nakamura, the melancholic start that builds so achingly slow is like being edged until you're begging for release—and with a hell of an intro from bassist Cain Williams and drummer Barrett Johnson at the halfway mark, the tempo doubles and you're riding the wave of an eargasm, a release you weren't sure they'd give you, only to take you back down again in sated outro bliss."

—*The Noise*

"The choice to self-title this album is a metaphor, a celebration of everything Final Revelations, like viewing their career through a kaleidoscope, tinted and honed by years in the industry. This is an older, wiser Final Revelations that knows who they are, battle-tested and unafraid to show their scars. It's a bittersweet ending, an overarching theme of escape laced throughout—escaping oneself, addiction, temptation, imposter syndrome, the trappings of fame, and most notably, escaping an industry that chewed them up and spit them out, only to come back swinging with an album that won't soon be forgotten by a band that helped shape an entire era of music."

—*Kerrang!*

"After years in the desert waiting for a new Final Revelations album, it would be too easy to get drunk guzzling down this album—but the band knew what they were doing when they crafted the track list. Little sips of what we've come to expect from them—heavy riffs, unrelenting energy, growls from hell, aggressive breakdowns, and infectious hooks. It's an album whose layers reveal themselves to you with each playthrough—and it's one we will be playing through, start to finish, for years to come."

—*Billboard*

"Whatever deal Dax made with the devil for those vocals must be up. That's the only reason they'd quit while still at the top of their game."

—YouTube comment

"How soon is too soon for a reunion tour? Asking for me."

—Reddit

CHAPTER THIRTY

Eighteen months later

"Sloane Donavan."

Tugging my press pass from my back pocket, I hold it up for the beefy man in the overtight black shirt that reads SECURITY.

He waves me through the barrier without consulting his clipboard. I've already been in and out multiple times at this point.

Undead Kings just finished their set, and the roadies are rushing to flip the stage for Final Revelations. The sky overhead groans, and I cast a wary look toward the roiling gray clouds. I cross my fingers that it holds off long enough for the guys to finish their set.

In the melee of backstage, I spot the blue hair of my intern, Murphy. She jerks her head in my direction. She's covering tonight's show.

I'm far too emotional tonight and far too close to the band now to write an unbiased piece. Even Gabe, Undead Kings' frontman, was getting choked up when I saw him backstage earlier—and they're not even the ones retiring. Thank god. I couldn't bear to lose two of my favorite bands in one year.

"You ready for this?" Murphy asks when I reach her.

I shake my head, staring wide-eyed at everyone running around backstage. I'm scared to blink, to miss a single moment of it. I can't believe this is the last show, that we're not waking up in a new city tomorrow to do it all over again.

The past year and a half has been a roller coaster, to say the least. The morning after Thanksgiving, I woke up to a stark email from John—You were right about the article. I'm running it with your edits. Fuck the haters. PS: Could you kindly let Robb know I'm making this right and to stop hounding me?—with an offer for a full-time staff-writer position attached. Trent—the alleged nepotism hire—was only ever an unpaid intern. John was never planning to pass me over. Despite the internet trolls' hot takes about me, the *Alternative Press* issues with my Final Revelations articles still did off-the-charts numbers. I'm not holding out hope for an apology. Final Revelations finished their album, which, upon release, quickly went gold, then platinum and hasn't slowed down in the months since. They put *Nixed* on their website as a pay-what-you-can setup, all the proceeds going to various nonprofits dedicated to helping those who struggle with the topics discussed on the album. Over the past year, the guys have given more interviews to more magazines, and Mike Song's shitty 2002 article is now buried six pages deep when you search "Final Revelations."

They started touring last year, traveling around the US through the summer and Europe in the fall. They took a break over the winter before doing a second US leg in the spring, and now they're back in Cleveland for their final show.

The final Final.

Dax got back into town yesterday, and we spent the afternoon alternately tangled up in each other and napping it out. But today...I've barely seen him. He was already gone when I woke up this morning. I don't fully know how to explain the energy in our apartment—*our* apartment. The concept is still a little foreign. I was basically living there anyway, but once my lease was up, I officially moved in while Dax was touring in the UK. But as I went about my morning routine in our condo this morning, my things amongst Dax's, his half-unpacked duffle at the base of our bed, I felt a trickle of excitement. No two days of our life have been the same—but we've figured out how to make it work, even when there was an entire ocean between us.

I'm sad to see this chapter of our lives close, but I'm also endlessly excited at the prospect of being boring and domestic together. Dax already has multiple requests to produce on albums, and I can't wait to see what he does, how he'll thrive in this new role, a new side of him I can't wait to discover. My new column launches next month, and I've spent the spring mentoring Murphy, who I convinced John to bring on as an intern a few months back.

But right now, I'm trying really hard to stay present, to soak it all in. "Ask me literally anything else," I say to Murphy. "Like this isn't the last night."

Murphy nods once, jerking her head toward where my friends are standing. They surprised me by showing up for this, insisting they wouldn't miss it. Drew is standing with his arm around Brooklyn, and she's tucked into his side, arms around his middle. "*What* is the real story there?"

I laugh under my breath. I will not be the one to undo their yearslong, *mostly* faked will-they-or-won't-they PR schtick. "No comment," I say, and Murph sighs. If only she knew the truth was much more interesting, that they're both desperately and devastatingly in love with other people.

"There you are." A zip of excitement shoots up my spine at the low, smoky voice. Dax's arms come around me, and I sink back into him on instinct. "I've been looking everywhere for you," he whispers in my ear.

Murphy immediately makes herself scarce.

"You've been busy," I counter. And he has. So many old friends have come out of the woodwork for today, so many people vying for the attention of Dax, Marcus, Cain, Barrett, and Jonah.

Dax hums noncommittally. "Yeah, but I thought I'd get to spend more of today with you."

I shrug. "We have tomorrow, and the next day, and the next day."

Dax presses his lips to the crown of my head, sighing contentedly. "Thank god."

He twirls my hair around his finger, twisting it off to the side before burying his face in the crook of my neck as he squeezes me tighter against him. "You wore this shirt the first time I saw you," he mumbles against my pulse point, making it jump. "Well...the second first time I saw you."

I angle my face so I can look at him. "Really?"

The brush of his lips against the hinge of my jaw gives me goose bumps. "At Battle of the Bands. My first thought was how I thought I was hallucinating. My second thought"—he places a kiss at the hollow spot behind my ear—"was how I wanted to do that."

I shudder at the low timbre of his voice. "No, it wasn't."

His laugh coasts across my cheek. "It was. I kept trying to find a way to casually touch you, to make sure you were real. I couldn't understand how the whole venue was going on like nothing monumental was happening. I never thought I'd see you again, and then...There you were. I felt like I'd been holding my breath for three years and could finally breathe again."

My fingers drag along his forearms wrapped around me, idly

tracing the shapes inked there. "When I kissed you—for the second first time—it felt like coming home after being gone for a long time."

Dax grunts, nuzzling his face in my neck. "I know that feeling too well right now."

Placing my hands atop his, I squeeze gently before spinning in the circle of his arms, stretching up onto my tiptoes to kiss him. "I love you."

He nudges my nose with his. "I love you." Dragging his mouth to my ear, he whispers, "This is my formal request to not leave the apartment for the next three days."

"Kinky," I murmur.

He laughs. It seems to come more easily to him now, laughing, smiling. "That, too, but also: naps."

"Very metal of you," I tease.

His lopsided smile fills me up.

"Dax," their stage manager calls, signaling it's almost time for them to go on. They've been playing a game of chicken with the impending storm all day, and the rush to stay on schedule is necessary if they want to finish their set.

Dax nods in acknowledgment before turning to me. "You watching from backstage?" he asks, already knowing that I won't. I wouldn't dream of wasting this final show by only half hearing it. I shake my head and he grins. "Going into the pit?"

I snort. "You know I prefer my nose unbroken. I'll be in the sound booth tent with Murph."

An unreadable expression crosses Dax's face.

"What?"

He presses a kiss to my forehead. "You'll see," he says, slapping me on the ass like he does before every show.

I arch a brow. "Alright. Have fun," I say, blowing him a kiss.

"Always do," he says, walking backward away from me.

I don't find out what he means until the fifth song.

"Cleveland," he says on a heavy exhale into the mic. His attention goes to the tented sound booth in the middle of the field, and I'm rooted to the spot. "This next song is my girl's favorite, and she wants to get in the pit."

I cannot fucking stand him. I love him so much.

"So," he says, wiping the sweat from his brow with the back of his forearm. "This is gonna be the softest shit we've ever done. Anyone who's ever wanted to get in the pit but been too scared—get in the fucking pit. And to make sure you all stay on your best behavior—"

The crowd's screaming is near deafening as Dax jumps down from the stage and approaches the barricade. Security watches him, too baffled to stop him.

"Open up for me, please." Like an undulating wave, the people near the front press back, parting like the Red Sea. "Good, good." He knows exactly what he's doing, how many people just captured that on video and will be listening to his low voice praise them on a loop.

A spotlight turns on, highlighting Dax as he hops the barricade and makes his way to the massive open space in the middle of the crowd.

"Sloane," he calls off-mic as he reaches the center of the pit. "C'mere, baby."

My face flushes, and I'm glad it's dark out. The sound tech nudges me out of the tented area, and I relent. The crowd parts, making a path from me to Dax. He grins when he sees me, beckoning me over with a finger. Once I'm within reach, his free hand comes up to cradle the back of my head, holding me steady as he kisses me fiercely.

On stage, Barrett drumrolls on a cymbal.

Breaking the kiss, Dax mumbles against my mouth, "I told you I'd get you in the pit."

I shake my head at him.

Turning toward the stage, Dax brings the mic back to his mouth. "Ready?"

Jonah, Barrett, Marcus, and Cain all nod in confirmation.

"Okay," Dax says, strolling around the middle of the pit, the spotlight tracking him.

The usual suspects who mosh have dutifully taken up residence at the edge of the pit, forming a protective wall, as people of all genders, races, sizes, and ages pour into the vacated space. It's the most diverse pit I've ever seen.

I can't believe no one has touched Dax, the person they all came here to see. He's undisturbed in the middle of hundreds of fans as they share this once-in-a-lifetime moment together.

"Can we dim this?" he asks, shielding his eyes. The bright white light switches to indigo, and he looks so beautiful, his edges bathed in blues and purples. "The lights are down. No one can see you. Dance however the fuck you want." The silence that follows as hundreds of people hold their breath, knowing exactly what comes next—

"LET'S GO!"

It starts to rain softly halfway through the song, but Dax doesn't leave, the guys don't stop playing, and the crowd doesn't seem to care. I have no idea what's coming next for Dax and me, but here in the middle of a muddy mosh pit with hundreds of people imperfectly dancing their hearts out, I'm not worried. Whatever we build together, if it's a fraction as beautiful as this, it will be epic.

ACKNOWLEDGMENTS

[*plays G note*] Welcome to the Thank You Parade:

First, I want to acknowledge how this book even came to be. In the fall of 2020, I wrote Sloane and Dax's first chance, a manuscript that was ultimately shelved. But just like Sloane and Dax, it was destined for a second chance. So, if you're a writer reading this, sometimes "no" simply means "not now," and that's okay. Keep going. Even if that book is the book of your heart. You contain multitudes, and you have more stories inside you than you know. *Keep going.* Now, I must thank all the people who indulged me in telling the story of my emo heart:

To my agent, Hannah Schofield—thank you for believing in me and being the biggest champion of my books. All the standing ovations for you.

To my editors, Junessa Viloria and Kate Byrne, thank you so much for believing in this book and for taking mosh pits so seriously. My unending gratitude to the teams at Forever and HQ who lent their time and talent, including but not limited to Jordyn Penner, Dana Cuadrado, Taylor Navis, Luria Rittenberg, Xian Lee, Grace Marshall, Elle Brown, and Rhiannon Morris. Thank you to Elizabeth McConaughy-Oliver for your thoughtful insights as Dax's authenticity reader. Any errors in Dax's representation are entirely my own. An extra special thanks to Daniela Medina for the art direction and Guy Shield for the gorgeous, gorgeous cover art.

Infinitely grateful for and in awe of the writing community. I'm so appreciative of anyone who has taken the time to yap with me and/or shout about my books online. You are rock stars. I especially need to thank the following: Alicia Thompson, Hailey Harlow, Courtney Kae, Tarah Dewitt, Rachel Lynn Solomon, Ande Pliego, Chip Pons, Ava Wilder, Lana Ferguson, Amy Buchanan, Heather McBreen, Anita Kelly, Jen Comfort, Alison Cochrun, Claire Laminen, Solange Bello, and Kristine Lopez.

I'd be remiss if I didn't thank the bands whose albums I had on repeat while drafting: Sleep Token, The Devil Wears Prada, Bad Omens, The Plot In You, Pierce The Veil, and last but definitely not least: A Day to Remember, whose "If It Means a Lot to You" got me through my first heartbreak. There are a dozen band names hidden within the prose of this book. Let me know if you spotted them.

To my mom, thanks for trusting teen me enough to drive all over the state to go see local bands. And to my dad—sorry we always made fun of you for listening to the same rock bands over and over because... yeah, same. To my brother, thanks for always being on top of how to hack an iPod into working in a car with nothing but a cassette tape.

All my love to my biffles, who loved me even when I was the angstiest teenager alive: Abby, Alisa, Ashley, and Lizz. Please never let me wear that much eyeliner ever again.

To Karrie, the Brooklyn to my Sloane, thank you for reading this story over and over, in its many, many iterations. Thank you for always believing in me. <3

My sweet pets: Basil, Paprika, Freya, and Odin—thank you for cuddling me so hard at my desk that I couldn't get up and had to finish this book. And no, it's not time for dinner yet.

To my husband, thank you for loving me (even when I make typos in your acknowledgments). Thank you for allowing me to mine your childhood for the Donavan sibling shenanigans. Mostly, thank you for loving me and chasing dreams with me. I love our life.

To you, dear reader. Your time is a gift. Thank you for choosing to spend it with me.

ABOUT THE AUTHOR

Erin Connor has been telling herself stories for as long as she can remember, and once she realized she could write them down and share them with others, there was no going back. She loves writing about messy women, platonic and romantic love, and happily ever afters.

Erin lives in the PNW with her spouse, two large dogs, two lazy cats, and more houseplants than she can count. When not exploring fictional worlds, she enjoys hiking, cooking, emo nostalgia, and slowly but surely actualizing her lifelong goal of becoming a forest witch.

You can find out more at:
Erin-Connor.com
Instagram @ErinConnorBooks